CHANGE IN PUTIN'S RUSSIA

Change in Putin's Russia

Power, Money and People

Simon Pirani

First published 2010 by Pluto Press
345 Archway Road, London N6 5AA and
175 Fifth Avenue, New York, NY 10010

Distributed in the United States of America exclusively by
Palgrave Macmillan, a division of St. Martin's Press LLC,
175 Fifth Avenue, New York, NY 10010

www.plutobooks.com

British Library Cataloguing in Publication Data
A catalogue record for this book is available from the British Library

ISBN 978 0 7453 2691 7 Hardback
ISBN 978 0 7453 2690 0 Paperback

Library of Congress Cataloging in Publication Data applied for

This book is printed on paper suitable for recycling and made from fully managed and sustained forest sources. Logging, pulping and manufacturing processes are expected to conform to the environmental standards of the country of origin. The paper may contain up to 70% post consumer waste.

10 9 8 7 6 5 4 3 2 1

Designed and produced for Pluto Press by
Curran Publishing Services, Norwich

Printed and bound in the European Union by
CPI Antony Rowe, Chippenham and Eastbourne

CONTENTS

PHOTOGRAPHS, FIGURES AND TABLES

Photographs

Figures

Tables

PREFACE

This book aims to introduce Russia in the 2000s to the general reader. It focuses on the economy, politics and society in the broad sense of those words, and devotes attention to trade unions, community organisations and social movements.

I have been writing about Russia as a journalist since 1990, when I reported on miners' protests in the Kuzbass coalfield. I have written about the workers' movement many times since. From 1997, I wrote mostly about the economy, occasionally in the *Observer*, but mostly in business publications including *Emerging Markets, Trade Finance, Financial News, Gas Matters* and *Metal Bulletin*. So I have had the chance to get to know about both labour and capital at first hand. Speaking and reading Russian, and writing an earlier book about workers' movements in the 1920s, has deepened my understanding.

This book is not reportage; it is an overview of the events and issues I think most important. I rely on books and articles by others, and the rich resources of Russia's media, as well as on my own research. However, there are important parts of the picture mentioned only fleetingly, such as Russia's foreign policy. And there's another caveat: like all observers, I know some parts better than others, and in particular, I know far too little of Russia beyond Moscow. In September and October 2007, after Pluto Press had agreed to publish this book, I tried to compensate for that, by visiting Izhevsk, Togliatti and Samara, and material from that trip appears in Chapters 5, 8 and 9.

The Introduction puts Putin's Russia in the context of the last 40 years of world history. Chapter 1 describes the transition from Gorbachev's Soviet Union to Yeltsin's Russia, and Chapter 2 brings the narrative to the point at which Putin took over. Chapter 3 presents a general picture of the Russian economy under Putin. The story of power and money relations is resumed in Chapter 4; the oil boom, and the bust that followed, is described in Chapter 5. Chapter 6 deals with politics in the broadest sense, Chapter 7 with human development issues, and Chapters 8 and 9 with social movements for change.

Where I use terms that deserve further explanation, these are marked with * or **, and a footnote is provided on the same page. The numbered endnotes, such as [1], refer to sources of information, which are listed at the end of the book. In the text I spell Russian names as they usually appear in the English language press. In the endnotes I use the Library of Congress transliteration system.

Finally, a note about sums of money. I have tried to keep references to these to a minimum, and to round figures up or down where appropriate – but, as in life generally, one can't avoid dealing with money all together. Most sums are given in dollars, the currency in which most international business is transacted. Some are given in Russian rubles. For reference, the exchange rates moved as follows:

Rubles to the dollar, average for the year

1996	5.1
1997	5.8
1998	10.0
1999	24.6
2000	28.1
2001	29.2
2002	31.3
2003	30.7
2004	28.8
2005	28.3
2006	27.1
2007	25.6
2008	24.8

Note that the ruble lost value against all currencies throughout the second half of 2008 and the first quarter of 2009. See page 107.

ACKNOWLEDGEMENTS

Many of the hundreds of people in Russia who have helped me to understand their country – friends, colleagues, labour and community activists, bankers, business people, officials and academics – might not want to be thanked here by name, for one reason or another. I sincerely thank them, all the same. I am particularly grateful to those who helped arrange my visits to Izhevsk, Togliatti and Samara in 2007.

Thanks also to Philip Alexander, Bill Bowring, Simon Clarke, Carrie Gibson, David Lane, David Mandel, Greg Muttitt and Vlad Mykhnenko, who kindly read and commented on parts of the text (but bear no responsibility for my views or my mistakes); Vicki Robinson, for the charts; Roger van Zwanenberg and all at Pluto Press and Curran Publishing Services; the Oxford Institute for Energy Studies and Jonathan Stern, director of natural gas research, for arranging our work in a way that allowed me time to complete this project; and others who helped in various ways including Christine Cooper, Chris Corrigan, John Crowfoot, Anouk Honore, Gavin Knight, Martin Mayer, Felix Pirani and John Spencer, and the staff of the British Library. My biggest thanks are to Monika, my partner, who has supported, rather than just putting up with, this project.

Photographs have kindly been supplied by *Den'* newspaper, Izhevsk; Tatiana Lokshina; RIA Novosti; and Reuters/RIA Novosti/Kremlin.

Simon Pirani

INTRODUCTION: PUTIN'S RUSSIA IN DEEP FOCUS

The relationship between power and money has changed fundamentally in Russia in the 2000s. So has the relationship between Russia's people, on one hand, and power and money on the other. This book describes these changes and offers a view about why they matter.

The dramatic clashes between the government and the billionaire oligarchs (politically influential businessmen) is an important theme. On one level, this was a battle between power and money, but it is more accurately described as a reordering of their relationship. The state disciplined the oligarchs in the interests of the property-owning class as a whole, and restored to itself the functions it lost in the chaos of the 1990s. Its power is not an end in itself, but a means of managing post-Soviet Russian capitalism and integrating it into the world system. Progress has been made to these ends largely thanks to Russia's economic revival, which was in turn made possible mainly by the rising price of oil, on which the economy so heavily depends.

Although the Russian state has since May 2008 been headed by Dmitry Medvedev as president, Vladimir Putin, the former KGB* officer, president in 2000–08 and prime minister under Medvedev, has been and is more influential. Many western commentators identify Putin's past in the security services as the key to his rule. By contrast, I argue that, while Putin's KGB background matters, it was the oil boom that was the really necessary precondition for the changes he has made. It follows that the end of that boom in 2008, and the impact of the world financial crisis on Russia, not only threaten to reverse much of the economic progress made, but

* The powerful security service of the late Soviet period. (See Glossary.)

will also be powerful determinants of what happens next in Russian society and politics.

Economic factors have shaped the relations between power and money and Russia's people. The oil boom raised average incomes, and restored the damage done to living standards by the 1990s slump. But it also exacerbated inequalities. And as the state became stronger and more stable, it also became more authoritarian, bearing down on unremittingly, even choking, the civil activity – by social movements, community organisations, trade unions, campaign and political groups, journalists and others – on which Russia's future so crucially depends. These movements and organisations working collectively to change people's lives and their country are a key theme of this book.

Russia is important to an international readership, in my view, for three major reasons. First, it was home to the Soviet social system that, for four or five generations, promised hope of a better future and then dashed those hopes. Second, the way that Russia has integrated into the world capitalist system since the collapse of the Soviet Union in 1991 tells us much about how that system works. Third, the challenges facing Russia's people in trying to change their country and their lives for the better have a bearing on social movements for change all over the world.

This Introduction puts Russia's story in the context of world capitalism and the forces of resistance to it. It places the 2000s, the Putin–Medvedev decade, in the context of the three previous decades of dramatic changes in capitalism and of the decline and fall of the Soviet Union, of which Russia was part until 1991.

The Late 1960s and 1970s: Growth Slows in the East, the Boom Ends in the West

Forty years ago, at the end of the 1960s, Russia was the largest of 15 republics that made up the Union of Soviet Socialist Republics (USSR or Soviet Union). Its capital, Moscow, was at the centre of a much larger group of countries, the 'Soviet bloc', that stretched from East Germany and Hungary in the west to Vietnam and North Korea in the east. China was a semi-detached partner, with similar ideology and economic practices, but an independent foreign policy. Across the whole bloc, all financial institutions (banks and so on), and most of industry and agriculture, were state-owned. The state – or rather, the bureaucratic elite that controlled the state – guided the economies by decree and took all investment decisions.

Currencies were non-convertible,* internal prices were controlled and foreign trade was a state monopoly. Western capitalism had no direct access. The profiteering and wealth accumulation that make capitalism tick were illegal, and derided by official ideology which deemed the Soviet system 'socialist' or 'communist'. The bloc was bound together by perhaps the most all-embracing system of political repression ever devised, under which only one party, called Communist or something similar, was legal. Non-political organisations (for example, trade unions) were strictly controlled, dissidents routinely imprisoned or worse, and the media comprehensively censored. The Soviet Union was seen as a second 'superpower' to rival the United States. It seemed invincible, both to most of its leaders and to most of its enemies. But the factors that would bring about its collapse in 1989–91 were already at work.

In the 1970s the Soviet Union appeared, to most outsiders, economically healthy, socially stable, and militarily equal to the United States. With hindsight, it was clearly none of these things. Outside the spheres of arms and space research, on which western observers concentrated, the Soviet Union lagged behind not only western economies but also East Asian ones, for example in technology and communications. Industrial development hit a plateau: from 1974, the US Central Intelligence Agency (CIA), which monitored the Soviet economy, reported zero or negative growth of labour productivity and industrial productivity.[1] The arms race with the United States was a heavy economic burden. Dependence on foreign trade for consumer goods and machinery was increasing. In terms of human development, the demographic improvements so noticeable in the 1950s and 1960s – an increase in life expectancy and decline in mortality rates – came to a halt. The improvement in living standards slowed down.

The Soviet Union's leaders believed that its economy could develop in isolation from world capitalism, and so did many people in the west. That turned out to be an illusion. From a twenty-first century vantage point it is evident that the crisis that shook international capitalism in the early 1970s, and the changes that followed, were among the causes of the Soviet economy's demise, and shaped the parasitic, vulgar and criminal forms of capitalism that sprang up in its place in the 1990s.

The early 1970s marked, first, the end of the economic boom

---

* That is, could not be more or less freely exchanged for other currencies. Exchange of the Soviet ruble was a tightly held state monopoly.

in the richest countries that had begun after the Second World War, and, second, the beginning of an unprecedented expansion of global financial markets, often termed 'globalisation'.[2] During the 1950s and 1960s, in the developed countries, economic output had risen – measured both in total, and per head of population – nearly twice as fast as at any time since the 1820s. Labour productivity had increased twice as rapidly as ever before. The turnaround came between 1968 and 1973. Economic growth measured by Gross Domestic Product (GDP) slowed and labour productivity growth slowed. By 1973, the economies of the United States and much of Europe were in recession; many of them suffered further recessions during the next decade.* As the real economy ran into trouble in many of the wealthiest countries, money capital gathered in ever-greater quantities in the financial sector. Instead of being returned to the spheres of production and commerce, where there was tougher competition for returns, this capital sought ways to grow financially. New financial markets appeared, in the first place the eurodollar markets, so called because they were based in London and other European cities, but shares, debts, currencies – and, as time went by, other ever more exotic financial instruments – were priced in dollars.

A key turning point in the financial markets' growth was the abandonment in 1971 of the link between the dollar and gold,**

---

* GDP is the most widely used measure of economic activity. It is the total market value of goods and services produced in a country (usually, per year), and is calculated as: consumption + gross investment + government spending + exports minus imports. As a concept, GDP reflects capitalism's priorities: that is, measures monetary value but takes no account of the external effects of economic activity, for example, on the environment, human development or welfare. So it treats as equal 1,000 barrels of $100 oil, a $100,000 Hellfire missile and $100,000 worth of medicines. It has other shortcomings: for example, it does not measure unpaid home work or the black market. A recession is usually defined as a period when a country's economic growth, measured by GDP, is negative for two or more quarter-year periods.

** Until 1971, under the Bretton Woods system established by the United States and other major powers at the end of the Second World War, dollars were exchangeable for gold at a fixed rate; other currencies in turn were fixed against the dollar. After the dollar–gold link was abandoned in 1971, there was no direct connection between the dollar, the international reserve currency, and underlying value formerly represented by the US gold reserves. The US monetary authority, the Federal Reserve, could and did henceforth issue dollars without this restraint.

and its replacement by a system – which many economists argue is not a system at all – of floating exchange rates. This created great opportunities to profit from trade and speculation in currencies, and by the mid-1970s, the volume of purely monetary transactions in offshore markets exceeded the total volume of world trade many times over. Transactions on the London eurodollar market alone were estimated to be worth six times the total value of world trade by 1979, and by 1986, 25 times. Along with this expansion of essentially speculative financial activity, there were major changes that impacted the real economy, including the rapid growth of, and intensification of competition between, transnational corporations. Mainly thanks to these, between 1970 and 1978 foreign direct investment* by the United States doubled, and by Europe trebled.[3]

Ordinary people may have been unaware of the vast excess of money capital sloshing around the globe, at a time when the end of the boom brought unemployment and other hardships. But they certainly noticed the worldwide inflation that resulted: thus the early 1970s was a time of constant strikes by industrial workers seeking to protect living standards from the impact of rising prices. Inflation was one of the principal factors that led the Organization of Petroleum Exporting Countries (OPEC), which represents the main oil producers in the Middle East and elsewhere, to levy a four-fold increase in oil prices in 1973. This produced an 'oil shock', with costs rising steeply for energy-importing countries, including most of the richest nations. Rich countries' leaders often held OPEC responsible for the recession of 1973–75 in the United States and Europe, but many economists think that is implausible. The 'oil shock' certainly had far-reaching consequences, though. It shifted the economic balance in energy markets towards the producers. Middle Eastern oil producers rapidly accumulated surplus funds, an estimated $80 billion of which soon arrived in the eurodollar markets and other offshore locations.[4]

The 'oil shock' came together with a turning of the political tide. US hegemony over the world capitalist system was seriously challenged for the first time since the Second World War. The world's largest non-OPEC producer, the Soviet Union – regarded as the United States's main strategic enemy – benefited from the sudden growth of its oil export revenues, as did Middle Eastern states. And the display of producer power coincided with the failure of

* Investment made directly into companies, as distinct from investment via share markets.

the United States's barbaric war in Vietnam and the humiliating withdrawal of its troops in 1975.

The 1980s: the United States Borrows Money, the Soviet Union Borrows Time

In the early 1980s, the largest world economies started out on a long period of expansion which – although punctuated by occasional recessions and in Japan's case by persistent stagnation in the 1990s – halted only with the 2008–09 recession. The United States, after a brief recession in 1981–82, embarked on a long period of growth. A key role was also played by the East Asian economies, which boomed without interruption from the mid-1980s until the Asian financial crisis of 1997.

This economic boom was accompanied by substantial changes in the financial system. The governments of Margaret Thatcher (British prime minister from 1979) and Ronald Reagan (US president from 1980) led a drive against market regulation. Banks were given greater scope to engage in financial speculation; derivatives, such as futures contracts, were put to speculative use;* and governments relaxed controls on the movement of capital across borders. The offshore tax havens, which until the 1970s had been the preserve of a few rich individuals, sucked in gigantic sums of money, notably from oil-producing countries and poor countries with weak financial regulation. In the early 1990s, much dubiously – or illegally – acquired capital would flow from Russia to these havens. The introduction of electronic trading, centred on the 'big bang' (computerisation) on the London markets in 1986, speeded up these processes. Foreign exchange markets, where currencies are bought and sold, mainly to speculate on their value, ballooned: between the early 1980s and the mid-1990s, the volume of business transacted grew an estimated ten times over, to $1500 billion a day.

---

* Derivatives is a collective term for complex financial instruments whose value is based on something else (the 'underlier'), which may be for example the value of a commodity, share or property, or an index. Many derivatives, such as futures and options, began life as a form of insurance, to hedge against changes in the underlier's value. But as international derivatives markets mushroomed over the last 30 years they engendered speculation. Securitisation is the packaging-up of financial assets (usually types of debt such as loans or mortgages) into tradable financial instruments. The instability of derivatives markets was a major element in the world financial crisis of 2007–08.

The 1980s was also a watershed in the relationship between the United States, the most powerful capitalist country, and the rest of the world. Previously, the United States had exported capital; now it started importing it. The US government, notwithstanding Reagan's rhetoric about tightening budgets, ran up the biggest state deficit the world had ever seen: in 1981–91 it rose from $74 billion to $300 billion, while the total national debt rose from $1,000 billion to $4,000 billion. The United States raised its interest rates above the level of inflation, to attract so-called 'hot' money. The higher interest rates, combined with falling prices of oil and other commodities, amounted to a punishment for poor countries that had borrowed in the 1970s, particularly in Latin America. That continent's interest payments on debt to rich countries rose from one-third of the value of its exports in 1977 to almost two-thirds in 1982. The process culminated in the debt crisis of 1982, when Mexico threatened to default on $70 billion worth of debt obligations.[5]

The Soviet Union and its satellites now came under pressure in two ways. The first was from the Reagan administration, which sanctioned a new round of nuclear armament – the 'Star Wars' missile system – and effectively challenged the Soviet Union to do the same. Whether Reagan knew it or not, he hit a weak spot, since in the course of the computer revolution in the west, the Soviet Union had fallen still further behind technologically. The Soviet leaders' bluff, which had served them so well through years of nuclear brinkmanship, was called. Soviet arms spending still accounted for 12–17 per cent of national income, and they could not afford to increase it.[6] The radical disarmament proposals made at negotiations in Reykjavik in 1985 by the last Soviet leader, Mikhail Gorbachev, were as much as anything a recognition of this economic reality. The defeat suffered by the Soviet Union in its last war, in Afghanistan (from 1979 to 1989), further underlined that Reagan's 'second cold war'* was one that Moscow could not win.

The second pressure on the Soviet bloc was economic. On one hand, the Soviet Union's trade with the west increasingly tilted towards the export of raw materials and the import of machinery and consumer goods – the classical trade profile of an economic

* The term 'cold war' was coined in the late 1940s to describe the tension between the United States and the USSR. After a period of 'détente' (that is, a thawing of relations) in the 1970s, tensions rose again in the 1980s as a result of the Soviet invasion of Afghanistan, and the US nuclear rearmament programme and deployment of extra missiles in Europe.

colony. In 1973–74, the Soviet Union was the second largest oil producer after the United States, and gained a windfall from the 'oil shock', just as the Middle Eastern producers did. But as prices fell again in the 1980s it felt the impact much more keenly. Between 1973 and 1985, exports of oil and gas accounted for 80 per cent of the USSR's hard currency earnings. Other oil exporters spent some of their windfall on Soviet weapons, which accounted for much of the remaining 20 per cent. The USSR spent its oil wealth on weaponry, to keep up with the United States in the arms race, and on imported goods to improve the living standards of its population. Machinery, consumer goods and food took up a greater and greater share of imports.[7]

The oil wealth was used to mask one of the Soviet Union's great failures, in agriculture. This huge country with rich land resources had failed to achieve self-sufficiency. By the 1980s, the USSR had to import 35–40 million tonnes per year of wheat, much of it from Canada and the United States. Then disaster struck. In 1983, Siberian oil output began to decline. It recovered briefly in 1986 and then continue its fall. And the price of the oil that was exported fell steeply – by 69 per cent in 1986 alone. The dollar, the oil trading currency, also fell in value. The terms of trade reversed against the Soviet Union disastrously. It began to borrow from western markets to pay for some imports. Soviet net debt to western governments and banks rose from a paltry $600 million in 1971 to $10.2 billion in 1984 and $37.3 billion in 1989; to this was later added many billions of dollars' worth of export credits that had been extended to the USSR by East Germany, which were owed to unified Germany.[8]

Given the size of its economy, the Soviet Union's debt burden was small beside those of Eastern European countries. They had been drawn into the maelstrom of international debt markets in the 1970s, when they borrowed dollars to buy western technology and consumer goods. Poland built up the largest debt, which had reached $41 billion by 1989. In the early 1980s, the attempt by Poland's rulers to impose substantial food price increases and other austerity measures, as part of a policy to meet their debt repayment schedule, helped trigger working-class protest. That led to the overthrow of Edward Gierek's government in 1981, and to the formation of the independent trade union Solidarnosc, which inspired dissidents and worker activists throughout the Soviet bloc. Debt repayment was also a mounting pressure on Hungary, Bulgaria and East Germany. The economic historian Giovanni Arrighi wrote:

> To make things worse for the south [i.e. the developing countries] and better for the west, third world states were soon joined in their cut-throat competition for mobile capital by second world [i.e. Soviet bloc] states. In taking advantage of the overabundance of capital of the 1970s, some of these states had moved quickly to hook up to the global circuits of capital by assuming financial obligations among the heaviest in the world. When capital became scarce again [i.e. in the 1980s] the Soviet bloc as a whole suddenly felt the cold winds of competition blowing. Bogged down in its own Vietnam [i.e. Afghanistan] and challenged by a new escalation of the armament race with the US, the atrophied structures of the Soviet state began to crumble.[9]

The Soviet bloc disintegrated: the Berlin Wall which symbolised it was taken down in November 1989. But neither it, nor the Soviet Union itself, collapsed because of external pressures alone. These exacerbated, and were exacerbated by, the economy's internal contradictions. In the Soviet Union, output growth slowed constantly. Industry was skewed on one hand towards the production of armaments, and on the other away from making consumer goods. That in turn aggravated the drastic shortages for which the Soviet economy was famous, and heightened demand for imports. With each decade, as the population became increasingly urbanised and educated, the 'economy of shortage' became less and less sustainable – as did the wall of censorship designed to cut people off from the outside world. Living standards stopped rising in the early 1980s. With retrospect, it is striking how completely the Soviet leaders deceived themselves, and most of the western elite, about the sustainability of their system. In reality, by the time Gorbachev proposed substantial reforms in 1987, it was already too late to save it. His attempts to introduce some market mechanisms into the economy nourished the embryo of the post-Soviet Russian capitalist class – bankers, traders and bureaucrats who used the openings created to make their first millions – but for most people simply made matters worse. Rapid inflation triggered a wave of strikes which swept the Soviet coalfields in July 1989, reviving the workers' movement. That, together with demands for secession from Ukraine and other republics, brought down the Soviet political regime. The Union was dissolved in December 1991.

The 1990s: Capitalism Arrives in Russia

Russia was by far the largest of 15 new republics to emerge from the Soviet Union. It is a multinational country of 160 or more ethnic groups, a federation of 83 administrative units (republics, autonomous territories, regions and so on). It has by far the largest land area of any country, stretching across eleven time zones. It kept the lion's share of the Soviet Union's wealth, including natural resources (oil, gas, minerals and metals) and industrial potential – but its population is falling, from 148 million in 1992 to 142 million in the late 2000s.*

From 1992, the seeds of capitalism planted in the last four years of the Soviet Union sprouted. Post-Soviet Russia's rulers, supported by the world's wealthiest countries and international institutions, set out to implement the transition to capitalism as rapidly as possible. Largely as a result of this, Russia rapidly sank into chaos. The breakdown of Soviet trading relationships, and the sudden imposition of price liberalisation and privatisation – 'shock therapy', as it came to be known – triggered the worst slump ever experienced in peacetime. Between 1990 and 1997, Russia's GDP shrank by about half. This was a profound human tragedy: millions were impoverished, and life expectancy plummeted as the last generation of Soviet working men, who suddenly faced unemployment, uncertainty and poverty, began to die in their 50s or even 40s.

Boris Yeltsin, who was elected Russian president in June 1991 and took Russia out of the Soviet Union at the end of that year, shaped a new political order in the midst of this slump. Yeltsin, supposedly a 'democrat', railroaded through a new constitution. Parliament disagreed; in 1993 he disbanded it, and then ordered the building to be shelled. The constitution was then accepted in a referendum which involved ballot-rigging on a large scale.**

---

* Russia accounts for just under three-quarters of the former Soviet Union's economy, measured by GDP, and just under half of its population (142 million out of 285 million).

** This constitution made Russia a presidential republic. The president has executive power. He appoints the prime minister and government, although his choice has to be approved by the national Parliament; he can veto (and has vetoed) legislation adopted by Parliament. Alongside the government is the National Security Council, another executive body appointed by the president, which covers security and other issues. The Russian Federation is made up of 83 administrative units, which have their own parliaments and their own governors or presidents. These are represented in the Federation Council, the upper house of the national

The character of Russia's federalism was decided in practice in Chechnya, the southern republic whose bid for secession Yeltsin answered with the murderous war of 1994–96. Yeltsin was throughout his two terms in office feted as a hero in the west, but most people in Russia associated him above all with the collapse of living standards. When he retired in 1999, his approval ratings had sunk below 2 per cent.

Russian capitalism was insane, in part, because it was being integrated into a world economic and financial system which was itself going crazy. As soon as Soviet-era regulations were removed, Russia suffered a gigantic surge of 'capital flight': at least $150 billion, much of it accumulated by the looting of state property, left the country. The international financial deregulation of the 1980s had created a system perfectly suited to the needs of the former bureaucrats, lucky entrepreneurs and gangsters who made the first Russian fortunes. They moved their millions to offshore tax havens. Some capital flowed into Russia, but it was far less than the amount that left, and it was mostly speculative lending.

The background to Russia's meltdown was a decade-long international expansion of capital flows to the 'emerging markets', a term that bracketed together developing countries and the former Soviet bloc. These flows went, above all, to East Asian economies, but were creating a bubble they could not sustain, alongside the bubble in the rising US stock market. In mid-1997 there was a crash of stock markets and currency values across East Asia – which in retrospect may be seen as the first shudder of the financial shake-out which would culminate in the 2007–08 crash. Russian politicians and their international advisers seemed not to notice the implicit danger. The cash-strapped Russian government kept issuing short-term treasury bonds* in a desperate attempt to balance its books, and these became the basis for a gigantic pyramid scheme, largely financed by international markets. This collapsed, inevitably, in August 1998. While the disasters that befell Russia in the 1990s may be explained partly in terms of the weakness of the Russian state following the Soviet collapse, this financial crisis was perverse

---

Parliament. The lower house of Parliament (the Duma) is directly elected.

* Treasury bonds are promises to pay, with interest, issued by a government. For governments, they are a way of borrowing money. For markets, they are a form of investment as safe as the government's reputation. US treasury bonds have long been seen as the safest form of investment.

proof that the causes also lay in the nature of the world financial system into which Russia was integrated.

The 2000s and Beyond

Putin succeeded Yeltsin in 2000. His Russia is different from Yeltsin's in two ways. First, Putin and his colleagues – not only former security services officers, but also economists and managers with a belief in capitalist modernisation – sought to pull the state apparatus out of the chaos of the 1990s. Of course, like elites everywhere, they wanted to make themselves rich. But more significantly, they wanted a state that would collect enough taxes to administer the country, which Yeltsin's governments had failed to do. Second – and this was a huge slice of luck for Putin and his colleagues – the prices of oil and other important Russian exports (gas, steel and other metals) began to rise at the very moment that they entered the Kremlin, and with one pause in 2001–02, continued to rise uninterruptedly until 2008. This provided the basis for an economic revival which, by 2006, returned Russia's economy to the level it had reached in 1990. Although Putin presided over a widening of the gap between Russia's richest and poorest, average living standards improved, recovering and overtaking the level of late Soviet times.

The commodities boom from which Russia profited so handsomely took place against the background of steady growth of the world economy. Demand for commodities was strengthened by a surge of industrialisation and urbanisation in China, and to a lesser extent India, which outstripped the boldest forecasts. With some exceptions – including most of Africa, and parts of Asia, which slipped even further into poverty – national economies grew and average living standards improved. But economic growth went hand in hand with an unprecedented expansion of cheap credit emanating from the wealthiest countries. When shudders went through the housing market and stock markets in the United States in 2007, some economists began to warn that a credit bubble had developed, and was unsustainable. The more far-sighted pointed to a new turn of the screw of financial speculation, in the shape of collateralised debt obligations, an opaque, unregulated market, through which mounting volumes of debt were repackaged and sold by financial institutions to each other.

In September 2008 the house of cards came crashing down – starting in the United States, at the centre of the world financial system. The US government, which throughout the 2000s had continued to champion market deregulation and derided state intervention, was forced to organise the largest state rescue of financial institutions in history. The world's largest insurance company, AIG Group, and two companies at the heart of the US housing market, were effectively nationalised. Hundreds of billions of dollars were pumped into banks and other financial firms. The aftershocks ripped through the world's financial system. The larger countries' governments had to dig deep into their pockets not only to support their own banking systems, but to rescue from default those of a swathe of small states, especially in eastern Europe.

Russia, now more closely integrated with the world markets than it had ever been, was harshly exposed. The rescue package for its financial system cost it about one-third of the oil money it had saved up for a decade. And the price of oil, which hit a peak in July 2008, sank. The crisis moved from the sphere of finance to the real economy, and at the time of writing a recession, deeper than any since the 1930s, was spilling out from the rich countries across the world. China's boom came to a halt; by February 2009, 20 million of its 100 million internal migrant workers had returned, jobless, from the cities to the countryside. Russia's real economy was hard hit, too. The construction industry practically ground to a halt. Steel mills and car plants laid off workers. Poverty loomed again for millions who had escaped it during the oil boom.

Social Change, Socialism and the Soviet Union

In considering the prospects of collective action for social change, a look back over 40 years yields important insights. A key legacy of the Soviet Union was the terrible damage its system of repression did to traditions of collective action, and to collective social and political consciousness. This shadow is now (in the late 2000s) drawing in, but has not disappeared by a long way.

In the post-war Soviet Union – in which everyone in Putin's Russia of middle age or over grew up – attempts to organise political activity outside the Communist Party (for example, street demonstrations) invariably met with heavy sentences in prison camps or, notoriously, psychiatric hospitals. Looking back from the age of the Internet, it is important to recall how the Soviet dictatorship monopolised information. Its control of the media was complete. Distribution of banned literature or the possession of any printing equipment, leaflets or petitions, could result in heavy punishment. The very idea of popular collective action, independent of the state's choking interference, was impossible to imagine before Gorbachev's time. At work, 'official' trade unions that worked hand in glove with industrial managers not only usurped all the collective functions that unions usually perform, but also helped to spy on dissenters.

The granting of political freedoms under Gorbachev – including the rights to free assembly, free speech and political organisation – marked a historic turning point. This produced a surge of social activity: for many journalists and human rights activists, the late 1980s were a golden age. But the 1990s had, in many respects, a numbing effect, as the legacy of subservience left by Soviet dictatorship combined with the shocking impact of the economic slump. Communities were battling for survival; trade union action mostly took the form of desperate pleas for payment of unpaid wages. Yeltsin's assault on Chechnya in 1994–96 was unpopular, but few had the energy to protest. In Putin's Russia there have been the beginnings of a renaissance of social movements, from this low base. But the part played by these abiding Soviet legacies needs to be kept in mind.

Another Soviet legacy that remains relevant in the twenty-first century is the perversion of the meaning of 'socialism'. The Soviet leaders described the economic system that evolved in the 1920s, in which the overwhelming majority of the economy was state-owned, as 'socialist'. The Soviet dictatorship was exercised in the name of the industrial workers and rural peasantry, and the dictators claimed that this 'socialist' economic system was exclusively to those classes' benefit. I understand by 'socialism' collective action, guided by collective decision making, to overcome exploitation, alienated labour and the state. From this point of view, the Russian revolution of 1917, in which millions of people sought to reshape their future, and thereby started the process that gave birth to the Soviet Union, was a gigantic historical landmark –but the Soviet system was never socialist. Nevertheless, for several generations of people in Russia and other Soviet republics, 'socialism' was the system they lived under. Many looked back at it from the chaos of the 1990s with nostalgia. And younger people in Russia often associate 'socialism' with the past, and are perplexed at the thought of a socialist future. The upshot is that, in social movements in Russia, the idea of socialism is surrounded with even greater confusion than it is in the west.

The international financial crisis of 2007–08, and the recession it has triggered, will produce new conditions for Russia's social movements, and their ideas, to develop. In the 1990s, the slump coincided with, and was to some extent caused by, the collapse of the Soviet system and of the certainties that went with it. Then, people reasoned that capitalism could not be worse than what they had lived under. But the economic troubles that lie ahead, in 2010 and beyond, will be for people in Russia much more clearly the product of capitalism and its inherent potential for crisis. It seems terribly likely, at the time of writing, that the crisis will cause a great deal of poverty and unemployment in Russia, and such hardships are as likely to undermine collective movements for change as to inspire them. But causes and consequences may become clearer. Twenty years ago, very few Russians could have imagined that world capitalism was the problem that needed to be overcome, and that humanity could supersede capitalism as a way of living – because that was exactly the claim made by Communist party propaganda, which people knew from their experience was all lies. Now, the false dichotomy between Soviet 'socialism' and western capitalism is receding further into the past, and the monstrous destructive power of twenty-first century capitalism is staring us in the face. It is difficult to say how people in Russia will react – but it will not just be more of the same.

1

FROM GORBACHEV TO YELTSIN

The changes in the relationships of power, money and people under Putin flowed from the upheavals during Gorbachev's reforms and the slump and chaos that followed the Soviet Union's dissolution. This chapter deals with the last Soviet years and the initial post-Soviet chaos, up to 1994; Chapter 2 covers the events leading up to the Russian financial crisis of 1998, and its aftermath.

SOVIET AND POST-SOVIET ELITES (1986–91)

The post-Soviet capitalist class grew in the womb of the Soviet bureaucracy. The baby was born in 1987; the bureaucracy nurtured it. The years 1988–91 were 'the most "golden" period for the elite politico-economic groups', during which the foundations of most of Russia's big fortunes and businesses were laid, Yegor Gaidar, one of post Soviet Russia's early prime ministers, recalled.[1] Bureaucrats converted apparatus power into capitalist wealth. By 1991, when the Soviet Union collapsed, the new rich already owned – as private, rather than state, property – an array of commercial banks. They were running the rapidly expanding private foreign trade and much domestic trade, and readying themselves to grab Russia's industrial assets.

The bureaucracy did not have a plan, worked out up front, for the transition. As controlled reform gave way to crisis, between 1987 and 1991, some bureaucrats were managing political change; some in the non-Russian republics, having benefited from the decentralisation of power from Moscow, were preparing for national independence; some, who foresaw or at least sensed that the future was capitalist, began securing power and wealth for themselves and their families in the new system. Some were doing all these things at once. And even for those who didn't move quickly at first, the access that their position provided – to information, to the corridors of power and to foreign-currency bank accounts – was decisive once the Soviet system began to unravel.

Young Communists, Bankers and Bureaucrats who went Capitalist

Key groups of people who went into business under the shelter of Gorbachev's economic reforms were young communist officials, bankers, and state enterprise managers who privatised whatever they were in charge of.

In mid-1986 the Soviet leadership gave a head start in business to officials of the Komsomol (the youth section of the Communist Party of the Soviet Union; see Glossary). Gorbachev had just abandoned his failed policy of speed-up, an attempt to tackle Soviet economic problems with a gigantic productivity drive. He adopted *perestroika* (restructuring of the economy), which meant in the first place loosening restraints on enterprise managers and giving them greater freedom of economic interaction, and allowing non-state trade to expand. Komsomol officials were licenced to set up quasi-state or non-state financial and trading organisations, which gained huge first-mover advantage.

In 1988, some restrictions on foreign trade and foreign currency trading were lifted, and the Komsomol businessmen were well placed to take advantage. Then cooperatives, the Soviet Union's most visible form of non-state business since the 1920s, were legalised. Komsomol officials created thousands of them. In August 1988, the USSR Council of Ministers fixed in law a range of tax exemptions and other economic privileges for Komsomol associations and cooperatives. In December that year, the legal basis was laid for internal tax havens or 'special economic zones', and by the summer of 1990, eleven such zones were operating. Private and 'hybrid' economic organisations accounted for 9 per cent of employment in the USSR by 1990, and 15 per cent by 1991. Probably the most successful Komsomol business, Menatep, formed the basis for Menatep bank, the foundation stone of the empire of Mikhail Khodorkovsky. He became one of the strongest oligarchs of the Yeltsin era, and would be singled out for punishment during Putin's campaign to rein in those oligarchs.

As *perestroika* speeded up and the USSR entered a serious economic and political crisis, the 'Komsomol economy' grew exponentially: its volume rose by 60 per cent per month in 1988–90, researchers at the Russian Academy of Sciences' Institute of Sociology estimated. By 1989 many organisations were counting their turnover in millions of dollars per year. The big money came from financial transactions. For example, Komsomol organisations could take state credits in foreign currency at the 'state' rate of 0.65 rubles to the dollar; so they simply borrowed, and changed the dollars back at 'commercial' rates of up to 18 rubles to the dollar.[2]

The Soviet leadership paved the way for another essential aspect of the Soviet-era capitalism with the banking reforms of 1987–88. These enabled state banks to be privatised by their managers and for other private banks to be incorporated. A first generation of banks, front-runners in accumulating state assets as they were shifted into the private sector, was created. As the USSR collapsed in 1990–91, huge chunks of the gold and money assets of the state, KGB and the Communist party drained into the private sector through these banks. There were three basic types:

1. Privately owned 'zero banks' started from scratch in 1988–90, some of whose owners became key oligarchs: Khodorkovsky's Menatep; Vladimir Vinogradov's Inkombank, founded with a small grant for a Komsomol housing project; and Vladimir Gusinsky's Most Bank and Aleksandr Smolensky's Stolichny Bank, both built up from Moscow construction co-ops. A second generation of 'zero banks', founded in the first couple of post-Soviet years, included Oneksimbank and MFK, both initiated by Vladimir Potanin.
2. Banks spun out of state banks. These could be attached to particular branches of industry, or originate from branches of large state banks. An example is Promstroibank St Petersburg (PSB), which flourished as a private bank in the 1990s, and was sold in 2005 to Vneshtorgbank, a large state-owned bank, for $577 million, in what was then Russia's biggest banking takeover.[3]
3. 'Pocket banks', usually originated in the finance departments of state enterprises, which could then use them for example to embezzle state funds, by transferring credits and resources from the enterprise to a private cooperative.

The state instituted a new system of privileges in 1987–90 by 'restricting many profitable activities to favoured groups' such as the Komsomol officials, Juliet Johnson, the historian of post-Soviet Russian banking, concluded. The private banks became 'intimately involved' in such activities, and facilitated the acquisition of state assets by their former managers. This allowed these key bureaucrats 'to ensure their own positions in the changing economy'. They then had a 'tangible stake in a more decentralised economic system' and supported Yeltsin's campaign to break up the USSR.[4]

The third aspect of the Soviet-era preparations for capitalism was the privatisation of state companies, and even whole ministries, by those in charge of them. These bureaucrats, known as the *nomenklatura* (see Glossary), turned such organisations into joint-stock companies and either put the companies' shares into their own or their fellow officials' hands, or left them in state ownership but entrusted control to their masters via management contracts or trust agreements.

The pioneer of *nomenklatura* privatisation was Viktor Chernomyrdin, the Soviet minister of oil and gas from 1983–89, who in 1989 persuaded the Soviet Council of Ministers to turn the gas industry ministry into a state-owned concern, Gazprom. This was turned into a joint stock company and partly privatised in 1993–94. Gazprom, Russia's biggest company then and now, remained partly state owned, and is to this day heavily influenced by the state. During the 1990s, it served simultaneously as a stabilising factor amidst economic collapse, by providing cheap gas at fixed prices to industry and the population; a power base for Chernomyrdin, who was prime minister from 1992 to 1998; and a honey pot plundered by its managers.

Another product of *nomenklatura* privatisation was Lukoil, today Russia's second largest oil company, put together in 1991 by Vagit Alekperov, who turned himself from acting petroleum minister to Lukoil's chief executive. In 1993 Surgutneftegaz, another of Russia's top six oil companies, was created in the same way by Vladimir Bogdanov, a former ministry official who became its boss.

Soviet–Russian Continuity and Discontinuity

To what extent, then, was the new Russian capitalist class the successor to the Soviet elite? There was discontinuity, for example, in the arrival of newcomers – in the first place, criminals who stole and then legalised wealth. But there was far greater continuity, in terms of the sources of wealth, control of it, and personalities. Research of the post-Soviet business elite by the British academic David Lane showed that among leading financiers, 25 per cent were former Communist Party and Komsomol officials and 56 per cent had backgrounds in the Soviet state apparatus. The figures were lower for industrial executives (16 per cent and 13 per cent), and slightly higher for heads of industrial and financial lobbying groups

(37 per cent and 56 per cent).[5] In the 1990s, former members of the Soviet elite owned and controlled most of the economy's commanding heights; in the 2000s, their dominance was eroded mainly by natural turnover or the appearance of new spheres of business.

During the 2000s, Putin and his colleagues have frequently referred to the 1990s as a time when Russia's wealth had passed into the hands of greedy profiteers, and presented themselves as reversing this trend. This argument – and the sight of oligarchs such as Khodorkovsky being sent to prison – has carried weight with people who suffered sudden and terrible poverty under Yeltsin. But while Khodorkovsky and a few others have been dispossessed, most political and business leaders – including those who acquired wealth just as Khodorkovsky did, by starting in Soviet times – have become richer and stronger.

An excellent example from the political sphere is Vladislav Surkov, deputy head of the presidential administration since 1999, and the person mainly credited with putting together the ideology of 'sovereign democracy' in which Putin has cloaked his authoritarianism. Surkov went into private business in 1987 at the age of 23, quitting the Moscow Institute of Culture, where he had been studying theatrical direction, to join Khodorkovsky's Menatep. Surkov was a leading light at Menatep until 1996. The following year he went to work for ORT, Russia's largest television channel, then controlled by Boris Berezovsky. In 1999, when Berezovsky was perhaps the most powerful man in the Kremlin, Surkov first became one of the organisers of Unity, the political party created from nothing that was instrumental in supporting Putin in 1999–2000. Then he got his job in the presidential administration.[6]

A good example among business leaders is Petr Aven, one of the oligarchs who has flourished under both Yeltsin and Putin. Aven had worked in the USSR's leading systems analysis institute, in 1989 became an adviser to the foreign ministry, and in 1991 head of the Russian federation's committee on foreign economic relations. From 1991 he was Russia's minister of foreign economic relations, and in 1994 became president of Alfa Bank. After 1998, Alfa became Russia's largest bank under private ownership. The Alfa financial-industrial group headed by Aven, Mikhail Fridman and Viktor Vekselberg, of which Alfa Bank is part, also took control of Sual, once Russia's second largest aluminium company, and TNK, one of Russia's largest oil companies, which in 2003 would merge with BP's Russian assets. When Putin became president in 2000, Aven called on him to combine monetarist discipline in economics with respect for the law, as Augusto Pinochet, the Chilean dictator, had. Pinochet had 'produced results for his country' and 'tried to enforce obedience to the law', Aven said, neglecting to mention that Pinochet also presided over the extrajudicial killing of thousands of political dissidents.[7]

These capitalist pioneers who started accumulating wealth under the protection of the Soviet elite have under Putin not only retained their wealth, but led public worship of the strong state.

Oppositions and Alternatives

As the Komsomol businessmen got rich, the Soviet workers – who, despite living in a 'workers' state', had because of repression not been able to organise collectively for decades – emerged as a social and political force. An all-USSR miners' strike in July 1989, sparked by anger over rising prices, soon became a sounding-board for a range of social and political discontents and rallied a movement which spread far beyond the mining towns. It led to the formation of the Independent Union of Mineworkers, the first Soviet trade union organisation since the 1920s that could claim to be independent of the state. There were further strikes in the pits in 1990–91, and lasting changes in terms of revived workplace activism. But most of the union's leaders became stalwart supporters of Yeltsin and embraced privatisation and other rushed 'market reforms'.

The sight of militant workers accepting, or even welcoming, privatisation was hard for many western observers – particularly anti-capitalists, and those who had seen working class interests damaged by privatisation in their own countries – to understand. Many western socialists had assumed that, once the Russian workers' movement found its voice, it would come to the rescue of state-owned property forms and resist the expansion of private capital. Whether the Russian workers *could* have done that is a moot point, but it seems clear that they did not want to. The miners' leaders, and most of the ranks, were in favour of state property being dismantled. Understanding why sheds light on the contradictions of the post-Soviet Russian labour movement.

The Soviet mineworkers had experienced hardship, ruthless speed-up and discipline in state-owned mines – and nowhere else. Their strike sought to right social injustices and to fix deteriorating welfare provision. It aimed to abolish workplace privileges for the Communist party and its members. Insofar as they addressed industrial policy, the miners' concern was to stop supplying coal to the Soviet government at fixed prices. They believed that the coal companies could sell at higher prices on the market, and use the proceeds to improve workers' living standards. If this could not be negotiated with Moscow, then coal should be exported, they reasoned. They had no experience on the basis of which to forecast the impact of international competition on their industry, let alone the slump and unemployment that capitalism would bring to the wider Russian economy. In their eyes, the hated Soviet institutions deserved to perish. The Russian workers' movement has learned much about capitalism, but could only do so subsequently.

In the western left, there were widespread illusions not only about what the workers' movement could rapidly achieve, but also about Gorbachev himself. Nearly all the western parties traditionally associated with the workers' movement expected in the late 1980s that the Soviet Union would somehow renew itself and open up new avenues of change. Most official Communist parties embraced Gorbachev's initiatives, and looked forward to some sort of 'reform socialism'; only once he abandoned the idea of holding the Soviet Union together was he condemned as a traitor. Trotskyists, who had long advocated 'political revolution' to overthrow the Soviet bureaucracy, were divided as to whether Gorbachev was friend or foe, but almost all saw hopes for what they called soviet democracy. Even in the social democratic parties (such as the Labour Party in Britain), 'reform socialism' and 'democratic socialism' became popular themes.

To this day, many believe that, had Gorbachev only been left to continue with his reforms, then the devastation of Russia in the 1990s could have been avoided, and a benign transition to some type of reform socialism achieved. For example Naomi Klein, the anti-capitalist journalist, wrote that Gorbachev was 'moving towards a mixture of a free market and a strong safety net, with key industries under public control'. His goal was 'social democracy on the Scandinavian model', but this 'peaceful and hopeful process' was 'violently interrupted, then radically reversed' by the strongest capitalist powers and international institutions. Klein recounted how US government and International Monetary Fund (IMF) advisers conspired with a small minority of ideologically driven officials to force 'shock therapy' on Russia, a process that culminated in 'extreme acts of terror' such as the invasion of Chechnya.[8]

Without taking anything away from such denunciations of Yeltsin and his advisers, I question the notion that Gorbachev could have offered a better alternative. First, there is no evidence that the Soviet elite, once having unleashed the destructive forces of the capitalist market on the economy, would have been able to put the brakes on. On the contrary, they had lost control of the process at least two years before the Soviet Union finally dissolved in 1991. Second, while Gorbachev was wowing his western admirers with talk of Scandinavian-style social democracy, many in his party machine were preparing for change by energetically privatising the state over which they ruled, in the ways described above. This is not to say that 'shock therapy', or such measures as bombing parliament or invading Chechnya, were somehow inevitable – rather, that the way was already being paved for them under Gorbachev.

The speed at which the Soviet Union collapsed, the extent of the economic and political rot that set in over decades beforehand, the force with which the winds of international capital blew over the mechanisms devised to obstruct them, and the ease with which sections of the elite abandoned Soviet ideology and used their power to assure their position in the new capitalist order, point to two conclusions. First, not only did the Soviet project have nothing in common with socialism, not only did it discredit the name of socialism by associating it with the horrors of dictatorship, but also there were such serious problems with its model of economic development that by the 1980s there was no real prospect that it could be reformed. Gorbachev and his allies, trapped by circumstances, could not realistically have chosen to press on, only perhaps to manage the break-up differently. The Soviet Union could not have been a bastion for twenty-first-century social change. Second, looked at from the standpoint of the history of world capitalism, there are respects in which the Soviet project turned out, notwithstanding its founders' intentions, to be above all the means to push through modernising processes that capitalism required in any case, to industrialise an agricultural country – or rather, a series of agricultural countries – and to prepare them to be reunited with the world market at a later stage. The same could be said of 'communist' China. In my view, it follows from this historical experience that movements for economic and social liberation in future need to place more emphasis on collective action and organisation as the motor of change than on the construction by elites of alternative economic systems.

YELTSIN'S RUSSIA AND THE WORLD (1992–95)

'Shock Therapy' and the Slump

In October 1991, Boris Yeltsin, president of the Russian Federation – then, and for two more months, a part of the disintegrating Soviet

Union – announced an economic reform programme that would become known as 'shock therapy'. It followed a recipe, developed in the United States in the 1970s to impose economic 'discipline' and poverty on Latin American states, of pushing through extreme free-market reforms rapidly, whatever the social cost. The state was to get as far out of the economic sphere as it could, and pull down barriers to the operation of the market and international capital. The main elements of Yeltsin's plan were:

- to abolish most price controls
- to free the ruble's exchange rate (that is, allow the international market to determine it) and loosen currency controls
- rapidly to liberalise trade and business regulation
- to privatise as much state property as possible, as quickly as possible
- to slash state subsidies and cut budget spending.

The programme was pushed through by a group of Soviet apparatus economists who had embraced the monetarist theories of the Chicago-based Milton Friedman* and hence were nicknamed the 'Chicago boys'. The group was led by Yegor Gaidar, first deputy prime minister from October 1991 and prime minister from June to December 1992, and Anatoly Chubais, who headed the state property agency. It was advised, pushed and supported by senior officials of the US administration and a group of like-minded American economists.

'Shock therapy', combined with a steep fall in trade with other former Soviet states, produced an economic meltdown unprecedented in peacetime in any major country. Between 1992 and 1998, gross domestic product (GDP) fell by 44 per cent;** industrial

* Monetarism is an economic theory according to which the supply of money is the key to changes in general price levels. From the 1950s, Milton Friedman and the so-called 'Chicago school' of monetarists argued that inflation could only be controlled by restricting the growth of money supply; they combined this argument with ideas about government playing a minimal role in the economy and giving free rein to market forces. Monetarism dominated the economic policies of the UK and US governments in the 1980s, and was seen as the right-wing response to Keynesian demand management policies favoured by social democracy.

** Supporters of 'shock therapy' point out that this statistic includes the cessation of unwanted production, such as of unused weaponry, to which production fell 56 per cent, slightly more than in the United States during the Great Depression; and capital investment fell to one-fifth of what it had been in 1990. Food production fell to less than half of the average in the late 1980s; the grain harvest fell from 99 million tonnes in 1993 to 48 million tonnes in 1998, way below what it had been before the First World War. Unemployment soared and more than 40 million people were pushed below the poverty line.

The most damaging 'shock' for many people in Russia was produced by price liberalisation in January 1992. The consumer price index rose 1354 per cent in 1992 and 896 per cent in 1993, and got back to double figures only in 1996. The state banks that held people's savings made no move to index link them, and they were obliterated. 'Liberalised trade' took the form of people standing on the streets selling their possessions in order to survive. While millions of families were thus crucified on the altar of monetarism, budget subsidies kept flowing to the bureaucrats who ran state-owned and heavily subsidised businesses, and were in many cases in the process of converting them to private ownership. Generous tax breaks were arranged for insiders: one of the more outrageous scams was the duty-free import of spirits and tobacco by supposedly non-profit organisations, which until 1995 enabled elite groups to corner key retail markets and cost the budget $4–5 billion a year.

The mass privatisation programme launched in December 1992 by Chubais also benefited the elites. All employees were issued with vouchers with which they were theoretically able to buy shares in enterprises: for example, those in which they worked. But those with money capital and information at their disposal were easily able to trick people with no experience of market-based personal finance. Vouchers were soaked up by managers to use in insider sell-offs or by illegal pyramid schemes. Within a year, 90,000 companies had been privatised, mostly by insiders and only 14 per cent of them via a public tender or auction. It was another step in the transformation of bureaucrats into capitalists.[9]

Supporters of 'shock therapy' have argued that the problem was not monetarist theory, but the Yeltsin team's failure to implement it aggressively enough, and his concessions to the *nomenklatura*. But there was never any prospect of Yeltsin turning on the bureaucrats:

---

one might reply that production could have been converted rather than trashed. The figure also takes no account of the large 'grey' (unrecorded) economy. Even so, the overall scale of the slump is not in doubt.

they were a vital bulwark of support. Peter Reddaway and Dmitri Glinski, authors of a history of Yeltsin's reforms, argued:

> The most clear-cut and realistic alternative to the Yeltsin–Gaidar reforms was the continuation and development of the anti-*nomenklatura* upsurge, ... which by the fall of 1991 had taken many of the levers of legislative power out of the hands of the ruling class through elections. It was on the crest of this democratic revolutionary wave that the new elite had been carried into the halls of the Kremlin. ... It was *fear of further change from below* ... that pushed the Yeltsin group towards a strategic alliance with the *nomenklatura* and Mafiya capitalists.[10]

Political, as well as social, chaos engulfed Russia in 1992–94. Government was paralysed by the stand-off between Yeltsin and his pro-market reformers, on one side, and parliament's collection of Communists, nationalists and bureaucratic and regional special interests on the other. Parliament rejected the reform programme and refused to approve Gaidar as prime minister. In September 1993 Yeltsin disbanded Parliament and announced he would rule by decree; the deputies voted to remove Yeltsin and occupied Parliament. On 4–5 October army and interior ministry tanks shelled Parliament, killing and wounding hundreds.* In December, the new Russian constitution was approved in a referendum marred by extraordinary levels of ballot rigging. In a parliamentary election conducted at the same time, protest was registered by voters deserting pro-Yeltsin parties and the Communists. The proto-fascist Liberal Democrats, led by Vladimir Zhirinovsky, received more than 10 million votes. The friction between president and Parliament would continue until Yeltsin retired in 1999.

International Support for Yeltsin

Russia's 'shock therapy' remains controversial internationally because of the support given to it by the major powers and international institutions. The United States in particular stands accused by the left of mobilising political and financial support for the reforms, with a cynical, anti-democratic disregard for the Russian people's wishes and welfare. US advice and support was lavished on Russia's

* The official count was 187 killed and 437 wounded. Independent and Communist party sources said the number of wounded especially was much greater.

'Chicago boys', backed up by a politically inspired programme of loans to Russia by the IMF.

In 1991, when Gaidar, Chubais and their associates joined Yeltsin's government, they began to meet with a group of Harvard-based economists including Jeffrey Sachs and Andrei Shleifer, and a lawyer, Jonathan Hay, who promised advice and support in what they saw as a unique opportunity to implement free market ideology. In 1993 the appointment as international undersecretary at the US Treasury of Lawrence Summers, also from Harvard, gave the group a powerful ally. An extraordinary procedure developed. The US advisers worked out policy measures with Gaidar, Chubais and their colleagues, which were written straight into presidential decrees. Every single significant economic decision of Yeltsin's presidency was implemented this way. Parliament was bypassed.

The Harvard group won control of most of the US government aid money directed towards Russia, spending more than $40 million and managing the distribution of another $350 million before 1996. The advisers set up organisations that straddled public and private roles, such as the Russian Privatization Center and the Institute for a Law-Based Economy, to hurry markets into existence. A handful of bankers helped. One of these, Boris Jordan, born into a family of White Russian emigrés in the United States and in 1992 a banker for Credit Suisse First Boston, recalled that, with Parliament bent on vetoing privatisation, 'Chubais approached me ... with a three month timetable to outwit the communists via a fast track privatisation programme'. Jordan, his partner Steven Jennings and a team of accountants and lawyers, worked 'literally day and night, sleeping in our offices a few hours', to launch the privatisation programme before Parliament met, thus pre-empting such democratic process as there was. 'What my grandfather could not achieve during the civil war, we were able to manage, by getting the state out of property ownership,' Jordan claimed. He and Jennings would go on to head Russia's largest investment bank, Renaissance Capital.

In some of the advisers, high-minded free-market ideology was combined with a prosaic desire to make money. A scandal erupted in the United States over investments made in the infant Russian stock market by Shleifer and Hay and others at a time when they were advising on market regulation. A legal action initiated by a US government aid agency ended in 2004 with a judgement that Shleifer and Hay had conspired to defraud the US government and had broken conflict of interest rules. Harvard, Shleifer and Hay paid the US government respectively $26.5 million, $2 million and $1–2 million, without admitting liability.[11]

Although 'shock therapy' was later criticised by some sections of the US political elite as extreme, it was very much in keeping with the logic of late twentieth-century capitalism. As global financial markets expanded, regulation had been undermined the world over, and poorer states urged to relax their defences against debt, punitive terms of trade and capital flight. The US advisers' contempt for Russian institutions was a natural corollary of this. And the political leaders of the capitalist world themselves used the IMF, a supposedly nonpolitical financial institution, first to help the extreme free marketeers in Russia frustrate their domestic political enemies, and then to prop up the Yeltsin regime financially.

In December 1991, Yeltsin had asked the leaders of the G7 group of the wealthiest countries for a stabilisation loan. Nervous about making a deal that could cause political trouble at home, they referred the request to the IMF. Russia became a member of the Fund in April 1992, by which time Yeltsin had already agreed with its executives on policy priorities on which loans would be conditional. These coincided with the Harvard/Gaidar plan: rapid privatisation and liberalisation, followed supposedly by macroeconomic stabilisation.* The IMF at first loaned relatively small sums to Russia – $2.5 billion in 1992–93 – and the annual rate of disbursement would be three times greater in 1994–98. But in the early period, on the basis of IMF plans, G7 political leaders made public promises of lavish support to Russia, carefully timed to support Yeltsin politically. For example, in April 1993 he arranged a national referendum, effectively as a vote of confidence for his economic policies. A few days before the voting, US president Bill Clinton publicly repeated promises of a $24 billion support package, only about half of which ever arrived, and then mainly in the form of export credits for western companies.

The IMF's strategy changed after the Russian elections of December 1993. Shaken by Zhirinovsky's success and the prospect of Yeltsin losing power, Clinton's Russia adviser Strobe Talbott called for 'more therapy, less shock'. Instead of promises of loans in return for assurances, the IMF now considered larger loans, with looser

---

* Macroeconomics is the branch of economics that focuses on the national economy as a whole. It deals with the stabilisation of economies by means of monetary policy (that is, decisions about how much of the national currency circulates, and exchange rules) and fiscal policy (that is, the state budget).

conditions. It came under pressure from the G7's political leaders to ignore its own rules to ensure Yeltsin's survival. The United States, the Fund's largest shareholder, won the argument that Russia's state finances should be propped up at all costs. John Odling-Smee, a senior IMF official who remained a staunch defender of its Russia policy, later acknowledged that the G7 wanted the IMF 'to lend in order to show support for [Yeltsin], even at times when economic policies or projects were not up to the standard normally required'. And so followed two gigantic loan programmes: of $6.8 billion in 1995, and $10.1 billion in 1996.[12] It would be exaggerating to describe what Yeltsin gave the IMF in return for the loans as a 'policy', but he did accept its dogma of 'fighting inflation'. This meant that, as Russia's new rich turned their fortunes into dollars, the economy was starved of rubles. That in turn produced a crisis of nonpayments, one of the main causes of Russia's 1998 financial crisis.

Capital Flight: The Ransacking of Russia

The true cost of Russia's integration into the world economy is best reflected in the gigantic wave of capital flight it suffered in the 1990s. Capital flight is the abnormal movement of money capital, caused by a country's economic problems and lack of faith in its government and financial system. Economists measure it in various ways: roughly, it is the transfer of assets denominated in one country's currency into assets denominated in a foreign currency, above and beyond normal trade and investment flows. It includes funds whose holders want to escape financial uncertainty or taxation, or who want to launder the proceeds of illegal activity.

In Russia's case, the flight capital included proceeds of oil and other export sales whisked into foreign bank accounts, revenues from legitimate and illegitimate businesses put out of the tax authorities' reach, and proceeds of large-scale theft of state property and other types of crime (for more details, see the box on page 30). Much of it went first to offshore tax havens, and some thereafter into the rich countries' financial and property markets. Capital flight was made easier by the rapidity with which liberalisation was implemented in 1992–93, before effective rules governing markets could be adopted or institutions set up to apply them.

Capital flight from Russia totalled $56–70 billion in 1992–93, and about $17 billion a year in 1994–98, according to research by a group of Russian and Canadian economists. That is $125–140

How the money got away

The main routes taken by capital flight in the 1990s were:

- bad debt, including payment for imports never received, or prepayment on fake import contracts
- nonrepatriation of the proceeds of exports
- manipulation of insurance and transport costs incurred on the export of oil and other high-earnings commodities
- establishment of trading partners in other former Soviet republics, and the export to them of ruble-denominated Russian goods then re-exported for dollars
- the violation of capital controls by banks controlled by big exporters and/or in the process of being bankrupted.[14]

billion in total up to 1998 – more than the aggregate capital flight from Brazil, Venezuela, Mexico and Peru in 1979–87, the years of the Latin American financial collapse. The Russian–Canadian team also produced estimates of internal capital flight, or 'dollarisation' – that is, the use of dollars instead of rubles for savings and transactions within Russia itself. Inside Russia, dollars comprised more than half of the money flow in 1992, and between a third and a half for the rest of the 1990s.

The flight capital was money that, in a successfully functioning capitalist economy, would be invested in the production of goods and services. Had a way been found to keep some of it in the country, Russia's entire loans programme would have been unnecessary. Each year, capital flight was equal to more than half of total budget spending. The whole IMF loan programme to Russia in 1992–98, $22.5 billion, was equal to little more than a year's capital flight. Neither did such capital inflow as there was compensate. When money started to flow into Russia in the late 1990s, it was mostly for speculation in the treasury bond market, rather than productive investment. So capital inflow rose to 44 per cent of capital flight in 1996 and 110 per cent in 1997, but two-thirds of these sums went into treasury bonds. The negligible sum of foreign direct investment into Russia for the seven years 1992–98, $11.6 billion, was equivalent to about six months' worth of capital flight. In the mid-2000s, some flight capital returned to Russia to invest in the oil boom –

although, even then, illicit flows out of the country continued (see Chapter 4, page 78).[13]

In short, the attempt to integrate Russia into the world market by 'shock therapy' sparked an unprecedented exodus of Russian capital, whose owners could not see quick returns in Russia and did not believe their property rights were secure. It almost destroyed investment in productive industry, and acted as a magnet for volatile capital flows seeking quick speculative returns from gambling on treasury bond interest rates and exchange rates.

2

FROM YELTSIN TO PUTIN

The return of capitalism to the post-Soviet space and the economic meltdown left Russia with the epitome of a weak state. The state almost completely abandoned its role as regulator of the economy, collected fewer and fewer taxes and could neither plan nor pay for its budget. As criminal gangs proliferated, the state effectively abandoned its monopoly on armed force. Powerful private interests in the legislature and executive obstructed the adoption of new laws and/or sabotaged their implementation. The two great dramas of 1994–96 – the Chechen war and the presidential election – were played out against this background. To survive these battles, Yeltsin struck a deal that turned a group of the strongest bankers and businessmen into the infamous oligarchy: they supported him politically and received valuable state assets in return. This chapter describes that deal, and its consequences; the impact of the 1990s slump on the Russian population; and the causes, and outcomes, of the 1998 financial crisis.

THE WEAK STATE AND THE OLIGARCHS (1995–96)

Russia's brutal, ill-prepared and unsuccessful war in Chechnya aimed to forestall secession by this republic of about 1 million people, which had resisted Russian rule ever since it expanded into the Caucasus in the late eighteenth century. Chechnya suffered especially savage repression under Stalin, who in 1944 ordered the deportation of the entire population, along with that of neighbouring Ingushetia. Chechnya had declared independence as the Soviet Union collapsed in September 1991, but Yeltsin had never accepted that. In December 1994, indiscriminate bombing of the Chechen capital, Grozny, followed by a disastrous and failed Russian attempt to take the city, killed many thousands. The war underlined the Russian state's perilous weakness. Some commanders and soldiers refused to fight; others traded weapons with criminals that ended up in the Chechens' hands; others engaged in barbaric attacks on civilians. After 20 months and a death toll estimated credibly at 50–100,000, Russia was defeated.[1]

Yeltsin was meanwhile fighting for political survival. His first term was due to end with the presidential election in mid-1996, and from early 1995 panic mounted in the political elite, and among his international supporters. The economic crisis and the war had reduced Yeltsin's approval ratings to single figures. The Communist candidate Gennady Zyuganov, supported by much of the state-owned industrial lobby, was a serious threat. Incumbents can usually influence elections by state spending to influence voters' attitude – and here was Yeltsin's biggest problem. The state was close to bankruptcy and incapable of collecting taxes. By 1996, election year, tax revenue had fallen to 29 per cent of GDP from 44 per cent in 1992 (and GDP had itself collapsed); only two-thirds of what was owing was collected, and half of that was in promissory notes and barter rather than cash. Twenty-six tax inspectors were murdered that year.[2]

Any government in trouble has three obvious places to borrow money: the international financial institutions, the banks, and the treasury bond market. The International Monetary Fund (IMF) stepped up with the loan programmes mentioned above. The domestic short-term treasury bond market took off. But the Yeltsin clique still needed rich backers who could not only supply cash for the government coffers but also finance an election campaign and ensure the right type of media coverage. Thus arose its pact with a group of Russia's most powerful bankers and businessmen, which formalised their political influence and made them into oligarchs: they grabbed chunks of Russia's rich natural resources industries under the 'loans for shares' scheme, and then united to ensure Yeltsin's re-election.

The Oligarchy

The 'loans-for-shares' scheme was devised by Vladimir Potanin, one of Russia's politically best-connected bankers. He had worked as a senior official in the Soviet foreign trade ministry in 1983–90, and used his connections there to launch a trading company, Interros. He also owned Oneksimbank and shared the finance company MFK with Mikhail Prokhorov. In 1995 he proposed that the government should lease oil and other companies to financial and industrial groups such as his own, in return for loans. Yeltsin's privatisation strategist, Anatoly Chubais, approved the plan. The auctions that selected the participants began in September 1995. The procedures were opaque, foreign bidders were excluded and nonapproved Russians elbowed out, the loans were never returned, and the companies were lost to the state. Most scandal-ridden was an $860 million deal that gave Khodorkovsky's Menatep group 33 per cent of Yukos oil company, and a further 45 per cent on lease. Menatep acted as the auctioneer and, through a shell company, the sole bidder; various auction rules were broken; and a rival group accused the finance ministry, which owned 10 per cent of Menatep, of investing in the deal. Potanin's banks also did well, picking up 51 per cent of Sidanco oil company for $125 million and 38 per cent of Norilsk Nickel, the biggest producer of nickel, platinum and palladium in the world, for $170 million.[3]

Another beneficiary of the 'loans for shares' scheme was the mathematician turned car dealer Boris Berezovsky, whose companies picked up a 51 per cent stake in Sibneft oil company for $100 million. Berezovsky had in 1993–94 joined Yeltsin's inner circle. In February 1996 at the World Economic Forum at Davos, Switzerland, an international gathering of politicians, bankers and businessmen, he was stung into action. He and other powerful Russians had watched with concern as Zyuganov worked the crowds: with Yeltsin's regime in meltdown, the international elite saw him as possibly the next president. Berezovsky now brought together Russia's oligarchs in what became known as the 'Davos pact'. They put aside their bitter differences, mostly caused by battles for property, to get Yeltsin re-elected in the June poll. Chubais, sacked from the government after the 'loans for shares' scandal, took charge of the campaign. Media was vital, and of the two national TV stations, Berezovsky effectively controlled the state-owned one, ORT, and Vladimir Gusinsky owned the other, NTV. Yeltsin was pushed to a second-round ballot in July, and narrowly beat Zyuganov.[4]

By the start of Yeltsin's second term, the contours of Russian property ownership were defined. The *nomenklatura* privatisation of 1989–91, the insider deals of 1992–93, and now the 'loans for shares' transactions, had put all the most profitable businesses in the hands of the oligarchs' financial and industrial groups and the Soviet managers turned owners. By the end of the 1990s, large private owners controlled roughly 35 per cent of Russian industry by sales – an ownership structure far more concentrated than in western Europe or the United States, or even in South Korea with its famous *chaebols* (industrial conglomerates).[5] While vast wealth had been transferred from the state to a tiny minority, millions of people were reduced to poverty, and the welfare state that might have helped them was wrecked by underfunding. This was the real tragedy of the transition to capitalism.

Many in the western financial elite, which has never been known for its humanitarian concerns, bitterly criticised the manner of Russian privatisation. They pointed to the yawning gap between the natural resources companies' potential market value and the prices at which they were sold. Financial analysts estimated that Gazprom was worth at least 100 times, and perhaps several hundred times, more than the 1992–93 privatisation prices of its shares had implied. In 1997 they estimated that the 17 largest Russian oil companies, which had gone private for total government receipts (including 'loans for shares') of less than $1.4 billion, had an aggregate market value of $17 billion.[6] These comparisons indicate how the Russian state sacrificed its finances for the oligarchs' sake, but need to be qualified. Russia was still in transition from the Soviet economy, in which aspects of the market were suppressed. The analysts' figures were *potential* market values in an embryonic market. Many Russian prices and asset values were still way out of kilter with international ones. (Thus the oligarchs, for all their entrepreneurial brilliance, were hard pressed to raise even the modest sums needed for 'loans for shares'. Some of them inveigled even more out of the state coffers, for example in the form of discounted treasury bonds, to pay for the deals.)

This leads on to a broader argument. Complaints about 'fairness' in the privatisation process often formed part of a discourse, reflecting western business interests aiming to profit from Russia, that ran through much western media coverage. Western business was concerned less about the Russian state being ripped off than about creating financial markets and ownership rules within which it could best work. It was sure it could gain by writing the rule books itself, as it had when the Harvard/Gaidar group was running things – and assumed, as did the IMF, that its methods are economically and morally superior. The Russian elite had different priorities: the 'loans for shares' auctions were designed precisely to cut a deal with the oligarchs and no one else. So western banks and oil companies were excluded, and doubtless aggrieved at losing an opportunity to outbid the oligarchs, as they could easily have done. Had the western companies participated, more money might have gone into the Russian treasury; the Russian oil industry might now be partly

A woman shows researchers the remains of Yarysh-Mardy village in Chechnya, which was destroyed and abandoned during the war, in December 2006. Photo: Tatiana Lokshina.

controlled by international oil companies, as Kazakhstan's is; and Russia's people might have as little to show for it as Kazakhstan's do. 'Fair' for western business is not 'fair' for Russian people – who, in this example, surely had nothing to gain in 1994–95 from any type of privatisation of the oil and metals resources companies. Western commentary on the battles of money and power in Russia always needs to be read with these issues in mind.

Criminality and Corruption

The near-collapse of the Russian state led to an unprecedented wave of criminal activity, and an abundance of sensationalist commentary about it. There is room here only to mention interpretations of it that make the most sense. The simultaneous breakdown of the state and expansion of private business activity brought into being a market in protection and other types of violence. Law enforcement agencies were in a state of collapse, and anyone starting a business – from humble street traders to bankers and industrialists – needed physically to protect their wealth. There was no effective judicial system, but ways of enforcing commercial contracts had to be found. The sociologist Vadim Volkov points to the appearance from the late 1980s of 'violent entrepreneurs', who offered to businesses both physical protection and 'enforcement partnership'. He shows how the gangs became 'violence managing agencies', with increasingly sophisticated relationships with their clients. Legal businesses not only paid protection money but also used criminal gangs to resolve disputes. The gangs often originated in sports clubs or Afghan war veterans' associations rather than the old Soviet criminal underworld, many of whose inhabitants failed to adapt to the new environment.

From the mid-1990s the strongest gangs began to convert themselves into legitimate capitalists. One example given by Volkov is the *uralmashskie* gang which operated around the Uralmash factory in Ekaterinburg. Former gang members acquired legitimate wealth and by 1999 had set up a political organisation that worked in the regional parliament. A similar process took place in the aluminium industry. In the mid-1990s, 'aluminium wars' between gangs offering protection to the owners of smelters in Siberia claimed 15 lives. But many gang members subsequently made the transition to legal business and politics. Anatoly Bykov, who started out as head of security at the aluminium smelter in Krasnoyarsk, western Siberia, and rose to become its chairman, epitomised this process. Despite having plentiful contacts in the gangs and in 2002 being convicted of murder, he went on to build a successful career as a local politician, businessman and president of the Russian boxing federation.

While the business–criminal nexus is often presented as an exclusively Russian phenomenon, during and after the 'aluminium wars' it also inevitably affected the business of the western trading companies that handled most of the exported metal. A representative of one trading company, AIOC, was kidnapped and brutally murdered. Another, the UK-based Trans World Group, became the largest exporter of Russian aluminium by the late 1990s. Its owners maintained that they had no knowledge of criminal activities by their business partners, and there is no evidence that they did. Bykov, who was a business partner of Trans World, was convicted of murder only after Trans World had sold its Russian business.[7]

Western commentators often claim that Russian criminality has a uniquely post-Soviet quality: that an alliance of former bureaucrats and criminals effectively criminalised the state. Stephen Handelman's book on the subject concludes that these 'comrade criminals' 'eclipsed all other social forces in Russia'.[8] In my view, this overstates the case, and slots in to a western discourse that removes responsibility from the 'shock therapists' for the chaos that engulfed Russia. Criminality thrives naturally, because it is economically logical, wherever capitalism is combined with weak regulatory institutions. (An obvious recent example is the proliferation of fraudulent schemes in the poorly regulated derivatives market. Few Russian gangsters could have dreamed of stealing $450 million, as Samuel Israel III did in this way, let alone spiriting away $50 billion as Bernard Madoff did.)

A related issue is corruption, accusations of which were and are regularly thrown at Russian businesspeople by their western competitors. Anders Aslund, the Swedish 'shock therapy' economist who worked with the Harvard/Gaidar team, argues that 'rent seekers', that is, former bureaucrats who profit more from control of cash flows than from western-type business activity, constitute the *main* obstacle to successful economic reform across the former Soviet Union. Other right-wing economists have incorporated similar assumptions into a broader generalisation about the inherently negative 'grabbing hand' of the state. Such normative arguments flow naturally from the belief that western capitalism's rules and methods could be imposed overnight on the former Soviet states (which was the basic method of 'shock therapy') – but take little account of the way that capitalism actually took shape. The market rules that developed over two centuries in western markets simply did not exist, and networks of personal contacts played a vital role in rebuilding an elite shattered by the Soviet collapse. This was an environment where personal, and therefore potentially corrupt, relationships thrived naturally. But, as in the case of the 'loans for shares' auctions mentioned above, western business viewed the way Russian business worked according to its self-interest. For large volumes of mobile capital to profit most effectively from Russia and other 'emerging markets', the essential thing was to establish capital markets on the US/UK model. Local ownership and local relationships, whether corrupt or not, stood in the way. Western business interests and institutions sought to remake Russia's markets in their own image, not because that was best for Russia's economy or its people, but, usually, because they thought it would maximise returns. And all too often, the western media saw corruption only where it was perceived to obstruct western business.[9]

SOCIETY SHATTERED

The hyperinflation, factory closures and impoverishment of families in the 1990s took a terrible toll on the physical and psychological health of millions. The safety net that survived from Soviet times, the welfare system, had holes ripped in it. This economic and social disaster was the main cause of a unique demographic disaster. People in Russia, especially men, suddenly started to die much younger, on average, than before. Between 1990 and 1995, life expectancy – one of the best indicators of human health and welfare – sank from 63.8 years to 57.5 years for men, and from 74.4 to 71.0 for women. The figures then began to improve again, by 1998 making up more than half the ground they had lost, before falling back during the 2000s. And while mortality (that is, the death rate) rose, the birth rate carried on falling, as it usually does in industrialised societies. More Russians were dying than were being born. The population declined from 148.6 million in 1993 to 142.0 million in 2008.[10]

Some key causes of the demographic decline were long term. Life expectancy in the USSR almost reached the same level as in the United States in the 1960s, but had fallen eight years behind it by 1984. The death rate had risen constantly. One problem was the Soviet health system, which had been very good at eradicating communicable diseases, but bad at providing preventive medicine. Another was alcohol. Men, in particular, died from the same respiratory and circulatory illnesses as in the west, but at a younger age. A stringent anti-alcohol campaign by Gorbachev affected mortality statistics in the mid-1980s; deaths postponed from those years may have exacerbated the crisis of the 1990s. But the central causes of that crisis were associated with the social disruption brought about by the Soviet collapse and the changes that followed. In total, there were 2.5 million excess deaths in Russia in the 1990s, the United Nations Children's Fund calculated. Deaths from fatal events – accidents, injuries, suicides, poisonings and drownings – rose sharply; so did deaths from heart disease. Researchers concluded that many of these deaths, as well as those from alcohol poisoning and cirrhosis, were linked to heavy drinking. The reappearance of tuberculosis in the former Soviet bloc, after decades of decline, and the spread of AIDS and of new multi-drug-resistant diseases, also played a role.[11]

The way that economic transition caused physical and mental illness, and many of the extra deaths, has been the subject of epidemiological and demographic research since the 1990s – although diehard defenders of 'shock therapy' continue to deny its role. In

2009, British researchers who reviewed economic transition and its effect on mortality in all the former 'communist' countries found a correlation between mass privatisation programmes, which had exacerbated unemployment and uncertainty, and higher death rates. They showed that four of the five worst countries in terms of life expectancy, including Russia, had implemented mass privatisation, while only one of the five best performers had done so. They concluded that mass privatisation, and the 'shock therapy' policies that encouraged it, ranked alongside other causes of extra deaths such as 'acute psychosocial stress', reduced access to good medical care, rising social inequalities, social disorganisation and heightened corruption.[12]

As well as the demographic crisis, the social cataclysm of the 1990s had two other special features. The first was the speed at which Russian society became less equal. This was unprecedented, and brought Russia in line with the most unequal societies in Latin America, researchers found. In 1992, the income of the bottom 10 per cent had been one-eighth of the income of the the top 10 per cent, but by 2000 it fell to one-fourteenth. By 2000, 42 million people (29 per cent of the population) lived below the poverty line.[13] The second feature was that, while poverty spread, hammer blows were struck at the often inefficient, but all-embracing, Soviet social welfare system. From 1990 to 1995 real spending on education fell by 40 per cent, and on health by 30 per cent. There was a chaotic rush to decentralise.

The collapse in the value of public sector wages, and the non-payment epidemic, led teachers and doctors to abandon their professions. The government scrapped the Soviet commitment to universal secondary education, and cash-strapped head teachers adopted selective admissions policies, leading to many children, especially adolescent boys, being denied access. In hospitals, free provision was reduced, willy-nilly. Hospitals began to levy payments for medicines, and poverty-stricken health staff routinely began to demand under-the-counter payment. Social welfare hit the bottom in 1996–97. Thereafter, the most extreme market reforms foundered on parliamentary opposition and the non-payment problem receded.[14]

A final point is that 'shock therapy', despite all its destructive power, left key aspects of the late Soviet system untouched. Vital social benefits survived: gas, electricity, water, public transport and other municipal services continued to be provided to urban residents for next to nothing. (The government only started to try to dismantle them in the mid-2000s, and this provoked post-Soviet

Russia's most widespread social movements, described in Chapter 9.) Furthermore, in those factories that survived the wave of closures, aspects of Soviet workplace relations persisted – authoritarian management focused on production targets, combined with paternalistic labour relations and nonmoney benefits (cheap food, childcare, health benefits, even holidays and so on). So slowly did these relationships give way to more typical capitalist ones that some researchers argued that the whole idea that Russia was in transition to capitalism had to be qualified.[15]

The Balance Sheet of Reforms

Even now, public debate rages internationally about 'shock therapy' and its consequences across the former Soviet bloc. Aslund, the 'shock therapy' economist, wrote several books during the 2000s in which he continued to insist that it was the right formula in all the former Soviet countries. Where it failed, that was because it was implemented with insufficient determination. His assumption that the damage done to Russia's people by 'shock therapy' was necessary and justifiable is, in my view, inhumane: 'A severe shock is needed at the level of both society and individual.... It is striking how many resisted change and for how long', he wrote.[16]

Leading economists both inside and outside Russia took up the cudgels against 'shock therapy'. Joseph Stiglitz, the World Bank's chief economist from 1997–2000 and winner of the Nobel Prize, emerged as one of its most vocal opponents. The increase in poverty and inequality was 'one of the most important failures' of Russian government and IMF policy, he argued. He contrasted the disastrous impact of Russia's 'shock therapy' with the improvement in the living standards of hundreds of millions of people during China's economic reforms. This comparison has also been made by the leaders of the Communist Party of the Russian Federation, and Russia's moderate reform economists, such as Leonid Abalkin, who had supported Gorbachev's reforms but opposed Yeltsin's excesses. They point out that the Chinese reform began in agriculture, a sector of the Russian economy left to rot by 'shock therapy'. The movement in China from collective production to the 'individual responsibility' system was a 'partial privatisation' on which the gradual introduction of market mechanisms could be built, Stiglitz wrote. 'The Chinese gradualist approach avoided the pitfall of rampant inflation' that marked Russian reform.[17]

The comparison with China certainly underscores the damage

done to Russia both by Gorbachev's chaotic, unplanned approach, and by 'shock therapy'. The Chinese Communist leaders opted for controlled integration with the world market from the early 1980s, when almost all their Soviet counterparts remained convinced that the Soviet economy could keep going in isolation, and truly became victims of their own propaganda. The Chinese leadership, having thus averted a Soviet-type collapse of the state apparatus – and simultaneously buried democratic aspirations by the suppression of the Tiananmen Square protests in 1989 – oversaw a transition based on a rapid industrial expansion which only began to slow down with the 2008–09 world recession.

But there are two problems with this argument, in my view. First, it presents far too rosy a picture of the expansion of capitalism in China, and says nothing about other paths that human development could have taken there. Second, it ignores basic differences between these two huge countries which guaranteed that capital would flow into China, but out of Russia. China has a population nearly ten times the size of Russia's, most of whom, even now, live in the countryside. This makes for a domestic market that, despite Chinese people's relative poverty, has greater buying power than Russia's. More important still, this is a gigantic reserve of labour power, much larger and cheaper than Russia's. A key driver of China's industrial expansion has been the migration of more than 100 million labourers into the towns, many to work under conditions of brutal exploitation. From the viewpoint of international capital, this is China's vital resource. In 2006 a World Bank report pointed out that labour productivity in Russia, measured by value added per employee, is higher than India's or China's – but 'low labour costs in these two countries give Russia a competitive disadvantage. For each dollar of wages, a Russian worker produces about half the output of an Indian or Chinese worker.'[18]

As international capital renewed its search for higher returns in the 1990s, the choice between China and Russia was easy to make. Not only were Russia's mechanisms of power in chaos, but its workforce was too small, and too well-paid, to compete with China's in investors' eyes. Furthermore, Russia not only had too few people, but also it had too much land over which those people were spread. Through the ages, the size of Russia's territory compared with its population has exacerbated the weakness of its state. In the context of the capitalist world economy into which both Russia and China were integrating, these objective factors, as well as policies, made a difference.

YELTSIN'S SECOND TERM AND THE FINANCIAL CRASH (1996–99)

The crisis that swept the Russian money markets in 1998 was an extension of the East Asian crisis in 1997. And all these events were tremors that preceded the international financial earthquake of 2007–08. The way for these events was paved by low interest rates in the world's largest economies, which had encouraged investors to move billions to emerging markets – at first to Latin America, but after the Mexican crash of 1994, increasingly to East Asia. Share prices, levels of debt and exchange rates became unsustainably high. In August 1997, the financial system in Thailand collapsed and triggered a run of crashes across East Asian markets. Volatile capital flowed out much more quickly than it had flowed in. What the US economist Paul Krugman wrote about the Asian countries also applied to Russia:

> They had become more vulnerable partly because they had opened up their financial markets – because they had, in fact, become better free-market economies, not worse, [and also] because they had taken advantage of their new popularity with international lenders to run up substantial debts with the outside world.[19]

In Russia, that indebtedness was driven primarily by the weakened state. After the 1996 election, key government and administrative posts were handed to oligarchs (Berezovsky, who joined the national security council, and in 1998 served briefly as executive secretary of the CIS, and Potanin, who was deputy prime minister for a year), and to extreme free-market reformers (Chubais, from July 1996 head of the presidential administration and from March 1997 first deputy prime minister in charge of economic policy, and Boris Nemtsov, who was put in charge of social policy and the energy complex). Chernomyrdin remained prime minister. They presided over three aspects of a deepening crisis:

- The nonpayments epidemic. The government and Central Bank – strongly supported by the IMF, in line with its dogma of 'fighting inflation' – had starved the economy of money, causing basic economic relationships to seize up. Government subsidies to or invoices from enterprises, enterprises' bills to each other, and millions of people's wages, were left unpaid for months and years. Noncash forms of payment – the barter of goods, offset arrangements, promissory notes or local government securities – rose from less than 10 per cent of all transactions in 1992 to 54–70 per cent in 1998, according to government statistics. Stories of workers being paid with boxes of shoes, or firms settling bills with stocks of machine components, filled newspapers. Nikolai Shmelev, one of the moderate reform economists, calculated that in 1992–95 prices had risen about 8,500 times, but the total money flow had risen only 230 times. Even accounting for the collapse of industry, the volume of money in circulation in 1996 was 15–20 times lower than required, he argued.[20]

- The state's inability to balance its books. The state was struggling to collect taxes, and things were made worse both by the nonpayments crisis and by the chaotic condition of the tax code. Nominal tax rates remained absurdly high, while special interest groups were handed out tax breaks which together exceeded the size of the budget deficit. A new code had been drafted in 1993, but got bogged down in parliament and was not made law until 1999. The government, having agreed with the IMF not under any circumstances to print more money, now depended more heavily than ever on the Fund's loans, and on money raised by issuing short-term treasury bills, known by their abbreviation, GKOs (see Glossary). The total volume of GKOs outstanding soared from $3 billion at the end of 1994 to more than $70 billion in mid-1998, just before the crash.[21]
- A speculative bubble was inflated by Russian and foreign banks at the state's expense. As interest rates rose, the yields (regular interest payments to investors) on GKOs rose, and new GKOs were issued to redeem previous ones. Foreign banks joined in. They bought up about one-third of all the GKOs in circulation, and arranged currency forward contracts with Russian banks to protect themselves against possible devaluation. In line with the IMF's anti-inflation dogma, the Central Bank repeatedly insisted that it would not allow the ruble to devalue, and in 1997–98 spent a large proportion of its reserves defending the ruble's high level in the international currency markets. The Russian banks were betting that this policy would not change.

In November 1997 the shudders emanating from East Asia combined with these domestic factors to produce disaster. Foreign banks sold $5 billion of their GKO holdings. They pulled money out of Moscow's still embryonic stock market, mostly composed of minority holdings in oligarch-owned companies, sending it into a year-long downward spiral. Oil and other commodity prices were falling, cutting into Russia's already meagre tax revenues. Government floundered: in March 1998, Yeltsin sacked Chernomyrdin from the premiership and replaced him with the inexperienced free marketeer Sergei Kirienko. In April–June 1998, after a temporary improvement, tax collection fell steeply. The GKO market had become a crippling burden on the state's finances, with debt repayment now accounting for 40 per cent of federal government expenditures. The government scrambled to raise money abroad, and in July the IMF announced a $22.7 billion rescue package supported by the World Bank and by Japan.

But by keeping the ruble artificially high and pouring ever-larger sums of money into the banking system via GKOs, the state was running a serious risk of bankruptcy. Something had to give way. On 17 August, the government announced a default:

- The ruble would be allowed to depreciate against the dollar.
- It froze its own ruble-denominated debt repayments and would restructure (that is, reduce and postpone payment on) GKOs.
- It froze certain private-sector foreign debts – including, crucially, those on currency forward contracts designed to protect foreign investors from the effects of a devaluation.

The process of integration into world markets was seriously disrupted. The Russian economy, which had just begun to grow, was pushed back into recession for another year. Many Russian banks – which had bet against the state defaulting, and lost – were effectively bankrupted. In most cases, their owners cut deals with the Central Bank to allow sustainable parts of their businesses to be transferred to new 'bridge' banks. Foreign banks bet, and lost too. They were left holding drastically devalued GKOs and losing billions on unfulfilled currency forward contracts. The biggest known single loss was Credit Suisse First Boston's $980 million.[22]

The crisis led to renewed criticism of the IMF's politically driven lending programme. Economists at the UN Conference on Trade and Development blamed the IMF for leading the Russian government into a blind alley with monetary and exchange rate targets. The anti-inflation policy had 'sowed the seeds of its own destruction' by creating a 'culture of non-payment and an intricate web of arrears'. The 'herd behaviour of international investors' had done much of the rest. The *Financial Times* commented that the IMF should not have lent money to Russia to support the ruble at an 'unsustainable' level – to which the economist Harry Shutt responded that this lending, combined with the absence of exchange controls on which the IMF also insisted, had:

> ensured that domestic interest rates [were] kept at astronomic levels. This in turn ensures that, as long as the exchange rate is kept more or less stable, ... holders of government treasury bills at interest rates ranging from 40% to 100% make super-profits, while local enterprise is strangled, government debt is pushed to ever more unfundable levels, public servants and pensioners go unpaid and millions more are subjected to destitution and premature death.[23]

As a result of the crisis, Yeltsin was forced into something of a retreat from 'shock therapy'. He sacked Kirienko as premier, and tried to bring back Chernomyrdin. Parliament rejected the candidacy. Foreign minister Yevgeny Primakov, more a friend of the state bureaucracy and the moderate reform economists than the free market extremists, became premier. His arrival coincided with a surge of anger among ordinary people about the loss of savings and consumer price inflation that resulted from the crisis. This climaxed in October 1998 with a brief revival of trade union protest. Millions of workers downed tools for a day of action and at least 1 million of them took part in demonstrations. Primakov sanctioned increased state spending, and in particular attempted to address the problem of unpaid wages and benefits. In a nine-month period the government coughed up about $2.4 billion in overdue wages, pensions and social benefits, about 12 per cent of its total budgetary spending.[24] This naturally made Primakov popular, and the Yeltsin clique – by 1999 casting around desperately for a successor to stand in the 2000 presidential election – conspired to sack him in May 1999. He was followed by Sergei Stepashin, who lasted three months, and then by Putin.

3

POWER AND MONEY: THE ECONOMIC FOUNDATIONS

Russia's economy was transformed during Putin's two terms as president (2000–08). Gross Domestic Product (GDP) grew by about 70 per cent, regaining in 2005–06, and then surpassing, the level it had reached in 1990 before the collapse of the Soviet Union. This chapter provides an overview of this boom, and shows how it was driven largely by exports of oil and other commodities. (Chapter 4 covers the changing relationship between state and private capital in the oil and gas sector, and Chapter 5 traces the boom in the wider economy and the recession that followed it.)

HOW THE ECONOMY CHANGED

One measure of the changes effected by the oil boom is the way in which Russia's state finances were turned upside down. When Putin took office, the Russian state owed about $47 billion to the 'Paris club' of state and quasi-state creditors (that is, foreign governments, the International Monetary Fund (IMF) and the World Bank). By 2006 every cent had been repaid, and debts to private creditors, mainly foreign banks, reduced from $84 billion to $35 billion, a small sum by international standards. Between 2000 and 2007, Russia's foreign currency and gold reserves grew 17-fold to $478 billion, then the third largest such pile of cash behind China's and Japan's. In 2004 a Stabilisation Fund was set up, comprising proceeds from oil exports held offshore with a view to long-term investment. This was and is one of the world's largest such sovereign wealth funds.* By 2007, it held more than $150 billion. In

* Sovereign wealth funds are state-owned funds that invest wealth over the long term, as distinct from foreign exchange reserves used by central banks for currency stabilisation and the management of liquidity.

January 2008 it was split into a Reserve Fund and a National Well-Being Fund, the spending of which became a topic of furious debate among Russian politicians.[1]

Another measure of the boom's progress is the change in living standards. The average wage rose more than fivefold in dollar terms, and most people in Russia in many respects regained, and in some respects surpassed, the material level they reached in the late Soviet period. The gaps between the rich and the poor, between the richest and the poorest, and between Russia's rich regions and poor regions, all continued to widen. (These issues are discussed in Chapter 7.) Nevertheless, for most families, the Putin presidency coincided with a continuous improvement in living standards. Russia's health, education and welfare systems began to recover from the disaster visited upon them in the 1990s.

The improvement in living standards is one of two essential elements of the political set-up that evolved under Putin: it is one of the reasons that, in electoral terms, Putin has been one of the most popular leaders in recent history. The other element is the authoritarianism with which the government has confronted political and social opposition.

The Russian financial system was shaken, and the economy thrown into recession, by the world financial meltdown, and the sharp drop in the price of oil that accompanied it, in 2008. Many of the gains of the preceding seven years have started to be undone. In 2008, $210 billion – more than one-third of the oil windfall – was spent supporting the currency and the banking system. In the real economy, the price of failing to diversify further during the boom began to be paid. The credit and property bubbles that accompanied the boom collapsed as quickly as they did around the world. At the time of writing, it is not clear how far this reversal will go.

Table 3.1 shows how the economy, and living standards, collapsed in the 1990s and recovered in the 2000s. The second two columns show the growth of GDP. (Note that prior to the dissolution of the Soviet Union in 1992, the Russian GDP figure is not an accurate reflection of economic activity.) The fourth column is GDP per capita, a statistic designed to reflect the level of a nation's wealth, as calculated by economists at the European Bank for Reconstruction and Development (EBRD); because it is calculated in dollars, it fell in 1998 as a result of ruble devaluation. The last three columns are statistics that reflect the well-being of ordinary people: average wages, the numbers living in poverty, and the numbers unemployed (using the International Labour Organisation's definition).

Table 3.1 GDP and living standards: down in the 1990s, up in the 2000s

Year	Real gross domestic prod. growth, year on year	GDP in billion rubles	Average GDP per capita in US $	People living wage in $/month of total pop'n	below subsistence, %	Unemp. % (by ILO definition)
1989	1.6	0.6	6202.8	n/a	n/a	n/a
1990	-3.0	0.7	8034.9	n/a	n/a	n/a
1991	-5.0	1.4	279.6	22.0	11.7	n/a
1992	-14.8	19.0	565.1	n/a	33.5	5.2
1993	-8.7	171.5	1135.5	n/a	31.5	5.9
1994	-12.7	610.7	1867.5	n/a	22.4	8.1
1995	-4.0	1428.5	2116.1	103.0	24.8	9.5
1996	-3.6	2007.8	2655.5	n/a	22.1	9.7
1997	1.4	2342.5	2750.3	n/a	20.7	11.8
1998	-5.3	2629.6	1802.2	n/a	23.3	13.3
1999	6.4	4823.2	1346.6	n/a	28.4	13.0
2000	10.0	7305.6	1788.7	79	29.0	10.5
2001	5.1	8943.6	2123.4	112.4	27.5	9.0
2002	4.7	10,817.5	2379.8	138.6	24.6	8.0
2003	7.3	13,201.1	2982.8	179.4	20.3	8.6
2004	7.1	16,778.8	4058.0	237.2	17.6	8.2
2005	6.4	21,665.0	5360.5	301.6	17.7	7.6
2006	7.4	26,882.9	6941.9	391.9	15.2	7.2
2007	8.1 (est.)	32,988.6	9062.0	532.0	13.4	6.1
2008	7.0 (proj.)	41,256.1 (proj.)	n/a	694.3	10.5 (est.)	6.3

The Beginnings of Recovery

What were the causes of Russia's economic recovery? Table 3.1 shows that the economy had started to pull out of the slump in 1997, but was set back again in 1998, the year of the financial crisis. The impact of the devaluation on ordinary people was negative. Prices of imported goods went through the roof. Most savers had long preferred dollars, and only 20 per cent of the population even had a ruble bank account – but anyone incautious enough to leave money in one lost heavily. And those who had borrowed in dollars while earning rubles suddenly found themselves with a debt that had quadrupled. Nevertheless, the devaluation, and other measures forced on the government and Central Bank by that crisis, helped to stimulate economic recovery. First, devaluation helped the raw materials exporters (the oil, gas and metals companies) on which the economy depended. The dollars for which they sold their products suddenly bought four or five times as many rubles with which to pay costs (labour, transport and so on). Second, devaluation helped Russian companies producing manufactured goods, including consumer items such as processed food and clothing: the prices of imported goods against which they had been competing shot up. Even regions with no raw material producers or financial centres started to catch up a little.[2]

Perhaps most important of all, the economy began to climb out of the vicious circle of barter and nonpayment of taxes that had paralysed it in the 1990s. Some economists argue that a key role was played, inadvertently, by the Central Bank. It was desperately short of foreign exchange with which to pay off government debts, and so changed the rules covering exporters' foreign currency earnings (that is, mostly dollars, in which most international commodities sales contracts are settled). Previously, exporters had been legally obliged to change 50 per cent of these earnings into rubles – but could do so through their 'own' banks, and/or outside Russia, which made the rule unenforceable. In September 1998 the Central Bank ordered that this 50 per cent of export earnings be exchanged at specific locations in Russia, and that it would itself have right of first refusal. Its aim was to build up its own foreign exchange reserves, but it also caused a huge influx of rubles into exporters' bank accounts inside Russia. Then, argue the US-based economists Michael Bernstam and Alvin Rabushka, enterprise export earnings started to make money available for tax remittances. The level of tax arrears stabilised in 1999–2001, and then fell.[3]

All these factors helped start the recovery, but they pale into insignificance besides rising oil prices, which kept it going. In 1998, international crude oil prices had sunk to around $12 per barrel, their lowest level for nearly 25 years. By 2000 they had more than doubled. They fell back to $22–23/barrel in 2001–02, and then started a relentless upward climb, breaking the $50/barrel barrier in 2005. In 2008 they passed $100/barrel and peaked above $130/barrel. This, more than anything else, explains the Russian economic boom. Russian oil production, which sank from 550–560 million tonnes/year in the late 1980s to a nadir of 305 million tonnes/year in 1998–99, began to climb steadily, reaching 491 million tonnes/year in 2007.[4] Billions of petrodollars flowed back to Russia, and Putin, by reining in the oligarchs, brought many of those dollars into the state coffers. Other commodity markets supplied by Russia boomed, too. The long-term contracts on which Russian natural gas is sold to Europe are linked to oil prices, so gas revenues surged upwards. And some of the factors that drove up oil prices – such as the rapid expansion of the Chinese and other Asian economies – also drove the demand for metals. The revenues from Russia's exports of iron ore, steel, aluminium, nickel and precious metals also rose substantially in the 2000s.

The central place of oil and gas in Russia's exports, and the riches they have provided for the state, are shown in Table 3.2.

From the standpoint of the Russian property-owning class, Putin managed this oil windfall well. His main achievements were:

- He reasserted state control over the oil and gas sector, in terms both of ownership and of tax take. This made it possible to stabilise the state finances.
- In the 2000s, Russia brought back some of the flight capital that had left, although there were also new outward flows. It attracted much more foreign investment than had come in during the Yeltsin period.
- These capital flows provided the basis for the evolution of the Russian stock market, which had been tiny under Yeltsin.
- The banking system was resurrected after 1998, with the oligarchs' 'pocket banks', glorified treasury operations and privatisation mechanisms now superseded by genuine banks that did the things that banks do throughout the capitalist world: borrow money from international markets, attract deposits, and lend to corporate and individual clients.
- Nonoil sectors of the economy – including markets in property, cars and other consumer goods and financial services – began to

Table 3.2 The role of oil and gas

	2000	2001	2002	2003	2004	2005	2006	2007	2008
Oil and gas exports									
Average export price of Russia's oil, $/barrel	24.0	20.9	21.0	23.9	34.1	45.2	56.2	64.4	91.2
Share of energy resources in export of goods, %	n/a	51.2	52.4	54.2	54.7	61.1	63.3	61.5	65.9
Total value of exports, $ bn, of:									
Oil	25.3	25.0	29.1	39.7	59.0	83.4	102.3	121.5	161.1
Oil products	10.9	9.4	11.2	14.1	19.3	33.8	44.7	52.2	79.9
Natural gas	16.6	17.8	15.9	20.0	21.8	31.7	43.8	44.8	69.1
The growing pile of cash									
Foreign exchange and gold reserves, $ bn,	27.97	36.6	47.8	76.9	124.5	182.2	303.7	477.9	427.1
including:									
stabilisation fund, $ bn end of year	–	–	–	–	18.7	42.9	89.1	156.8	225.1*

* In 2008 the stabilisation fund was divided into the reserve fund and the national wealth fund, which at the end of the year contained $137.1 bn and $88.0 bn respectively.

Sources: Central Bank of Russia web site (total value of exports), and World Bank, Russian Economic Report, nos. 1 and 16 (all other figures).

develop, attracting the excited attention of European corporations, for which Russia's population amounts to a market much less developed, and potentially much larger, than they have at home.

None of these changes would have been possible without the rising price of oil and the way that that strengthened the hand of Russia and other producers in the international economy.

THE SHIFTING BALANCE OF OIL POWER

Russia's renaissance as the world's second-largest oil producer after Saudi Arabia, and the steady oil price increases that strengthened producer countries' bargaining position, coincided with another important shift in economic power – away from the privately owned international oil companies (IOCs) based in north America and Europe, towards national oil companies (NOCs), controlled by or linked to the state, based in producer countries. The balance had shifted towards NOCs before, in the 1970s, when some producer countries nationalised oil, and the Organization of Petroleum Exporting Countries (OPEC)* responded to the world economic crisis with price increases. In the 1980s, the pendulum swung some way back towards the IOCs; in the 2000s, it moved in the opposite direction again, towards the NOCs.

The IOCs accounted for most of the world's oil reserves (that is, amounts in the ground that could be produced) until the 1970s, and most production until still more recently. By 2005, NOCs that did not allow any foreign ownership controlled 77 per cent of the world's proven oil reserves, and partly or fully privatised Russian companies controlled another 6 per cent, a major study showed. ExxonMobil, BP, Chevron and Royal Dutch-Shell, the four largest IOCs, ranked 14th, 17th, 19th and 25th in the league table of companies by reserves, far behind Middle Eastern, Russian, African and Latin American competitors.[5] The world's gas reserves are just as unevenly distributed: three countries – Russia (25 per cent), Iran

* OPEC is a cartel, which agrees production quotas, comprising the six large Middle East oil producers, four African producers, Venezuela and Ecuador. It accounts for more than one-third of world oil production. The Soviet Union, and then Russia, stayed out of OPEC to retain independent bargaining power.

(16 per cent) and Qatar (14 per cent) – have more than half the total.

The IOCs are responding to these trends by redoubling their increasingly desperate search for ways to make up the shortfall in their reserves. This drive is supported by governments, who continue to subsidise the oil and gas industry globally, for example through tax breaks on development, which run at about $200 billion a year, compared with $33 billion in support to renewables and nuclear energy. The drive for reserves has pushed oil companies in to the expensive, environmentally perilous business of developing Canada's tar sands, from which oil products can be produced; to brave near-civil war in the Niger delta area of Nigeria; and to follow the US and UK armed forces into Iraq, which has the world's third largest oil reserves after Saudi Arabia and Iran.[6]

For producer countries, the IOCs are not completely dispensable, since they have a good share of the available technical expertise. And as easy-to-access oil gets used up, and reserves get successively more difficult to produce, these skills are at a premium. Nevertheless, during the 2000s the IOCs' reserves hunger, combined with high oil prices, put oil producer countries' governments – including Russia's – in a uniquely favourable bargaining position. Across the world, producer countries sought to improve the terms on which they allow IOCs to participate in producing their oil.

Power and money: Vladimir Putin, then president (left), and the aluminium magnate Oleg Deripaska at a business conference in Vietnam in 2006. Photo: RIA Novosti.

This issue was at the heart both of the Russian state's tussles with foreign oil companies, and indirectly of its clashes with Yukos and other privately owned Russian companies. But this is an international phenomenon. In 2007, the Venezuelan NOC unilaterally raised its stake in foreign-controlled projects in the Orinoco oil field. In 2007–08, Libya renegotiated agreements with French, Italian and Spanish oil companies to give its NOC a greater share of projects in the country. Headline writers fond of the idea of 'oil nationalism' focus on such actions by governments politically hostile to the United States, but friends of the United States have demanded a bigger share of the pie too. Algeria, for example, in 2007 tore up a deal with the Spanish energy group, Repsol, to develop a gas field, deciding it could do it more profitably itself. Kazakhstan, the former Soviet Union's second-largest oil producer – which has been generally more welcoming than Russia to US and European companies – in 2007 renegotiated the production sharing agreement (PSA) with a group of foreign companies covering the Kashagan oil field in the Caspian Sea. The foreign companies will pay more tax, and Kazmunaigaz, the Kazakh NOC, will increase its share. NGOs monitoring the oil industry argue that the Kazakh treasury still gets a raw deal. But the episode shows that producer countries, regardless of political colouring, are seeking a bigger share.[7]

The Demand for Russian Oil and Gas

The relative decline of the IOCs mirrors big changes in early twenty-first-century capitalism. As the oil-guzzling economy has expanded in recent decades, seeking new means of reproducing capital and ratcheting up the danger of global warming, it has used up many of the oil and gas reserves in areas most securely under the strongest capitalist powers' political control. One symptom of this problem is the IOCs' reserves hunger; another is the rich countries' failure to reduce their dependence for year-by-year purchases of oil and gas on a limited group of producer countries, many of which they see as unreliable or hostile. From this standpoint, the emergence of Russia from the Soviet Union in 1992 was a potential boon: a source of energy supplies independent of the Middle Eastern producers and OPEC. From 1998, as oil demand and prices rose – and Russia pulled out of its slump and began to recover shortfalls in oil production – the rich countries began to see Russia as an increasingly important source of non-OPEC oil, and to wonder whether its production growth could be sustained over the longer term.

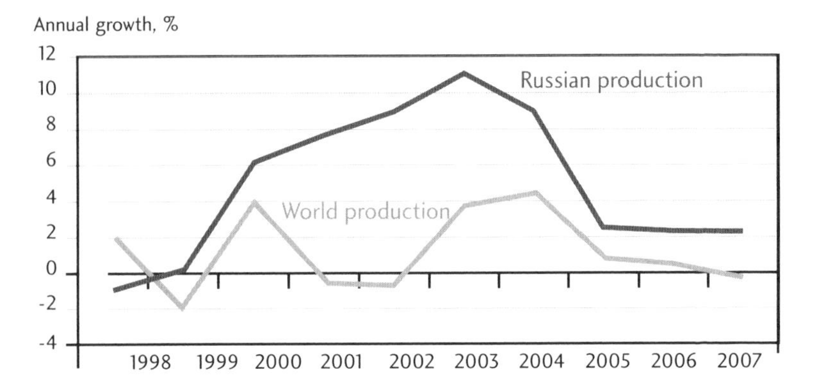

Figure 3.1 Russia and world oil production growth, 1998–2007
Source: *BP Statistical Review of World Energy.*

From 1998 to 2004, as world oil production grew at snail's pace, partly because of the IOCs' reluctance to invest, production in Russia and other former Soviet states rose rapidly. In those seven years, 60 per cent of incremental global oil supply – that is, of the amounts being added to the total – came from the former Soviet Union (mainly Russia, Kazakhstan and Azerbaijan). Russia's production rose steadily for a decade, from 304 million tonnes (8.6 per cent of the world total) in 1998, to 491 million tonnes (12.6 per cent) in 2007. Russian and world production growth are compared in Figure 3.1.

The former Soviet Union will likely remain both the largest source of additional non-OPEC oil, and the largest oil producing region outside OPEC, for a long time – but OPEC's share of total production will probably increase again in the coming decades. Economists at the Organisation for Economic Cooperation and Development (OECD), the rich countries' club, argued in 2006 that this was 'a matter of concern', since the OPEC countries could always decide collectively that there is 'no incentive to increase output so rapidly', limit production, and take profit from higher prices. This 'prospect of rising dependence on OPEC – and in particular on Middle Eastern OPEC' made developing supply from non-OPEC countries including Russia 'even more important' in order to weaken OPEC's hand, they said.[8]

The conclusion? Despite rich country governments' talk about cutting production of carbon-heavy energy, and the Kremlin's talk about reducing over-dependence on oil exports, both sides hope that Russian oil and gas production will rise in the coming decades. The

Russian government's Energy Strategy, covering the years to 2030, projects a constant increase in output. That in turn begs another question – about how the large-scale long-term investments necessary to produce and deliver the oil can be assured. (See box.)

Oil and gas investment

The debate around investment in production and pipeline infrastructure throws light on the tensions between oil and gas companies, the Russian government and international institutions. In the early 2000s, the Russian oil companies pumped easy-to-produce oil, as fast as they could, from fields that had been explored, supplied with infrastructure and started up in Soviet times. The expensive business of exploring and developing new fields was postponed. Capital expenditure in the oil fields tripled between 1999 and 2003, but most of that went into low-cost opportunities to boost output at existing fields – the 'low-hanging fruit', as a report by the International Energy Agency, which represents consumer countries, called it.[9]

This was the naked profit motive at work. The greatest production increases were achieved by companies such as Yukos and Sibneft, owned by financiers who – correctly, as it turned out – feared that their rights to the property were not secure in law. The companies' harshest critics accused them of using slash and burn methods. 'Aggressive recovery' techniques for pumping additional oil out of existing wells had helped 'to improve short-term results at the expense of the future', analysts at Alfa Bank argued. They noted that after five years of leading the world (1999–2004), Russian production growth fell back after 2005 to 2–3 per cent. During 2005–07 capital expenditure continued to rise, but only because it was racing to keep up with soaring costs. This approach could only postpone, but not reverse, the natural decline in production, which happens when fields start to run out of oil. Investment was also needed in pipelines.[10]

Similar dilemmas faced the gas industry. Gazprom's largest fields in western Siberia have been in natural decline since the 1990s. Gazprom maintained output largely thanks to a new field that started up in 2001, Zapolyarnoe. But both Gazprom and the government continually hesitated to commit resources to the only project large enough to replace western Siberian gas in the long term, on the Yamal peninsula in the far north. And no wonder: it will cost more than $20 billion and involves settling scarcely inhabited wastes north of the Arctic circle and building pipelines across permafrost.[11] At the time of writing, with the recession depressing demand for gas, worries about getting Yamal ready in time have eased. As long as demand, and energy prices, stay down, the debate about long-term investment may be pushed into the background. But it cannot and will not go away.

Meanwhile a quarrel between Gazprom and the oil companies over investing in gas pipeline infrastructure has exacerbated one of Russia's most serious environmental problems. The oil companies could produce substantial amounts of gas, if pipelines were put in place. This includes associated gas, which comes out of the ground with oil and is currently flared (burned off at the wellhead). Such flaring is one of the international oil industry's dirtiest habits: the gas is almost pure methane, which produces a stronger greenhouse effect than carbon dioxide. But building infrastructure to take the gas away, store it or pump it back into the ground is difficult and expensive, so flaring is practised internationally to keep oil production costs down. Putin said in 2007 that Russia was flaring 20 billion cubic metres (bcm) a year, and had to stop. But things could be even worse. A research group that measured flaring with satellite imaging reported that Russia had probably overtaken Nigeria as the world's biggest flarer, and in 2004 may have flared up to 50 bcm of gas, more than France's consumption.[12]

RUSSIA AND THE RESOURCE CURSE

While the oil boom has made Russian power more assertive, and tilted the economic balance towards it and other energy-producing states, it has also masked failure to address other economic weaknesses – specifically, the poor state of agriculture and the machine-building and processing industries. Economists have been disputing whether Russia is prone to the 'natural resource curse'. This concept describes a situation in which abundant natural resources* may produce short-term benefits, such as big export revenues, but potentially damage long-term economic development. Economists define the 'natural resource curse' in various ways, but usually point to three manifestations of it:

- the way that dependence on natural resources export revenues puts a national economy at the mercy of external factors, in particular the unpredictable level of those revenues
- the 'Dutch disease',** that is, the negative economic effect of a natural resource boom on other sectors of an economy, and especially the way that big export revenues strengthen a country's currency, making manufacturing and agriculture less competitive and reinforcing dependence
- a range of social and institutional effects, including exacerbation of social inequality, greater corruption, and 'rent seeking' (in this context, efforts by elites to grab control of export revenues); some authors have argued that oil revenues undermine democracy.[13]

It is difficult to compare Russia with other petrostates (states whose economies are based on oil exports) because of its so obviously exceptional history. Between the 1920s and 1940s, Russia, then within the Soviet Union, underwent rapid industrialisation and politically and militarily became a great power. Other petrostates that benefited from recent oil booms (Saudi Arabia, Iraq, Libya, Indonesia, Venezuela, Nigeria and so on) were less industrialised, and are not great powers. Nevertheless, the three phenomena listed above clearly apply to Russia to some degree. First and foremost, while average living standards have risen substantially during the oil boom, inequalities of all kinds have increased. Some types of corruption have increased too. Russia has also suffered from the 'natural resource curse' if measured by narrow economic criteria. The proportion of export revenues from oil and gas sales has grown constantly, and a big chunk of what remains is from other raw materials exports, mostly metals. This made it possible to turn the ruble into a strong, internationally convertible currency – which in

* 'Natural resources' here refers to resources provided by nature, and mainly those with a high market value – oil, gas, metals and minerals, but also coal, coffee and other agricultural products. Natural resources understood more widely includes land and other renewable resources.

** So called because the expression was coined to explain the effect of North Sea gas production on the Dutch economy.

turn exacerbated the competitive disadvantages suffered by Russian manufacturing and agriculture.

Russia has applied the best practices economists have come up with for managing the huge build-up of petrodollars, that is keeping them in offshore funds as a safeguard against future oil price falls and for use in state-led development projects. A large chunk of those funds was spent in 2008 to stabilise the financial system. But in terms of stimulating other areas of the economy, let alone tackling inequalities, the government has largely missed the chances provided by the oil boom. Putin acknowledged as much in 2008, when he said Russia had 'still not yet succeeded in breaking away from the inertia of development based on energy resources and commodities'. The state is 'weighed down by bureaucracy and corruption and does not have the motivation for positive change', he added.

Western critics have related Russia's 'natural resource curse' to its model of state-led capitalist development. Some of them say that the 'curse' has been exacerbated by increasing the state's role in the oil and gas sector, since that has opened the door to corrupt and 'rent-seeking' behaviour by bureaucrats. The implication is that Russia would be better off opening the oil and gas industry to majority foreign ownership. That might boost the IOCs' earnings, 'but would it benefit Russian workers and consumers, and lead to lower levels of corruption?', the economist Peter Rutland wrote in response to such arguments. 'Neighbouring Azerbaijan and Kazakhstan have pursued such a path, but are hardly models of democratic accountability.'[14]

The 'natural resource curse' discussion usefully highlights the damage that oil-producing nations, including Russia, do to themselves by prioritising energy exports. But in my view it leaves out of account two relevant issues. First, it is not inevitable that Russia's, or any other country's, natural resources will forever be owned by private capital or by a state that serves its interests. If the presence of a property-owning class in society is seen as immutable, then the 'natural resource curse' discussion is limited to considering how individual states might overcome the problems created by that class's control of resources, such as social inequality and corruption. For those who remain optimistic that society can do better, and supersede the power of the property owners, compelling solutions to such problems will be found in the context of collective management and control of resources.

Second, Russia is a petrostate not just because natural resources exports feed the wealth and power of its elite, but also because the oil and gas-consuming countries in north America and western Europe have continued to gulp down those fuels ever more rapidly, and have encouraged newly industrialising countries such as China and India to follow oil and gas-intensive paths of development. But the 'natural resource curse' discussion usually assumes that the demand from the world economy for oil, gas and other natural resources will remain constant or increase, always placing in front of resource-rich nations the temptation to rely on exports to an unhealthy degree. Why? It is pretty universally accepted first, that the oil and gas-guzzling model of capitalist development will, within a few decades, present the danger of horrible and largely unpredictable environmental change, and second, that long-term economic development depends on prioritising energy saving and the development of noncarbon energy sources.

In the long term, the sort of fundamental changes needed in the rich countries, in any case, to minimise the risk of climate change, should also reduce demand for hydrocarbons and remove the incentives to invest in their production. I seriously doubt that capitalist economies can make such adjustments, given that they have so many opportunities to profit from energy-intensive industrial expansion. That is why carbon pricing and taxing schemes are being introduced at a pace environmental scientists regard as ruinously slow. Capitalism's inability to face these issues amounts to another convincing reason why it should and could be overtaken by a more just form of society. And lasting solutions to the 'natural resource curse' will surely be found in the course of such a change.

4

POWER AND MONEY: THE STATE, OLIGARCHS AND OIL

Putin and his collaborators pulled the Russian state out of the chaos of the 1990s and centralised it. They moved against the Yeltsin-era oligarchs in the interests of the property-owning class as a whole – a process that climaxed with the Yukos affair of 2003–05. An important part was played by the *siloviki* (former military and security services officers brought into government: see Glossary). They strengthened state control of, and the tax taken from, the oil industry, and used it to redefine Russia's relationship with its former Soviet neighbours. But, as I suggest in the next section, they were only one part of a team which also includes market reformers seeking to develop Russia's economy along capitalist lines. The character of the cooperation between *siloviki* and market reformers has been obscured in the western media. Whereas in the 1990s, it used caricatures of corruption and criminality to portray Russian capitalism, in the 2000s there was a new stereotype to play with: a grab for state power by the security services. Some newspapers painted lurid pictures of a regime of 'spies'. The London *Daily Mail* warned that 'the ruthlessness and ingenuity of gangsters and terrorists' has combined with Russia's 'superpower' resources to pose 'a profound threat to our way of life'.[1] In contrast, I describe in the next section how Putin was promoted to succeed Yeltsin not by a sinister KGB conspiracy, but by an alliance of Yeltsin's cronies, *siloviki* and 'market reformers'. Putin brought *siloviki* into the state apparatus to help reverse the damage done to it in the 1990s – but that state was, and is, far from being a 'superpower'.

ENTER THE MEN FROM THE KGB (1999–2002)

When the Soviet Union was dissolved in 1991, the KGB had more than half a million employees. Spying on Soviet citizens and foreign governments was only one of the KGB's jobs. It also policed the USSR's thousands of kilometres of borders; coordinated the repression of dissidents; and ensured the security of transport links and state communications – huge tasks under a dictatorship that relied on limiting freedom of movement and depriving citizens of information. In the early 1980s, the KGB's remit for combating 'economic crime and corruption' brought it into sharp conflict with other sections of the Soviet elite: it famously targeted the Soviet leader Leonid Brezhnev's daughter, Galina, and her criminal associates.[2] The KGB came out on top. When Brezhnev died in 1982, he was succeeded as Communist party general secretary by Yuri Andropov, who had for the previous 14 years been the KGB director. Andropov's war on the Soviet mafia, waged from the pinnacle of the hierarchy, was a precursor to Gorbachev's reforms.

The KGB's leaders, like their colleagues in government, the Communist Party hierarchy and the military, witnessed the effects of those reforms with growing apprehension. In 1991, as Ukraine and other Soviet republics declared independence, Andropov's successor as KGB head, Vladimir Kriuchkov, together with the defence and interior ministers and other conservatives, attempted to stall the process. On 19 August 1991 they set up a 'state emergency committee' and announced that they had deposed Gorbachev, who was on holiday. Only Gorbachev and his most avid defenders still insist he had no part in it: he had three months earlier given the KGB sweeping new powers, and there is plentiful evidence that he knew of the coup plotters' plans and may even have indicated approval. In any case, the coup failed. The attack by protesters on the statue of Feliks Dzerzhinsky, the founder of the Soviet security forces, outside the KGB's Moscow headquarters, became the iconic image of the defeat of the coup. In October 1991, Gorbachev abolished the KGB and replaced it by three separate agencies. In post-Soviet Russia these were superseded by the foreign intelligence service, the presidential security service and the ministry of security. The federal security service (FSB) emerged from the latter, after several reorganisations, in 1995.[3]

Yeltsin dispensed with Kriuchkov and a few other senior *chekisty* (that is employees or former employees of the KGB and FSB: see Glossary). But he skilfully deployed the bulk of the organisation to defend his power – further proof, were it needed, of the hollowness of his claims to be a 'democratic' hero. *Chekisty* rose to the highest positions. In 1993–96 Aleksandr Korzhakov, head of the 4,000-strong presidential guard, successor to a section of the KGB, ran a 'kitchen cabinet' in the Kremlin and supervised Yeltsin's every activity, until he was sacked at the start of Yeltsin's second term. Yevgeny Primakov, foreign minister in 1996–98 and prime minister in 1998–99, moved into government from the helm of the foreign intelligence service, successor to the KGB's foreign intelligence directorate.

The explosion of private wealth, and orgy of looting from the state, in the early 1990s had as powerful an impact on KGB officers as on the rest of the Soviet elite. They, too, wanted their piece of the pie. Their contacts, exceptional understanding of institutions, and training in economics, research and information gathering, made many of them well placed to get it. It was survival of the fittest, and they were often fitter than others. The main paths into business for *chekisty* were:

- Before the Soviet Union dissolved, KGB officers engaged in *nomenklatura* privatisation – the establishment of private businesses grafted on to state structures – as described in Chapter 1. In 1990, some *chekisty* opened a semi-private cooperative, ANT, which secretly exported Soviet weaponry. In the early Yeltsin years, similar plays on the KGB's expertise were legally sanctioned.[4]
- High-level *chekisty* quit state service and ran security or information services in the oligarchs' empires. Those oligarchs who claimed most loudly to be champions of 'democracy' employed *chekisty* with the most fearsome CVs. Filipp Bobkov, former head of the KGB directorate that specialised in hunting Soviet dissidents, took charge of the research department of Vladimir Gusinsky's Most Bank. Another veteran of that directorate, Aleksei Kondaurov, worked for Yukos, Khodorkovsky's oil company, from 1994 until 2003, and then entered parliament as a Communist deputy. Others went freelance.[5]
- A large contingent of middle and lower-ranking *chekisty* went into banks' and companies' security departments or private security firms. In 1995 ex-KGB men were estimated to account for half of all security firms' workforces, with former internal affairs ministry and military officers making up the rest. (In 2002 the private security sector regulator estimated there were more than 280,000 registered security staff, and more than half that number again who were unregistered – less than one-seventh of the number in the United States.)[6]
- Other *chekisty* simply went into business. An example is

> Aleksandr Lebedev, who worked in foreign intelligence in the 1980s and in 2008 was Russia's 39th richest man; by 2008 he controlled shares in banks, leasing companies, 30 per cent of the national airline Aeroflot and 1 per cent of Gazprom. To Lebedev's credit, he is also a 49 per cent shareholder of *Novaya Gazeta*, the only significant liberal opposition newspaper that survived until the late 2000s. In 2009 he bought the London *Evening Standard*.[7]

There was no doubt that greed was a major factor in the motivation of *chekisty* who moved into business. But that was not the whole story. Many viewed themselves as upholders of the national interest. There seems no reason to doubt the sincerity of Igor Goloshchapov, head of a private security firms' business association, when he told a western journalist:

> In the 1990s we had one objective: to survive and preserve our skills. We did not consider ourselves to be separate from those who stayed in the FSB. We shared everything with them and we saw our work as just another form of serving the interests of the state. We knew that there would come a moment when we would be called upon.[8]

It would be pushing things too far to say that the *chekisty* have a shared ideology. But along with ideas such as Goloshchapov's about state service, they do seem overwhelmingly to have embraced the perceived virtues of capitalism as a social system. For all the hundreds of times this author has heard, or read about, *chekisty* – from Putin down to the humblest bodyguard – privately or publicly praising capitalism, he has never heard them advocating Soviet-style nationalisation.

The Handover from Yeltsin to Putin

Putin was elevated to the presidency not by a KGB plot, but by Yeltsin's corrupt entourage. Putin had quit the KGB and joined its 'active reserve' in 1991. The future president returned from East Germany, where he had been posted, to his native city, St Petersburg. There he joined the team of administrators around Anatoly Sobchak, a pioneering right-wing 'market reformer' and mayor of the city in 1991–96. In 1996, Sobchak narrowly failed to get re-elected. Pavel Borodin, head of Yeltsin's presidential administration, encouraged Putin to move to Moscow, and Aleksei Kudrin, an economist from St Petersburg who headed the Kremlin's chief inspection directorate, helped find Putin a job. (Kudrin would go on to serve as Russian finance minister from 2000.) Putin then rose rapidly: he was appointed Borodin's first deputy in May 1998, and director of the FSB in July 1998.

By this time the Yeltsin clique was working obsessively to find a suitable candidate to take over as president at the elections in 2000, and the prime minister's job was the best place to put him. In May 1999 Yevgeny Primakov had been sacked from that post, and joined Moscow mayor Yuri Luzhkov in building a parliamentary opposition to the Yeltsin clique. Primakov was replaced by Sergei Stepashin, another candidate being considered to replace Yeltsin. He in turn was discarded in favour of Putin. The consensus among Kremlin-watchers is that Putin had the full support of Yeltsin's most powerful cronies: that is, Berezovsky, Yeltsin's daughter Tatiana Dyachenko and future son-in-law Valentin Yumashev, and Aleksandr Voloshin, Borodin's successor as head of the presidential administration.[9]

When Putin started as president, he relied, above all, on three groups of people to refashion the state apparatus:[10]

- *siloviki* whom he appointed to key posts
- his former colleagues from St Petersburg, and especially the market reform economists and administrators
- veterans of Yeltsin's administration, who were gradually eased out during Putin's first term – most notably Voloshin, who finally quit in 2003.

The *siloviki* who rose rapidly with Putin included Igor Sechin, who in the mid-1980s served as a military interpreter in Mozambique and Angola, a post that would normally have been open to KGB officers only. Sechin worked in Sobchak's team in the early 1990s, followed Putin to Moscow in 1996, and served as deputy head of the presidential administration throughout Putin's presidency. Sechin became a key figure in the drive to bring oil and gas assets back into state ownership, and in 2008 became deputy prime minister for energy and industry.

Another key figure is Viktor Cherkesov, who worked in the KGB from 1975 and headed the St Petersburg FSB from 1992 to 1998. He was brought to Moscow by Putin when the latter briefly headed the FSB in 1998, was appointed presidential representative to the North West Federal District in 2000, and moved from there in 2003 to head Russia's anti-drug-trafficking agency. In Soviet times Cherkesov worked in the KGB directorate that undertook surveillance of dissidents, and in 1996 supervised the notorious prosecution of Aleksandr Nikitin, a navy captain who had blown the whistle on nuclear pollution in the Barents Sea.[11]

The Petersburgers who have largely directed economic policy under Putin have been no less an important part of his team. Dmitry Medvedev, who succeeded Putin as president, was among them; so was German Gref, a legal adviser to Sobchak's city administration in the early 1990s, who served under Putin (2000–07) as the minister of economic development and trade, guiding privatisation policy and other pro-market reforms, and in 2008 took over as chairman of state-owned Sberbank, Russia's largest bank. Kudrin has been the longest survivor, and remains finance minister at the time of writing.

In many ways the story of Putin's presidency has been one of the state regaining the strength that it had largely lost in the 1990s. The *siloviki* have played a key role in this, and, in the process, become stronger as a group in comparison with the economic reformers. Exaggerated misreporting of these processes is widespread. For example the journalist Edward Lucas claims that the KGB has thereby 'seized power in Russia'. Yuri Felshtinsky, a close associate of Berezovsky's, writes of an 'experiment' by the Russian 'secret police' aimed at obtaining 'absolute control over Russia and its resources'.[12] In response, I offer the following points:

- None of the nominally democratic states of western Europe and north America has ever been thrown into an economic crisis as deep as Russia's in the 1990s, or suffered an analogous collapse of the tax system. That collapse threatened the Russian state's ability to carry out many of the state's typical functions in capitalist society, such as providing frameworks for the economy and protecting private property. The assault on the oligarchs and the expansion of the state's role in the oil and gas sector was above all a response to these extraordinary problems.
- Even after that attack, the state's role in Russia's oil and gas sector remained less significant than it is in many countries that provide the western powers with both oil and political cooperation – including Saudi Arabia, Kuwait and Mexico, where 100 per cent state-owned companies dominate. What has really irked the western elite is the lack of respect for private owners' 'property rights'.

- While the *siloviki* often instinctively opt for state control and initiative, their attachment to such methods is no more ideological than the attachment to 'free market' dogmas of US Republicans. It was they who, when US capitalism ran into significant problems of its own in 2008, undertook the biggest series of state takeovers in history (of the AIG insurance company and others) and the biggest state-supported bank rescue in history.
- The *siloviki* have left key areas of economic policy, such as the liberalisation of markets, to the economic reformers. Conflicts between the two groups are more often about spheres of interest being threatened than about matters of principle. Both sides agree that the state's job is to provide the best possible working conditions for Russian capitalism.

What the *siloviki* brought to the Russian state was not the threat of wholesale 'Soviet style' nationalisation, nor totalitarianism, but ways of adapting Soviet methods of administration and control to the needs of the new, twenty-first-century, Russian capitalist class.

How Putin Consolidated Control

During Putin's six months as prime minister and his first two years as president, his priorities were to centralise the state apparatus, to regain control of key taxpayers starting with Gazprom, to widen the regime's fragile base of popular support, and to isolate and silence political opposition where necessary.

Ten days before Putin took over as premier, the republic of Dagestan, which borders Chechnya, was invaded by Islamist militants. This put a weapon in the Kremlin's hands: within a month, it had launched the second Chechen war. Putin travelled ostentatiously to the front line and talked tough on television to boost his popularity ratings. Against this backdrop, Berezovsky's political manipulators created from scratch a pro-Kremlin parliamentary party – Unity. This assured success in the parliamentary elections in December 1999 and the presidential poll in March 2000, and provided a political base for Putin that Yeltsin had lacked for most of his presidency. Once elected, Putin reversed the centrifugal motion of Russia's federal state and subordinated regional leaders materially and politically to the centre. He divided Russia into seven federal districts and appointed presidential representatives – most of whom, and most of whose deputies and staff, were *siloviki* – to bring the 83 subjects of the federation to heel. These political processes are discussed further in Chapter 6. Here the focus is on the battle, fought simultaneously, to reinforce state control over Gazprom, Russia's biggest company. This was the first step towards taking back from the oligarchs some of the natural resources wealth they had grabbed in the 1990s.

Gazprom's unique position in the 1990s was mentioned in Chapter 1. While the oil barons profited from exports, Gazprom sold most of its output domestically, effectively subsidising the economy with gas that was cheap, and often not paid for. In return for this support, the state lavished political favours and business opportunities on Chernomyrdin, his successor as Gazprom boss Rem Vyakhirev, and their management team. But in 1998–99, as political paralysis overtook the Yeltsin administration, a real danger materialised that control over Gazprom would slip out of the state's grasp. First, Chernomyrdin lost the prime minister's job and thereby his presidential ambitions. Next, in 1999, Vyakhirev deserted the Kremlin gang and joined the opposition led by Luzhkov and Primakov. Under Chernomyrdin's government, the state's 38 per cent share in Gazprom had been transferred to Vyakhirev in trust, and people in the Kremlin feared the state might never get it back. In June 1999, shortly before Putin was appointed prime minister, Vyakhirev had contrived at a Gazprom shareholders' meeting to limit state representation on the board, in defiance of a government instruction. In August, as soon as Putin took over as prime minister, the *siloviki* persuaded Vyakhirev to abandon his opposition stance.

Another essential weapon in the opposition's armoury was NTV, then the only nonstate national television channel. It was controlled by the oligarch Vladimir Gusinsky. He gave its exceptional team of journalists free reign to provide relatively balanced news coverage, which was easily the best available to most people in Russia. It was an effective counterpoint to the defamatory campaigns against Luzhkov and Primakov being run by the other national station, ORT, which was controlled jointly by the state and Berezovsky. Within days of Putin's inauguration as president on 7 May 2000, his administration turned fire on Gusinsky's business empire, including NTV. On 11 May, armed prosecutors raided the offices of Media Most, Gusinsky's media holding company, in connection with alleged offences related to the privatisation of a video company. On 13 June, prosecutors arrested Gusinsky and jailed him for three days on fraud and tax offences. It was a turning point: the new president was warning the oligarchs, both privateers and heads of state-controlled companies, that no one was untouchable.

Vyakhirev had been friendly to Gusinsky before Putin's arrival, but he now abruptly joined the attack. By a twist of fate, Gazprom had in 1996–97 – probably as a gesture of thanks to Gusinsky for his support in getting Yeltsin re-elected – bought 30 per cent of Media Most and stood as guarantor of a $262 million loan from Credit Suisse First Boston to NTV. Once the Kremlin moved against Gusinsky, Gazprom used these links to put pressure on him. After Gusinsky's spell in jail, he signed a deal handing effective control of Media Most and NTV to Gazprom-Media, a Gazprom subsidiary. He fled Russia to Spain, where he has lived in exile ever since. The episode marked not simply the end of Gusinsky's empire, but the break-up of the Kremlin–oligarch alliance that had ruled Russia since the mid 1990s. Soon afterwards, in October 2000, Berezovsky also fell out with Putin, sold his shares in ORT and most of his shares in the Sibneft oil company to Roman Abramovich, and moved to London. (Abramovich, very much a Berezovsky protégé in the late 1990s, went on to become one of the richest men in the country and in 2003 owner of Chelsea Football Club.)

In January 2001 Putin met with a group of the oligarchs and laid out the new rules of the game. They were to invest in the economy, pay their taxes, and keep out of politics. There would be no special favours; the state would remain equally distant from all the oligarchs.[13] Of course this did not actually mean that the Kremlin would cease to work with oligarchs, or cease to have favourites. But the relationships built in the 1990s could no longer be taken for granted. The political power, having hit its nadir in 1998–99, was on its way up; it had re-established some semblance of popular support; by its treatment of Gusinsky it had shown it would not take orders any more from the super-rich; now it was ready to claw back tax revenues and property that had been so generously sacrificed to the oligarchs by Yeltsin.

Two issues were raised, but left unresolved, by the Kremlin –Gusinsky–Gazprom drama. The first was whether NTV would continue to provide most Russian homes with an alternative view of the news. The Kremlin had promised it would – but that did not happen. In April 2001 its board, now controlled by Gazprom, dismissed as director Yevgeny Kiselev, the station's most prominent anchorman, and replaced him with the banker Boris Jordan. Three quarters of NTV's journalists quit in protest. Attempts to sell Gusinsky's share to Ted Turner, the US media magnate, failed, and Gazprom-Media took complete control. Although NTV news had lost its cutting edge, it remained relatively independent. But in October 2002, Chechen militants took hostage a theatre audience in Dubrovka, Moscow, and law enforcement agencies stormed the theatre, causing at least 129 civilian deaths. NTV's critical coverage was publicly lambasted by Putin. Thereafter, resignations and self-censorship almost completely extinguished controversial news content.[14]

The second, much deeper, problem was control of natural resources revenues. The Kremlin, having dealt with Gusinsky and broken with Berezovsky, was ready for a fight. It started at Gazprom. Having encouraged Vyakhirev to dispossess Gusinsky, the Kremlin now dispossessed Vyakhirev. He retired in May 2001 and was replaced by a Petersburger, Aleksei Miller, who had served briefly as deputy energy minister. In September 2001, Miller cleared Vyakhirev's old guard out of the company's management. Among their replacements were *chekisty* and financiers who had worked with Putin in St Petersburg. War was declared on a multitude of corrupt schemes. In November, in a speech to Gazprom employees in Siberia, Putin asked why the production units sold gas at such low prices to trading intermediaries, enabling private firms to profit handsomely at Gazprom's expense. 'Where does the difference go? Where's the cash?' the president demanded. The asset-strippers were on notice. Yakov Goldovsky, boss of Gazprom's petrochemicals subsidiary Sibur, was jailed in January 2002 and only released nine months later, after abandoning a plan to float off Sibur on the cheap. Vyakhirev's son Yuri was sacked as head of Gazprom's lucrative export arm. Assets sold off cheaply to companies in which senior managers had shareholdings were returned to Gazprom.[15]

By mid-2002, the Kremlin had turned Gazprom from a potential financier of dissent into a powerful bastion of its own. Next came the battle for oil.

THE STATE TAKES CHARGE OF OIL AND GAS (2002–07)

Putin's campaign against the oligarchs culminated with the arrest in 2003 of Mikhail Khodorkovsky, the break-up of his oil company, Yukos – then Russia's largest – and the return of its assets to the state sector. This action was the axis of a broad shift towards greater state control of economic sectors deemed 'strategic' and a greater role for the *siloviki* in the state apparatus. The state struck a mighty blow at the tax avoidance and evasion schemes of the 1990s, and increased substantially the amount of tax revenue collected. The anomaly of a major oil-producing nation without a flagship national oil company was ended: Rosneft, transformed by absorbing Yukos assets, became that company. The Kremlin let foreign oil companies know that their Russian party was over, and drove a much tougher bargain on gas supplies to Russia's neighbours.

The Yukos Affair

The attack on Yukos began in July 2003 with the arrest of Platon Lebedev, chief executive of Khodorkovsky's holding company, Menatep, on charges of stealing a share in a fertiliser company in 1994. Then Menatep's head of security, Aleksei Pichugin, was arrested and charged with two murders. And in October 2003, gun-toting security men surrounded Khodorkovsky's private plane as it touched down in Novosibirsk, and he was arrested and charged with fraud, embezzlement and tax evasion. At first it was not clear that the Kremlin sought to break up Yukos, but things soon moved in that direction. In November Sibneft, Abramovich's oil company, unwound a $3 billion deal to merge with Yukos which had been agreed on just before Khodorkovsky's arrest. In December the tax authorities claimed from Yukos $3.5 billion for underpaid taxes in 2000, plus penalties. During 2004 they sought another $13.5 billion for succeeding years. They effectively spurned Yukos's offers to pay the bills: in fact they made that impossible, by obtaining freezing orders on the main owners' property. In December 2004, the giant oil-producing company Yuganskneftegaz, the jewel in Yukos's crown, was sold at a bankruptcy auction. In May 2005 Khodorkovsky and Lebedev were sentenced to nine years' imprisonment. Former Yukos vice president Sergei Aleksanyan, also jailed, was severely maltreated: the prison service denied him medical treatment for 14 months after he was diagnosed with AIDS, and ignored rulings by the European Court for Human Rights on that issue. Most of the rest of Yukos's owners and executives fled Russia.

The attack on Yukos did not appear to follow a predetermined plan. In the months after Khodorkovsky's arrest, it seemed that the company would be allowed to keep functioning under new, private ownership. Members of the Putin team had other ideas, though, and during 2004 they began to thrash out plans for bringing its assets into state ownership. Sechin, one of Russia's most powerful *siloviki*, joined the board of Rosneft, the only sizeable oil company to remain in state hands, and in July 2004 became its chairman. In September the government announced that Rosneft would be merged with Gazprom to create a world-class energy company. Such a behemoth would rival Saudi Aramco, Exxon-Mobil and the rest, and be a favourite candidate for taking over Yukos's production assets. But things didn't go as planned. A cloud was thrown over the auction of Yuganskneftegaz, the most important of these assets, by legal actions in the United States by Yukos's exiled bosses. That probably worried Gazprom, which had a large number of foreign shareholders, and it did not bid even indirectly for Yuganskneftegaz. Instead Yuganskneftegaz was sold for $9.3 billion to Rosneft, via an unknown shell company.

The 'Rosneft party' and the 'Gazprom party', arguably the two most powerful Kremlin factions in Putin's second term, now squared up to each other. The planned merger between the two companies collapsed amid ill-disguised acrimony, in March 2005. Rosneft, with Sechin's backing, then set out to replace Gazprom as the state energy industry flagship. In September 2005 Gazprom hit back, establishing a foothold in the oil industry by buying control of Sibneft from Abramovich. In 2006 both companies raised billions of dollars by selling their shares on international markets. Then Rosneft went on a gigantic shopping spree, scooping up production companies, oil refineries and trading firms that had belonged to Yukos. In 2007, Rosneft became Russia's largest oil producer. It continued its rivalry with Gazprom, but more importantly, both companies together helped tilt the balance against the oligarchs. Four of the most powerful oligarchs of the 1990s – Khodorkovsky, Berezovsky, Potanin and Abramovich – had been driven out of oil. State-owned Rosneft and Gazprom, together with the Kremlin loyalists who owned Surgutneftegaz and Lukoil, and the Russian and British owners of TNK-BP, now dominated.[16]

Most Russian people either supported the assault on Yukos, or felt indifferent, opinion pollsters reported. One survey registered a 67 per cent majority for 'some type of renationalisation' of assets sold off in the 1990s.[17] Senior politicians played to those powerful emotions on television – but the claim that the Yukos case heralded an all-out attack on the 'free market', repeated countless times in the foreign press, simply never added up. The assault on Khodorkovsky came in the midst of a continuing wave of privatisations: in the oil sector it was preceded in 2000–03 by the privatisation sales of Onako and Slavneft, and the TNK–BP merger. It was followed by the sale of the state's remaining

7.6 per cent stake in Lukoil to ConocoPhillips for $2 billion in September 2004. And while the state's role in some 'strategic' sectors was strengthened in 2005–08, this went alongside further large-scale privatisations, such as those of power and municipal services. The objective of the attack on Yukos was to *re-order the relationship between power and money.* The limits within which the oligarchs had to work were made very clear. For the state, property rights were not sacrosanct as they are in the west, but conditional. Tax avoidance was scaled back. Financing opposition political parties, or launching strategic projects such as privately owned oil pipelines without state sanction would not be tolerated. Khodorkovsky had done both.

Khodorkovsky was embraced in some US and European political circles as an anti-authoritarian hero, and even set out a liberal capitalist credo in open letters from prison. But the banks that formed the main nexus between Russia and international markets could not have cared less. With oil prices moving upwards and interest rates moving downwards, they were pouring money into Russia with indecent haste. The banks had queued up to lend money to Yukos because of its massive reserves, the principal measure by which financial analysts judge oil companies. When the reserves were unceremoniously grabbed by Rosneft, they queued up there too.

During the hiatus when Yukos had lost Khodorkovsky but looked set to stay in business under private ownership, in December 2003, a syndicate headed by Société Générale lent $1 billion to Yukos, a very large deal by the then prevalent market standards. A year later, Yukos defaulted on the loan as it sank under the state offensive. The banks had to claim on guarantees made in the name of Yuganskneftegaz – which by then belonged to Rosneft. But now it was Rosneft that every Moscow-based western banker was desperate to win as a client – and Rosneft that needed to borrow billions to refinance the purchase of Yuganskneftegaz. The banks were tripping over themselves to exit their relationship with Yukos: one, HSBC, sold its share of Yukos debt to hedge funds, one of which was run by business partners of Rosneft's. And in September 2005, a syndicate headed by ABN Amro and Barclays put together a $2 billion deal for Rosneft, which helped pave its way to the sale of its shares on western markets. The fact that Rosneft had bent international lending rules, by breaching covenants on earlier loans while borrowing for the Yuganksneftegaz purchase, was quietly forgotten.[18]

The Tug of War over Tax

The Yukos affair sent a clear signal to the other oil companies that they would be expected to pay more tax in future. Senior government figures not only hinted that other 1990s privatisations might be reviewed, but also made clear that they intended to curtail tax avoidance schemes that had flourished under Yeltsin.

The state's difficulties in collecting taxes during the 1990s were discussed in Chapter 2. In 1999 the new tax code, which had been bogged down in parliament for years, became law. At the same time, export duties on oil, gas and metals, scrapped in the mid-1990s, were reintroduced. During his first term, Putin undertook a further overhaul of the tax system. In January 2002 the mineral resources extraction tax was introduced, paid by oil, gas and minerals producers on the basis of physical volumes of output. It replaced a range of royalties and excise duties, and aimed to counteract tax avoidance schemes. Putin's tax reforms also had a centralising effect: revenues were switched away from regional budgets to the federal government.[19]

The government and tax authorities targeted schemes using transfer pricing (that is, setting the prices assumed to be charged by one part of a company to another part of the same company lower, or sometimes higher, than market prices, to avoid tax). In the 1990s these schemes had worked like this. (The company names are imagined and prices indicative.) An oil production company, Ivan Oil of Tyumen, would produce oil at a cost of $4.50/barrel. This would be sold to Ivan Trading of Kalmykia (one of Russia's onshore tax havens) for $5/barrel. Ivan Trading of Kalmykia would sell the oil to Ivan Trade of Switzerland at $20/barrel, and this company would take hedging risks and arrange transport, and receive $21/barrel. The ultimate beneficiaries of the trading companies also owned the production companies. Most taxes were paid by Ivan Oil of Tyumen, and Ivan Trading of Kalmykia's 300 per cent mark-up was completely, or almost completely, tax free. As the oil holding companies (Yukos, Sibneft and so on) took shape, the production and trading companies were brought under one corporate roof, while transfer pricing and other 'tax optimisation' schemes remained. When I interviewed Khodorkovsky in 2000, he emphatically defended the schemes, under which Yukos was at that time buying oil from its subsidiaries at one-twentieth of the market price. At that stage, the schemes were accepted by the authorities as legal; only in 2005, when the book was thrown at Yukos, did Russian courts start to find otherwise.[20]

In 2005, economists at the World Bank estimated the cost of transfer pricing to Russia at about 2 per cent of GDP, that is $6–9 billion per year in 2002–03.* The Russian state audit chamber reckoned that legal tax avoidance schemes by oil companies only were costing the budget $2–4 billion per year.[21] The tax ministry, having demanded arrears from Yukos, now examined the other oil companies' payments. The companies loudly promised they would meet outstanding claims, and, where necessary, voluntarily renounce tax avoidance measures. Oligarch watchers noted that Sibneft, then controlled by Abramovich, had done better at saving its shareholders' money than Yukos. Analysts at Alfa Bank reckoned that in 2001, at the high tide of tax avoidance, Sibneft paid just 9 per cent of its total turnover in taxes, compared with 15 per cent by Yukos and 21 per cent by TNK International, while the oil companies most loyal to the state, Lukoil and Surgutneftegaz, paid 31 per cent and 25 per cent respectively.[22]

In March 2004, while Khodorkovsky was awaiting trial, Abramovich's Sibneft received a demand for $1 billion in taxes owing from 2000–01, although this was later reported to have been halved. The economist Nikolai Petrakov accused Sibneft of using transfer pricing via Kalmykia, plus other tax avoidance measures involving an association of disabled employees. TNK-BP was presented with a $1 billion bill for back taxes from 2001, relating to TNK's liabilities before its merger with BP. The tax authorities did not excuse the oil companies most loyal to the state, either. The audit chamber reported that in 2001 Lukoil had made 75 per cent of its oil sales through trading companies based in the tax havens of Kalmykia, Uglich and Baikonur (Kazakhstan) – although by that time the company had already voluntarily paid the taxes it said it saved in 2001 via the Baikonur scheme – $103 million.[23]

How did all this change the relationship of power and money? Three points stand out:

- The oil and gas sectors started paying a great deal more current tax, putting the state finances on a solid foundation for the first time since the late 1980s.
- There was still room for tax avoidance.

* These economists noticed that transfer pricing was so ubiquitous that it distorted Russia's official GDP figures. They estimated that 11 per cent of GDP that should have been attributed to the oil and gas sector, and 2 per cent to other sectors, was instead marked 'trade', because the income was reported from trading instead of producing companies.

- Capital flight, the curse of the Russian economy during the 1990s slump, continued to grow during the oil boom.

The oil and gas sectors' tax payments rose steadily throughout Putin's first term, and nearly doubled between 2003 and 2004, as shown in Figure 4.1.

These payments laid a solid basis for the state finances during Putin's second term. And as a result of Putin's efforts to centralise the state apparatus and retrieve power from regional governors, a greater share of these tax revenues went straight to the federal budget. Federal tax revenues rose from about 2.3 trillion rubles in 2004 to more than 6 trillion rubles in 2006, while the taxes paid to regional governments fell from 1.7 trillion rubles to less than 500 billion.[24] Figure 4.2 shows how revenues into the federal budget grew, and what share of these were from oil. It also shows how the fiscal surplus (that is, what was left in the state's pocket after paying all its outgoings for the year) grew. Much of this was paid into the oil stabilisation fund.

The scope for tax avoidance remained, and classic transfer pricing schemes continued to operate. For example the aluminium producer Rusal has legally avoided tax by way of transfer pricing ever since it was set up in 2000 (see the box on pages 79–81). Rusal brought together aluminium assets controlled by two of the Kremlin's favourite billionaires, Oleg Deripaska and Abramovich. Deripaska later bought out Abramovich's stake, and in 2006 merged Rusal with its smaller competitor Sual and the Russian aluminium assets of the Swiss-based commodities trading firm, Glencore. This was

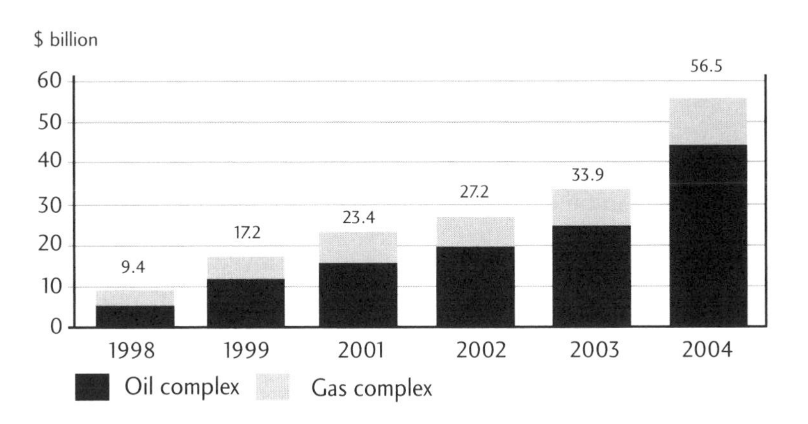

Figure 4.1 Rising oil and gas tax revenues 1999–2004
Source: VEDI (http://vedi.ru).

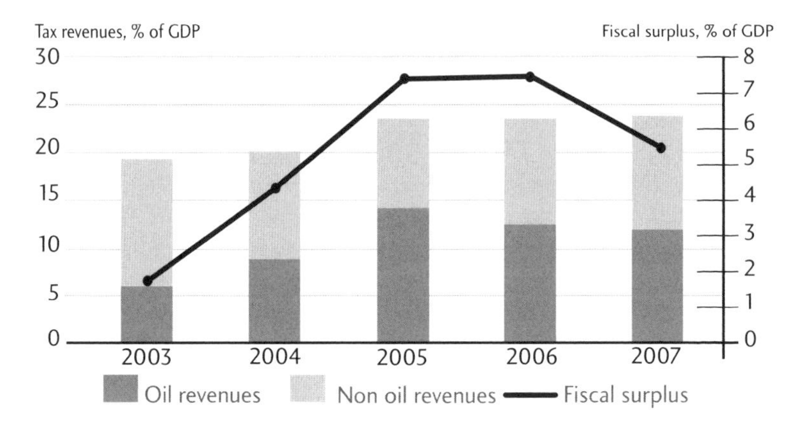

Figure 4.2 Oil revenues boosting the fiscal surplus, 2003–07
Note. Federal budget only, regional budgets excluded.
Source: finance ministry/Alfa Bank Research.

Russia's biggest-ever corporate merger; the company created, UC Rusal, became briefly the world's biggest, and then second biggest, producer of aluminium.

Capital flight continued on a large scale. It had been the scourge of the Russian economy in the 1990s (see Chapter 1, pages 29–31), and in the 2000s continued – despite the fact that the Russian economy was recovering and investment capital was coming in. Economists at the Global Financial Initiative, a US-based NGO, found that Russia's capital flight in 2002–06 was the world's fourth largest, behind China, Saudi Arabia and Mexico, rising from $17 billion in 2002 to $38 billion in 2003, $53 billion in 2004 and $55 billion in 2005, before falling to $16 billion in 2006. 'The lion's share' of flight capital was from Russia's corporate sector, which doubled its borrowing while 'at the same time moving retained earnings offshore, out of the reach of the state', economists at Fitch, the ratings agency, wrote in 2005. One key cause of capital flight was Russia's growing oil wealth: earlier research on Middle Eastern oil producers showed that capital flight rises along with the price of oil. Another factor was that the Yukos affair, and property owners' fears of further tax claims, probably encouraged them to spirit funds out of the country.[25]

Redoing the Deal for Foreign Companies

The Russian state, having regained control of oil wealth it had ceded to the oligarchs, fought to claw back concessions made to

Transfer pricing in the aluminium business

Russia's aluminium producers have reduced their tax burden by concentrating cashflows in trading firms instead of production units. This arrangement is called tolling.

The main inputs for aluminium are alumina, which is refined from bauxite (a mineral), electric power and labour. The Russian aluminium smelters have always had to import most of their alumina, but usually enjoyed the competitive advantage of cheap hydropower from dams on Siberia's huge rivers.

Under tolling schemes, a trader buys the alumina, which remains its property up to the point at which it is processed. When the aluminium is ready, that too becomes the trader's property. Both items stay on the trader's balance sheet. The production company receives a processing fee – so it doesn't have to buy alumina, but doesn't get to sell the aluminium either.

Tolling was devised in the United States in 1979–81, not as a method of tax avoidance, but as a means of giving trading houses greater control over financial flows. The recession of those years, combined with high energy prices, threatened aluminium makers in the northwest United States with bankruptcy. The traders had access to cash. They paid the processors (smelters) a fee, and stood to win or lose from aluminium sales. They won.

In the early 1990s tolling was adopted in Russia, with bad results for the tax authorities. Domestic demand for aluminium had collapsed, and alumina supplies were disrupted. Western commodities traders soon saw the potential for exporting Russian aluminium – and used their access to credit to tilt the market in their favour.

The traders tolled aluminium in Russia (that is, brought the alumina to the Russian smelters, paid them a processing fee, and took the aluminium). The producers' costs were slashed, and so were their revenues. Their tax bills fell as a result. Western traders such as Trans World, AIOC and Glencore handled almost all Russia's aluminium exports. The arrangement gave them a strong hold over the smelters – until the late 1990s, when Russian business groups became strong enough to establish their own offshore trading companies. They began to toll the aluminium themselves, accumulating offshore the proceeds that had previously gone to the western traders.

In 1999, when Deripaska was battling for control of the industry with Trans World and their partners, he said: 'Those that can't work without tolling should sell their factories.' His company, Siberian Aluminium, even ran a poster campaign against the practice. But when Rusal was put together by Deripaska and Abramovich in late 2000, it used a string of offshore trading subsidiaries, such as Rual Trade of the British Virgin Islands, to borrow money from western banks to fund tolling schemes.

As a result, Rusal's shareholders (mainly Deripaska and Abramovich) benefited from the company paying far less tax. The banks preferred an offshore revenue stream to use as collateral for loans. The tax collectors lost out. For example the Krasnoyarsk aluminium smelter, one of the biggest, reported – and paid tax on – turnover of $397 million in 2001, its first full year as a Rusal subsidiary. That was about $461 for each tonne of aluminium produced, compared with world prices in that year of $1,300–1,500/tonne.

In 2003, as the clouds gathered over Yukos, tolling faced significant opposition. Vladislav Reznik, deputy leader of United Russia, the pro-Putin party, argued that the budget was losing $176 million a year, mainly from Rusal and its smaller competitor, Sual. But when he proposed abolition of tolling, he could not garner a single vote in Parliament except his own. The aluminium industry had lobbied effectively. Resource Industries, a US consultancy which helped invent tolling in the 1980s, was among those that wrote to the government.

By 2005, with aluminium prices booming, Rusal's turnover had risen to $6.65 billion (compared with $3.9 billion in 2002) and its profit to $1.65 billion (compared with $840 million in 2002). But 60 per cent of the revenue stayed offshore and Rusal's trading subsidiaries tolled the aluminium. The turnover of Rusal's Russian subsidiaries could not have exceeded $620 million, and the profit tax they paid was a mere $149 million.

In July 2008, the Russian audit chamber made a new proposal to scrap tax breaks on cross-border tolling. The auditor, Sergei Agaptsov, complained that it was costing the budget about $410 million a year.

Wherever the extra revenues went, bauxite miners at Rusal's

Sevuralboksitrud mine complex felt that not enough went to them. In March 2008, 123 of them staged a week-long underground sit-in, demanding a 50 per cent increase and an end to compulsory Saturday working. Rusal claimed the miners earned an average of 35,000 rubles ($1,250) a month, but the union insisted that face workers earned only 26,000 rubles ($930), and journalists reported other underground miners taking home as little as 10,000 rubles ($360) after fines and deductions. The dispute dragged on, unresolved, through the year.[26]

foreign oil companies. This was part of the international turning of tables described in Chapter 3. A key target was the production sharing agreement (PSA) covering the Sakhalin II oil and gas project in the far east of Russia. The unusually generous terms conceded by Russia in the 1990s were effectively renegotiated. In 2007, Shell, which headed the consortium operating the project, retreated before mounting pressure from the government and regulators, and arranged the sale of a 50.1 per cent share to Gazprom.

Sakhalin island, 9,900 km east of Moscow, will be a key provider of oil and gas to Asia for many decades to come. Japan, Korea and Taiwan, which do not have a single big oil and gas field between them, are looking to Sakhalin. So is China. Development of Sakhalin's resources, mostly offshore, began in Soviet times, and during the 1990s six exploration and production projects were launched. The two that have progressed farthest, Sakhalin I and II, have been developed under PSAs. The Sakhalin II PSA was signed in 1994 between Russia and a consortium headed by Shell, Marathon Oil of the United States and the Japanese industrial conglomerates Mitsui and Mitsubishi.

A PSA is a commercial contract under which an oil and gas field may be explored and developed over a fixed period. Usually, the state retains ownership of the resources, while the investor – very often, and in Sakhalin II's case, a consortium – bears responsibility for exploration and production, and either puts up or borrows most of the money for it. In large projects – and Sakhalin II is one of the largest ever – there is a first, development phase, taking several years and costing billions of dollars, before substantial quantities of oil and gas are produced. At the next stage (that is, during the first few years of production) a PSA will typically allow for most of the revenue (named 'cost oil') to go back to the investor, to repay costs incurred. Subsequent revenue ('profit oil') is split between the investor and the state under a prenegotiated formula. But the Sakhalin II PSA, Russia's first, was far from typical. It was signed in 1994 when the state's fortunes had hit rock bottom. The result was an agreement uniquely favourable to the investor – 'the best PSA terms you will ever get in Russia', as Stephen McVeigh, the consortium's chief executive, put it – and unusually damaging to the state's interests. Its critics pointed out that:

- The agreement abandoned the usual formula, that once costs were recovered, an agreed proportion of 'profit oil' would go to the host country. Instead, it provided for the consortium not only to recover its costs, but to achieve a 17.5 per cent real rate of return on its capital.
- Unlike most PSAs, there was no annual cap on the amount that can be considered 'cost oil' in the early years of the project.
- Unlike most PSAs, there was no clear definition of what expenditures can be included in calculating cost oil and profit tax.
- Instead of being limited to a fixed term, the PSA is renewable, if the consortium wishes, after 25 years.
- Whereas most PSAs generally cover exploration, as well as development and production, exploration of Sakhalin II was complete before the agreement was signed.

The Sakhalin II PSA was sharply criticised by the state audit chamber and many of Yeltsin's political opponents, and in 1995 a PSA law was adopted, placing stringent restrictions on future agreements. In 2004–05, against the background of the Yukos affair, the mood in Russia's ruling circles shifted towards the idea of retrieving the state's perceived losses on Sakhalin II. By then, Shell had increased its stake and taken over from Marathon as the project operator. It claimed that Russia would do well from the deal. But the energy economist Ian Rutledge concluded, on the contrary, that the PSA was 'disadvantageous' to Russia. The government's patience was sorely tested by the thought that it would see barely a kopek from Sakhalin for many years. It ran out when the consortium's cost estimates for phase two – which involved building pipelines, oil terminals and a gas liquefaction plant – were revised upwards, from $8.5 billion to $10 billion in 2004 and $22 billion in mid-2005. The PSA did not strictly limit costs, or specify with the usual precision the method of calculating them, meaning that even more years would pass before the state received any revenue. While the ballooning costs reflected skyrocketing prices of labour and materials, it also seemed that the consortium had underestimated technical challenges.[27]

Throughout 2006 Russia's regulatory agencies intensified pressure on the consortium. The audit chamber criticised its selection of suppliers. The environmental regulator suspended permits. In November 2006, Shell conceded defeat. The PSA remained, but a 50.1 per cent stake in the consortium was sold to Gazprom. It was widely reported that a secret deal between Shell and the government included a compromise figure on costs. A flood of western press commentary denounced the government, but it had simply shifted the balance of the PSA back towards the state.

In 2007, another project run by foreign investors, at the Kovykta gas field in east Siberia, came under pressure from regulators. Again, the project operator, in this case BP, ended up in June 2007 by agreeing to bring Gazprom into the project as a majority shareholder. In this case, the key issue was that BP had hoped to export gas from Kovykta to lucrative Far Eastern markets, but found that Gazprom was not prepared to contemplate relaxing its monopoly on gas exports. A further dispute, in mid-2008, centred on TNK-BP, the oil company created in 2003 by a merger of the oligarch-owned TNK and BP's Russian assets; this ended with BP employees seconded to the company being sent home and its BP-appointed chief executive Robert Dudley being replaced.

Despite all this, foreign investment in Russian oil and gas has grown uninterruptedly. It is easy even for attentive newspaper readers, regaled with stories of threatened nationalisation, to lose sight of this fact. The sector accounted for most of the $85 billion in inward investment in 2006–07. Foreign shareholdings in Gazprom, Rosneft and other companies have soared. Strategic investors (that is, foreign oil companies) remain keen. BP reacted to the Kovykta and TNK-BP disputes by announcing that it intended to increase its strategic focus on Russia, and by appointing to the board of TNK-BP former German chancellor Gerhard Schroder, a good friend of Putin's. Since 2006, Gazprom's German partners, BASF and EON. Ruhrgas, have both taken shares in the Yuzhno-Russkoe gas field. In 2007, when Yukos's assets were being sold off at auction under bankruptcy courts, a group of oil and gas fields was snapped up for $6.83 billion by Enineftegaz, a holding company owned by the Italian energy groups Eni and Enel – although this deal was closely linked to these companies' long-standing relationship with Gazprom, which had option agreements to repurchase the stakes.[28]

The Russian state has asserted its dominant role in oil and gas. But it has not turned its back on foreign companies any more than it has on its domestic oligarchs.

THE 'ENERGY WEAPON'

The oil boom has split western elite attitudes to Russia more or less in two. Political relationships cooled, as Putin and his colleagues, emboldened by the oil windfall, responded angrily to attempts to expand US political and military power. But economic relationships warmed: Russia remained an 'emerging market' – a very attractive one too, as long as oil prices kept rising – and, especially in 2005–07, capital flooded in.

Putin's political relationship with the United States and its allies had begun with a rapprochement: after the terrorist attacks on the United States on 11 September 2001, Russia agreed not to obstruct US efforts to put military bases in central Asia, and the United States turned a blind eye to Russian human rights abuses in Chechnya. But soon afterwards, Washington went on a military and diplomatic offensive in Eastern Europe, withdrawing unilaterally from the Anti Ballistic Missile treaty in 2002, and encouraging membership in the NATO alliance for Baltic and central European states. In 2004–05, US support for NATO membership applications by Georgia and Ukraine – where western-facing governments had come to office shortly after the 'Rose' and 'Orange' revolutions respectively – further infuriated Moscow. The bad blood came to the boil in February 2007, when Putin denounced US attempts to create a 'unipolar world'. But every year, notwithstanding the foreign policy ups and downs, foreign lending and investment into Russia increased.

The western countries' approach was most deeply divided in the energy field. The international oil companies were anxious to strengthen relationships with Russia, and as discussed above, were even willing to make commercial concessions in order to join partnerships to develop energy resources. But the western political establishment began to worry that Russia would use its energy resources to pursue strategic or political goals – the 'energy weapon'. Russia's 'emergence as an energy superpower' would have a long-term impact in the first place because European countries will 'begin to think twice before saying "no" to Russia', Marshall Goldman, who advised US president George Bush on energy, wrote.[29]

These worries focused on the natural gas trade. To understand why, readers should bear in mind the difference between oil and gas. Because oil is liquid, it is much easier than gas to transport. Oil is sold, more or less, on one global market. Gas, on the other hand, has to be sent through a pipeline under pressure, stored or liquefied. Buying pipeline gas requires a long-term commitment, and contracts often last 25 years. In the 1970s, Germany helped to build huge pipelines that brought gas from Siberia, and started buying Soviet gas that came through them. Other European countries joined in this largest of western–Soviet trades. Over the decades, it became more and more important for both sides. It has always provided Gazprom with most of its revenue, and, by the 2000s, was providing one quarter of the European Union's gas supply.

While this trade suited European energy companies, it worried some politicians. Throughout the 2000s, more and more European Commission reports and newspaper articles have urged that Europe reduce its dependence on Russian gas. Proposals to build pipelines to bring gas from alternative sources have so far foundered, because the possible suppliers (Turkmenistan, Iraq, Iran and so on) have neither proved politically friendlier to Europe than Russia, nor been able, for various reasons, to consider the sort of long-term commitment that would justify investing billions in pipelines. The worries in Europe might well have faded, had it not been for the very real political and economic problems that arose over Russian gas supplies, not to Europe, but to its former Soviet neighbours.

Soviet industrial expansion in the 1970s and 1980s was geared to cheap gas, and when the Union broke up, Russia's neighbours found themselves over-dependent on Russian gas imports. Ukraine, in particular, relies on gas piped from or through Russia for more than three-quarters of its needs, and in the 1990s built up huge debts for supplies. The tragedy, or irony, of the post-Soviet break-up is that 80 per cent of Russia's supplies to Europe are piped through Ukraine. So in every dispute over payment, Russia threatens to cut off Ukraine's supplies, but backs down because it needs Ukraine's help to get volumes through to Europe without being stolen or delayed on the way.

Two things brought Russia's gas disputes with its neighbours to a head in the mid-2000s. First, gas prices in Europe started rising steeply (they are correlated with oil prices), and Gazprom managers demanded an end to discounts for former Soviet customers, which were now costing billions. The second was that the 'coloured revolutions' increased political tension between the Russian,

Georgian and Ukrainian governments. Moscow demanded higher prices more quickly from Georgia and Ukraine, while continuing larger discounts to Belarus, in exchange for a deal under which Gazprom bought a 50 per cent share in its gas pipeline. In the course of haggling, supplies were temporarily halted to both Belarus (in 2004 and 2007) and Ukraine (in 2006). Supplies to Georgia were disrupted, in disputed circumstances, in 2005.

In January 2009, with the world recession looming, Gazprom facing a disastrous drop in sales revenues all round, and Ukraine mired in a deep economic and political crisis, their dispute over gas prices veered out of control. Gazprom cut off Ukraine's supply. Ukraine made payments late and threatened to divert European volumes for its own use. After a complex 'who did what' argument, the entire Ukrainian gas transit system was shut down for two weeks, leaving 17 European countries short of gas or, in some cases in the Balkans, without it all together.

This stand-off convinced European politicians who believed in the Russian 'energy weapon' that they had just been hit by it. But that interpretation still made little sense. As the oil boom ended and the slump began, Gazprom was not less reliant on European export revenues, but more so. Why antagonise your best and biggest customer? Probably because the Kremlin – which, after all, has the final word on Gazprom's export strategy – decided that punishing Ukraine was an aim worth risking European irritation, or even anger, for. But even the drivers of the dispute with Kiev were more about money than about power. Recessions have long caused governments to lash out at economically weaker neighbours, and this was no exception. Moscow wanted to end the Soviet legacy of cheaper gas for Ukraine – and the pro-NATO leanings of its president, Viktor Yushchenko, simply increased its appetite for a fight. Moscow's reactions are those of a government embracing capitalism and integrating into the world market: this logic, rather than the idea of an 'energy weapon' against Europe, explains its actions during the 'gas wars'.[30]

5

POWER AND MONEY: FROM OIL BOOM TO BUST

Russia's oil boom underpinned an economic revival, albeit a partial and uneven one. Manufacturing and processing industries picked up – not only oil-linked businesses such as pipeline construction, but machine-building and manufacture too. The retail trade, and consumer-oriented industries such as production of cars, household goods and food products, flourished. Capital markets and banks acquired more solid foundations. There were flaws: in particular, Russian companies built up high levels of debt. In 2008, oil prices hit their peak and started to fall. The boom began to unravel. Capital flowed out and the stock market plunged. The international financial meltdown of September 2008 whipped away the credit that had helped Russian industry grow. In 2009 Russia was sinking deep into recession. The first part of this chapter describes the boom, and the second part the bust.

THE OIL BOOM (2002–07)

When Putin took over as president in 2000, Russian capitalism was a pretty strange hybrid. The oil, gas and metals industries were becoming immensely profitable. Some of the crippling economic distortions of the 1990s were being overcome. The nonpayments crisis receded after the 1998 devaluation, and tax revenues rose. But some parts of the economy were still in the doldrums and, eight years out from the dissolution of the Soviet Union, Russia lacked the structures most other capitalist countries have to finance the economy (that is, effective banks and stock markets). There were banks, but many of them were little more than ramshackle conduits for oligarchs' cashflows. There were stock markets too, but few shares were available on them, because the most successful companies were controlled by handfuls of individuals, usually through opaque offshore structures.

The Capital Markets

During Putin's first term, as the battle with the oligarchs raged and the oil money started to flow, corporate Russia set about establishing real capital markets.* The largest companies began in the early 2000s to list substantial proportions of their shares, on both Russia's own exchanges and those in London, New York and Frankfurt. And some banks began seriously to do what they do in other capitalist countries: attract deposits from savers and use them to finance corporate activity or households.

Table 5.1 shows how the Russian stock markets have grown. In 2000, the total market capitalisation** of the companies listed was a paltry $40 billion, roughly 1 per cent of the analogous figure for the London stock exchange. But by 2005 the Russian figure had grown tenfold, to about $400 billion. In 2006–07 it leapt up again, to more than $1.2 trillion. The Russian Trading System (RTS) stock exchange's index reflects the changing value of the shares that are quoted, rather than their volume. The increase in the number of shares available for trading is reflected in the last two columns, which record transactions in which shares were newly listed on the stock markets, and the amounts these sales raised.

Russian companies and banks, as well as issuing shares, also sold large numbers of bonds – both eurobonds, which are traded internationally, and bonds denominated in rubles. The volume of the ruble bond market grew 25 times from 2003 to 2007, reaching $39 billion in mid-2008; the volume of bonds issued by regional governments grew similarly, to $9 billion.[1]

* The methods by which companies raise capital boil down to variations on two: selling shares, and borrowing. Shares can be traded privately, or on stock exchanges; privately owned companies often decide to issue freely traded shares in order to raise extra capital. Borrowing can be done directly from a bank, but companies – and national and local governments – also issue bonds (essentially IOUs redeemable over a period of time). Capital markets are the places where shares, bonds, and financial instruments that reflect their value, are traded.

** The market capitalisation of a company is the total value of all its shares (the average price at which a share changes hands, multiplied by the number of shares). The figures in Table 5.1 record the aggregate market capitalisation of companies listed on Russian stock exchanges, including shares held by government or other large owners.

Table 5.1 Russia's stock market boom, 2000–08

Year	Total market capitalisation $ billion, end of year	RTS index performance %	Equity issuance	
			No. of issues	Amount raised, $m
1996	n/a	142	1	111
1997	n/a	98	–	
1998	n/a	-85		
1999	n/a	197	1	52
2000	40	-18	1	323
2001	71	81	–	–
2002	102	38	2	220
2003	172	58	1	14
2004	206	8	5	620
2005	400	83	12	4926
2006	966	71	15	17,654
2007	1216	19	29	32,862
2008	350	-72	4	1690

Sources: Deutsche Bank, Moscow; Finam website (www.fin-rus.com) (market capitalisation); RTS website (market performance); UralSib bank estimates (equity issuance).

Russia's largest state-owned companies gave a big push to the domestic capital markets and their integration with world markets. In 2005, after the Gazprom–Rosneft merger was called off, the Russian government pushed ahead with plans to sell more Gazprom shares outside Russia. First it consolidated its own stakes and brought them up to 50.1 per cent, to ensure that control remained in its hands. Then in December 2005 it abolished restrictions, imposed in the 1990s, that 'ring fenced' locally traded Gazprom shares and permitted foreign ownership only of a limited number of special shares traded on international markets.* The world's largest banks, finance houses and pension funds rushed to buy Gazprom shares, effectively expressing faith in the Petersburgers and *chekisty* running Gazprom to provide a good return on their investments.

* In the early 2000s, because of the restrictions, prices of Gazprom's internationally traded shares were up to ten times higher than prices of the locally traded ones. After the 'ring fence' was abolished, the prices converged. That meant a handsome profit for canny western investors who had effectively got their hands on locally quoted shares, through 'grey schemes' – which adhered to the letter but not the spirit of Russian law – under which they owned financial instruments that indirectly reflected the value of the locally listed Gazprom shares.

Within months, Gazprom's market capitalisation rose above $250 billion, more than ten times what it had been in 2003, making it the world's third biggest company by that measure. In mid-2006 it was Rosneft's turn: it arranged an initial public offering (IPO)* of its shares on the London and Moscow markets. It did less well than it had hoped, but still raised $10.5 billion, twice as much as all the Russian IPOs in the previous year put together. In May 2007 there followed a similar London–Moscow IPO by state-controlled Vneshtorgbank, Russia's second largest bank, which raised $8 billion.

Most of the capital Russian companies raised on the stock markets in 2006–07 came from foreign investors. Senior politicians often talk about creating a shareholding middle class – but that was easier said than done. Take the case of Rosneft. As a result of its IPO, Rosneft acquired 150,000 individual Russian shareholders, and in June 2007 several thousand of them attended its first ever public shareholders' meeting in Moscow. Igor Sechin, chairman of Rosneft, *chekist* par excellence and deputy head of the presidential administration, made his first ever public appearance. But he struggled to answer angry protests by small investors, including oil industry families who had ploughed in their savings, about the 'miserly' dividend paid. Hans Jurg Rudloff, chairman of Barclays Capital, who represents western financial institutions on the Rosneft board, supported Sechin energetically and urged patience. Shareholders responded that they would have got better returns from savings accounts.[2]

As the capital markets expanded, Russia's banking system also revived on firmer foundations. The government's market reformers, including Aleksei Kudrin, finance minister, and Sergei Ignatiev, Central Bank chairman from 2002, saw a healthy banking system as critical to the growth of Russian capitalism. The first task was to attract savers. That was tricky: the 1998 crisis had left people deeply suspicious of banks, and the savers hung on to their cash dollars. The Central Bank tried to tighten regulation, but business groups that used banks to manage their funds resisted changes fiercely. Loopholes in the law allowed ownership to be concealed and dodgy banks to avoid failure. Minimum capital requirements (a standard regulatory measure in most countries) were not imposed

* An IPO, or flotation, is the transaction by which shares in a company formerly owned privately or by government are first made available on stock markets.

until 2004, and then only on newly founded banks. Nevertheless, as the oil boom gathered pace, some banks – such as state-owned Sberbank (originally the Soviet savings bank), Vneshtorgbank (originally the Soviet foreign trade bank), Gazprombank and Bank of Moscow, and privately owned Alfa and MDM – saw there was money to be made in real banking. In 2003, crucially, deposit insurance was introduced. In July 2004, a mini-run on some banks put backbone into the system. Some small banks folded, but Alfa, the largest privately owned bank, survived rumours that it was in trouble, and came out stronger.[3]

From there the banking sector expanded rapidly. From 2000 to 2007, bank assets rose from one-third of GDP to two-thirds, and the lending portfolio from 12 per cent of GDP to 39 per cent. Lending to individual consumers boomed – and that was new for Russia, since middle class borrowing in the 1990s had been negligible, and almost all from foreign banks. In 2005–07, the floodgates opened: from January 2005 to June 2007, the banks disgorged $127 billion in personal loans, $35 billion in mortgages and $26 billion in car loans. This was very much part of the international credit bubble. Banks advertised interest rates of 20–30 per cent, but hiked them up to 50–70 per cent with commissions and charges, until regulators clamped down. The bad debts were minuscule compared with those in the United States, but they multiplied – until the 2008 crash. There was a property bubble, too: although a mortgage remained out of most Russians' reach, real estate prices rose by 40 per cent in 2006 and 30 per cent in 2007. Prime Moscow property was as dear as that of New York or London.[4]

Was this just an oil boom and a credit bubble, then? No, it was more:

- This was a consumer boom. Ordinary people started to go shopping in a way they never had before: millions splashed out on cars, household goods and holidays. In 2000–06, real disposable incomes grew by 11.4 per cent per year. Russia's food retailers were still far behind Wal-Mart and Tesco, but very much in the same league as Latin America's largest.
- Once companies and households had money to spend, they gave impetus to manufacturing, trade and construction. GDP growth shifted towards goods and services produced for Russia itself, World Bank economists asserted at the end of the boom, in 2008. 'There is a clear shift away from resource extraction and towards trade and construction.' From 2003 to 2007, construction and

retail trade grew by 14 per cent and 13 per cent per year respectively, far faster than the economy as a whole. Manufacturing expanded: in 2006–07, production of steel-making and metallurgy equipment soared, but so did that of cranes, bulldozers and trucks for construction and rubber and plastics products, often for domestic use.

- Russia experienced a surge in productivity, which many economists consider to be the most important aspect of economic growth. Higher productivity – in part due to industrial capacity that lay idle during the 1990s being brought back into use – drove higher output.[5] Only agriculture failed to get out of the doldrums, although in 2007 several large agribusiness groups had consolidated farm holdings and begun to invest.

The State's Alliance with Private Capital

Putin and his colleagues took advantage of Russia's boom to refashion further the alliance between state and private capital. They seemed to grope towards a strategy rather than work it out in advance, but five trends became clear:

- In 'strategic' industries (for example, arms manufacture), they repeated the approach taken to oil and gas, of creating strong, state-owned corporations.
- In other important economic sectors, and in the Russian regions, they initiated team work between the state and the surviving oligarchs.
- The government pressed on with privatisation and liberalisation in power, municipal services and other sectors.
- The government encouraged alliances with foreign investors.
- Friends and colleagues of the Putin team began to flourish in private business.

The drive to bring 'strategic assets' into *state corporations* spread from the oil sector to other parts of the economy. Atomstroiek-sport, which specialises in nuclear construction, was bought by Gazprombank in 2004; a clutch of helicopter and aviation builders by state-owned Oboronprom in 2005; and machine builders and metals companies by other state entities. Russian Technologies, headed by Sergei Chemezov, a friend and colleague of Putin's, was formed in November 2007 and soon became a leader among state corporations. Although its core business is high technology, it took control of more than 400 companies, including arms exporters, machine builders and chemical manufacturers, and has taken over big private-sector firms including VSMPO-Avisma, the titanium producer, and the Avtovaz car factory (see below).[6]

Alongside these corporations are the surviving *oligarchs' business groups*, which frequently tied into the state's plans for economic development. An example is Oleg Deripaska's holding company, Basic Element, which controls the aluminium company Rusal and insurance, construction and manufacturing businesses. It has played a big part in state-sponsored projects such as the development of Sochi in preparation for the 2014 Winter Olympics, and the industrial regeneration of Lower Angarsk region in eastern Siberia, where Deripaska also controls hydropower and aluminium assets. The oligarchs' boom-time cooperation in such investments marked a sharp contrast with the 1990s, when they invested barely anything outside the natural resources sector and kept revenues offshore.

The Kremlin and its favoured oligarchs also strengthened their presence in Russian regions, elbowing local elites out of the most profitable sectors and breaking up regional fiefdoms. The Udmurtiya republic in the northern Urals is a good example. Its prize assets are the oil companies Udmurtneft and Belkamneft. In 2000, Udmurtneft was owned jointly by the Udmurt republic and a string of offshore companies apparently controlled by business partners of the Udmurt president, Aleksandr Volkov. Belkamneft's owners were the republic; Bashneft, an oil company based in nearby Bashkortostan; and a clutch of offshore companies linked to Viktor Khoroshavtsev, leader of United Russia in Udmurtiya. But these local oligarchs sold up to national oligarchs. In 2001 Mikhail Fridman's Alfa group took control of Udmurtneft, and Sistema, a holding company linked to Moscow mayor Yuri Luzhkov, bought into Belkamneft. In late 2008, after further ownership changes, Belkamneft looked set to be swallowed by Deripaska's group. Meanwhile, in 2006 Udmurtneft was sold, in a deal strongly supported by Putin, to Rosneft (51 per cent) and Sinopec of China (49 per cent). The dispossessed local oligarchs moved on, to the oil products and trading business, and into construction and property, where close links with local government gave them a competitive edge.[7] Their rapacious acquisition of land provoked battles with local communities (see Chapter 9, pages 180–2).

Putin completed major *privatisation and liberalisation* programmes left unfinished by Yeltsin – notwithstanding periodic claims in the western press that he was bent on renationalisation. These included one of the biggest privatisations in world history: the break-up of the state-owned electricity monopoly United Energy Systems (UES), the sale of more than $40 billion of assets to Russian and foreign buyers, and the liberalisation of the electricity market. The process, which took five years up to the dissolution of UES in June 2008, was overseen by Anatoly Chubais, the arch-privatiser of the 1990s. It left Russia's generating companies in the hands of foreign owners including E.ON, Enel and Fortum, and Russian ones including Lukoil, Gazprom and Norilsk Nickel. The electricity market liberalisation stimulated plans to raise tariffs for electricity, gas and water, and privatise municipal services, which are discussed in Chapters 7 and 9.

Putin also encouraged *alliances with foreign capital*. The car industry is a good example. The government has given Russian carmakers limited help in competing with imports, but has also welcomed the foreign manufacturers. Sales of Russian cars ran at around 800,000 per year in the 2000s, but faced stiff competition from used imported cars, sales of which reached 500,000 in 2002. The government slapped a 25 per cent duty on these, but drivers who preferred the imported models usually opted to pay the extra. By 2006 foreign models outsold Russian ones for the first time: sales hit 1.2 million, including 250,000 foreign models made in Russia. The government changed tack, and told importers they would qualify for relief from import duty if they built factories in Russia that could produce 25,000 vehicles per year. There was a scramble. Ford, Toyota and Nissan set up near St Petersburg. Renault started building Logans near Moscow at the old Moskvich factory; Volkswagen is due to set up in Kaluga.[8]

Another intriguing alliance with foreign capital was concluded at Avtovaz in Togliatti, Russia's – and the world's – largest car factory. In the 1990s it had fallen under the sway of oligarchs and criminals. Boris Berezovsky established a close partnership with Avtovaz director Vladimir Kadannikov in the late Soviet period, and Berezovsky's Logovaz car dealership became the sole distributor of the Avtovaz-made Lada. The factory also attracted criminals, who pillaged and on-sold cars. Togliatti became a centre for some of Russia's strongest criminal groups and a police investigation in 1996 uncovered 65 contract murders of managers or dealers, presumably committed during turf wars over Avtovaz production. When the *siloviki* moved into government, Avtovaz was a natural target. In 2005, the state corporation Rosoboroneksport (a forerunner of Russian Technologies) bought a controlling stake in Avtovaz, and offered 25 per cent plus one share to western strategic partners. Renault won a fierce bidding war and bought in for more than $1 billion.[9]

Another significant trend in the 2000s has been the *success in private business of some of Putin's associates*. One example is Gennady Timchenko, whose trading firm, Gunvor, was by mid-2008 shipping about 30 per cent of Russia's oil and oil products, with a turnover of up to $43 billion in 2007, implying that it is the world's fourth-biggest oil trader. Gunvor exports oil produced by all Russia's largest companies except Lukoil. Timchenko, who *Forbes* magazine reckoned was worth $2.5 billion in 2007, worked with Putin in a St Petersburg trading company in the late 1980s and sponsored the future president's judo club. Timchenko has categorically denied that his past friendship with Putin underlies Gunvor's success. He has said that Gunvor's meteoric rise is due to effective work with clients.

In 2008 Bank Rossiya, which grew quickly to become Russia's 36th largest, attracted media attention for its manifold indirect links to Putin. Its largest shareholder, the then dollar billionaire Yuri Kovalchuk (with 28.3 per cent of the shares), and another shareholder Nikolai Shamalov (12 per cent), were business partners of Putin's in the 1990s. Timchenko of Gunvor and Mikhail Shelomov, a son of Putin's cousin, control shareholdings of about 9 per cent and 12 per cent respectively. Another Putin associate on the bank's board is Matthias Warnig, who served in the East German secret police, the Stasi, and in the 1990s ran Dresdner Bank's St Petersburg office, before in 2006 becoming managing director of North Stream, a joint venture between Gazprom and European energy companies that is building a new gas pipeline from Russia to Germany.* Rossiya's success in acquiring the assets of former state-controlled companies has caused public discussion – and drawn allegations from Putin's most vocal opponents that Rossiya's business empire has gained at the expense of the state and, specifically, of Gazprom. In 2004–05, via a complex succession of deals, Rossiya took control of Sogaz, an insurance company formerly controlled by Gazprom; Sogaz bought a finance firm, Lider, that manages investments for Gazprom-linked

* Warnig's case is exceptional. Former Stasi officers are usually shunned by business in Germany, in contrast to Russia, where a KGB service record is usually a career asset. Warnig has said he met Putin in October 1991, although a Wall Street Journal investigation suggested the two met in the 1980s in Dresden, where they served their respective agencies.

Gazfond, Russia's largest private pension fund; and in May 2008 Sogaz bought from Gazprom-Media a controlling stake in *Izvestiia*, one of Russia's best-established newspapers.[10]

Plenty of millionaires, too

By the end of the oil boom, Russia's propertied class had well and truly taken shape. A substantial population of dollar millionaires complemented the better-known billionaires. The 2008 financial crisis eroded, but usually did not destroy, their wealth.

In March 2008, at the peak of the boom, the *Forbes* rich list counted 87 Russian billionaires. All the top ten were oligarchs of 1990s vintage, and for all the discussion about the Kremlin diverting business opportunities to its close friends, only a handful of those were on the list.

In 2009 *Forbes*'s Russian billionaire count had fallen to 32 – and their collective wealth had slumped from $471 billion to $102 billion. Oleg Deripaska (2009 wealth estimated at $3.5 billion) had slipped to tenth place from first, where he was replaced by Mikhail Prokhorov ($9.5 billion). Roman Abramovich ($8.5 billion) was second; Lukoil boss Vagit Alekperov ($7.8 billion) replaced Aleksei Mordashov of Severstal ($4.3 billion) in third.

Russia's dollar millionaire population rose to 136,000 in 2007, according to the Capgemini World Wealth Report – 96 for every 1 million people, compared with 989 in the United States, 31 in China and 11 in India. Other estimates of millionaire numbers, which may include undisclosed wealth, are higher. While the billionaires are mostly main shareholders in large natural resources companies, the millionaires are concentrated most visibly in the financial sector.

Russian bankers' salaries went 'through the roof' in 2007–08, *Institutional Investor* reported. Igor Shekhterman, managing director of RosExpert, a headhunting firm, said he knew 'a few people who have gotten $10 million plus options guaranteed for two or three years'. When the US banker Eric Kaufman left the Swiss bank UBS to head the investment banking business at Alfa, Russia's largest privately owned bank, his annual salary was reported as $20 million, a figure he commented was 'exaggerated'.

In 2007 the Moscow investment firm Troika threw a late summer lawn party at the historic Kolomenskoye estate. Ruben Vardanyan, chief executive, arrived by parachute and distributed $10 million in early bonuses.

For the millionaires' children, London is the place to be, working in the City or studying for a business administration degree. One highlight of the social calendar is the 'Moscow Motion' party: tickets are £400 and girls in bikinis are lowered from the ceiling to pour champagne.[11]

The Cross-Border Debt Mountain

There was a sharp rise in capital flows to all 'emerging markets' during the oil boom: these flows soared from $90 billion net in 2002 to about $600 billion net in 2007, according to IMF estimates. Russia was one of the main beneficiaries. This was the ultimate 'hot money': it came in despite the fact that many 'emerging market' economies had savings that could have been used for investment; and it came largely in the form of bank loans to banks, a survey by economists at the Bank of International Settlements noted.[12] These capital flows, driven by low interest rates in the United States and Japan, were part of the unsustainable credit bubble that would burst in 2008, triggering the world economic crisis.

Figure 5.1 shows the net flow of capital in and out of Russia, in the private sector (as opposed to the state sector), as recorded by the Central Bank. This includes money brought in or out for loans, investments and other financial transactions. It also includes the 'net errors and omissions' category from the balance of payments, and receipts from trade that are not repatriated: both these items are usually assumed to be flight capital. In the 1990s net capital flows, measured in this way, were negative to the tune of about $20 billion per year, largely as a result of capital flight. In the early 2000s, capital flight continued (see Chapter 4, page 78), but large amounts of capital also started to come into Russia, so the net outflow was sharply reduced. In 2006–07 the inflow surged upwards, as it did in most 'emerging markets' – but the net outflow in 2008, most of it in the last quarter, after the Wall Street crash, was greater than the net inflow in the two preceding years.

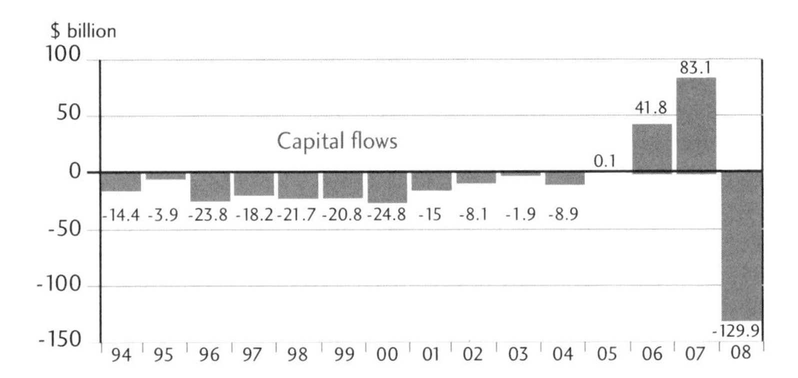

Figure 5.1 Net private sector capital flows in and out of Russia, 1994–2008
Source: Central Bank of Russia website.

The capital flows into Russia during the oil boom were almost all in the form of loans, rather than investment. In 2005, debt accounted for more than three-quarters of the total inward flow; by early 2008, it accounted for more than five-sixths, economists at the World Bank reckoned. So while the Central Bank and government, following best market practice, accumulated nearly $600 million in foreign exchange reserve accounts – the world's largest such cash pile after those of China and Japan – Russian companies and banks built up foreign-currency debts on nearly the same scale.

The total debts outstanding grew relentlessly, from $33.8 billion from companies, plus $14.2 billion from banks, at the end of 2002, to $299.6 billion and $198.2 billion respectively in September 2008. The foreign lenders became more and more profligate. At the beginning of the oil boom, banks would typically charge Russian borrowers a 3–4 per cent margin on top of the interest rates they were paying to fund themselves, for a maximum of five, and more often three, years. They would also insist on complex security structures under which the loan repayments were paid directly (for example, from oil export revenues, into special offshore accounts). By the end of the boom, the banks were queuing up to throw multi-billion dollar loans to Russian banks and companies, for longer periods and on more flexible terms, often with margins of less than 1 per cent.[13]

This giant lending spree was accompanied by an increase in the share of the Russian banking system owned by foreign banks, from 9 per cent in 2001 to 22 per cent in 2007. At the height of the oil boom, the US investment banks returned to Russia. They had by and large quit Moscow after the 1998 crash, leaving specialist fund managers to play the stock markets and European banks to concentrate on corporate lending. But the big boys returned as the debt mountain piled up: Morgan Stanley established a presence again in 2004, Goldman Sachs reopened its Moscow office in January 2007 and Merrill Lynch arrived a year later.[14]

Although capital flows were dominated by debt, direct investment in Russia still grew to way above the minuscule levels of the 1990s. Funds invested in Russia rose as a proportion of the total invested in 'emerging markets', from around 3 per cent in 2001 to nearly 10 per cent in 2007. Russia remained behind Brazil and India, and even further behind China, but it counted. At the height of the oil boom, inward investment was measured in tens of billions of dollars: $32.4 billion in 2006 and $52.5 billion in 2007, according to the Central Bank. Most of this money went into the energy and power sectors. The largest deals were investments of $5.5 billion by E.ON of Germany, and $2.2 billion by Enel of Italy, into power companies, and the $5.8 billion Italian investment into Yukos's gas assets, mentioned in Chapter 4. On top of this was portfolio investment (that is, via stock markets). Another key element of the investment boom was the return of Russian-owned capital. Up to 40 per cent of the flows registered as inward foreign direct investment arrived from Cyprus, the Virgin Islands, Luxemburg and other havens of Russian flight capital in the 1990s.[15]

Russia's integration into world markets was not a one-way process. As its corporations became wealthy, they invested abroad. In 2005 Lukoil spent $2.1 billion on Nelson Resources, a Canadian company that owns oil fields in Kazakhstan. In 2006, the Russian steel producer Evraz spent $2.3 billion on the US Oregon Steel Mills. In 2007 the Renova group, controlled by Viktor Vekselberg, spent $1.2 billion buying 80 per cent of Energetic Source, an Italian energy company. The largest cross-border deal of all was the $3.6 billion merger of Glencore's aluminium assets with Rusal in 2006.[16]

All these developments in the real economy were tangible enough. But it was the debt built up by banks and companies during the boom that became Russia's crucial problem when the financial crisis and recession arrived.

THE WORLD CRISIS TAKES ITS TOLL (2007–09)

In December 2007, when Putin nominated Dmitry Medvedev his chosen successor, the fault lines along which any international crisis would spread to Russia were already clear to see. The economy had been transformed, the oligarchs brought under control, and the state finances put in order. Some flight capital was returning; so were many young, educated people who had emigrated. But manufacturing and processing industries were only just getting back on their feet. Investment levels remained low – just 21 per cent of GDP in 2007, compared with India's 34 per cent and China's 42 per cent – and heavily skewed towards the oil and gas industries.[17] The boom would only last as long as the high oil prices and the cheap cross-border credit. It turned to bust in two stages. First, capital was sucked out of Russia, from late 2007 by the early tremors of the international financial crisis, and from mid-2008 by the falling oil price. Second, the Wall Street meltdown in September 2008 turned the retreat of capital from Russia and other economies into a rout, and threw the world economy into recession. Russia's foreign exchange reserves offered some defence against falling oil prices, but only limited shelter from the destructive force of the capital outflow and the recession.

The End of the Oil Boom

The trigger for the international crisis was the bursting of the US housing bubble in 2006. It became clear that billions of dollars lent in the form of subprime mortgages would never be returned. The ripples spread through the financial system, and in February 2007 the world's largest bank, HSBC, declared potential losses of $10.5 billion on subprime mortgages. The dominoes kept falling from then on. It became widely known that black holes of unrecoverable debt had spread through the vast, opaque and unregulated derivatives market, to which all major financial institutions in the United States and Europe were exposed. Money ran scared from US markets, seeking safer boltholes: in 2007, some of it moved into oil, food and other commodities markets, giving a last upward turn of the screw to prices. In March 2008, Bear Stearns, one of the 'big five' Wall Street investment banks, collapsed, and was bought by JP Morgan Chase with state support.

In early 2008, Russia was still enjoying the final few months of record and ever-increasing oil prices, but suffered a significant outflow of capital, which reversed just once, in April, before gathering pace again. In May, the Russian stock market hit an all-time high: its aggregate market capitalisation was $1,450 billion. By mid-September, before Wall Street imploded, it was worth less than half of that, and by the end of the year, less than a quarter, $350 billion. Many of the oligarchs' fortunes, tied up in their companies' shares, were cut down to size. The top 25 people on *Forbes* Russia's rich list lost an estimated $230 billion between them.

The Russian stock market's value often rises and falls in line with the prices of oil and other commodities – and they were the key factor in this, its biggest-ever fall. In July 2008, oil prices hit a high, $147 a barrel, and then plunged, reaching $34 a barrel at the end of the year. But there were other reasons why Russia's stock market fell faster than other comparable 'emerging markets'. Western investors' general jumpiness was aggravated by fears of a 'Yukos mark two' (that is, unpredictable government intervention against the oligarchs and their companies). The dispute over control of TNK-BP, mentioned in Chapter 4, was at its height. In June Putin – now appointed prime minister by Medvedev, who took over as president in May – publicly accused the steel company Mechel of tax evasion and price gouging. Mechel's value sank from $15.2 billion to $10.5 billion in a day, and the Russian stock market as a whole lost $60 billion the following week. After the government made mollifying noises, most of these losses were recovered.

In August 2008, Russia fought a two-week war with Georgia over the disputed territory of South Ossetia, its first military conflict with a former Soviet neighbour. One of the biggest surges of capital outflow for a decade ensued. In the first week of trading after the conflict, the Central Bank recorded a $16.5 billion reduction in its foreign exchange reserves – the second largest one-week fall since records were started in 1998 – attributed mainly to foreign investors withdrawing from the stock market. This rush from rubles into dollars was partly due to exchange rate movements but mainly because of perceived 'political risk'.[18]

The Financial Crash

The second phase of the crisis in Russia, and across the world, was triggered by the meltdown in mid-September 2008 of the US financial markets, the heart of the globalised system. The crucial turning point was the US government's refusal on 15 September to bail out Lehman Brothers, one of Wall Street's four remaining investment banks, which then went bust. The US and international banking system seized up: the interest rates banks charge to each other quadrupled, and lending stopped. Stock markets plunged. This was by far the most serious financial crisis since the 1930s. In the week after the Lehman bankruptcy, rich-country governments mounted an unprecedented rescue operation, during which central banks bought up an estimated $2.5 trillion of debt and damaged assets and pumped another $1.5 trillion or so into the system. The biggest US insurance company, AIG, was effectively nationalised. The evaporation of the 'big five' investment banks was completed, with Merrill Lynch being sold to Bank of America and Morgan Stanley and Goldman Sachs converting to commercial banks.

The 'emerging market' economies now faced a financial emergency imposed from above. George Soros, the billionaire fund manager, wrote in October 2008 that 'there has been a general flight for safety from the periphery back to the centre'. In the 'emerging markets', currencies had dropped against the dollar and yen, some precipitously. Interest rates and credit default premiums (that is, the interest rates paid by lenders to insure against the bankruptcy of borrower governments or companies) had soared. Stock markets had crashed.[19]

In Moscow, short-term liquidity – the money that banks and

'Our children want to eat!' Workers at the Volfram mine complex, the main employer in Svetlogore village in the Russian far east, demanding payment of wages arrears, April 2009. Photo: RIA Novosti.

financial institutions lend to each other day by day – dried up, as it did across the world. Chaos ruled Russia's stock markets, which were closed 15 times in September and October. Western financial institutions wanted to pull back from Russia in a hurry and Russian borrowers looked immediately vulnerable. When the merry-go-round stopped in September, Russian companies owed $296 billion to foreign lenders, and Russian banks owed a further $198 billion. Opportunities for refinancing and rolling over debt had vanished. Russia's largest native investment bank, Renaissance Capital, was the first to fall victim to the crisis. In a $500 million deal wrapped up on 23 September, its owners sold a 49.9 per cent share to the oligarch Mikhail Prokhorov – who was cash-rich, having in April, after a bruising battle with his co-owner Vladimir Potanin, sold up his 25 per cent share of Norilsk Nickel to Oleg Deripaska's Rusal. Renaissance's owners accepted a price far lower than they had hoped to receive during talks a year earlier. One of them, the Yeltsin-era financial markets pioneer Boris Jordan, said the crisis was characterised by the 'incredible growth of the volume of [banks'] debt by comparison to the level of their capital'.[20]

Russian corporate borrowers were sweating too, particularly because in many cases they had pledged shares as collateral for loans – only for those shares' value to plunge and for lenders to exercise margin calls: that is, their right to immediate repayment. Rusal, which had earlier in the year taken a $4.5 billion loan from a group of western banks, to finance its acquisition of Prokhorov's Norilsk stake, faced such a dilemma. In October 2008 it was rescued by a loan from Vneshekonombank, the state development bank; the 25 per cent stake in Norilsk Nickel was made over to Vneshekonombank as collateral. The Alfa group, controlled by Petr Aven and Mikhail Fridman, benefited from a similar deal: Deutsche Bank called in $2 billion worth of loans to Alfa as a result of a fall in value of the collateral, a 44 per cent holding in the telecoms company Vimpelcom. Vneshekonombank took over the $2 billion loan, again guaranteed by the Vimpelcom shareholding.[21]

Under the Russian authorities' rescue package for the financial system, up to $130 billion – about 10 per cent of GDP, compared to 5 per cent in the case of the United States – was made available to recapitalise banks and raise bank deposit insurance guarantees. The Central Bank issued $35.4 billion of subordinated debt financing, almost all to three state banks to support liquidity. A further $11.5 billion – including the Rusal and Alfa loans mentioned above – was disbursed in the last quarter of 2008 via Vneshekonombank, to help businesses make foreign loan repayments. China, which sees Russia as a valuable source of oil supplies long term, also offered valuable support to Russia's state-controlled energy companies: in March 2009 it presented a $25 billion loan package to oil producer Rosneft and the pipeline company Transneft, in return for guaranteed deliveries of oil over the next 20 years.[22]

A longer-term rescue package, designed to deal with the economic recession and stimulate business activity, was announced in November 2008. After discussion in government it was accepted by Parliament, in the form of a revised budget, in April 2009. It was decided to spend 1.4 trillion rubles ($42.6 billion) on a range of measures, including social welfare programmes and support for industries deemed essential. Tax cuts of 2 trillion rubles or more will be implemented, in order to stimulate spending, and the government will run a budget deficit for the first time in the 2000s. The government listed 295 'systemically important enterprises' that will receive support under the plan, with attention focused on the consumer sector, machine building, agriculture and construction.[23]

In the aftermath of the Wall Street meltdown, Putin and Medvedev complained that Russia and other countries would now pay for a crisis largely created in, and mismanaged by, the United States – and were slated by western commentators.[24] Without denying or vulgarising the fundamental causes of the crisis, I would say that the Russian leaders had a point. The fall in oil prices, one of the immediate sources of Russia's economic problems, had little to do with US policy directly. But the financial meltdown was clearly exacerbated by decisions taken in the United States. It unfolded against a background of overproduction and overaccumulation of capital – deep and long-term problems associated with the way that capitalism has expanded over a quarter of a century. But the insanity of market deregulation made the proliferation of derivatives markets easier. And the policy of keeping US interest rates low contributed in turn to the dot-com bubble and the housing bubble, each of which ensnarled the world financial system in a greater net of debt.

The Global Recession Bites

The financial crisis, having emerged in the strange world where sharply dressed bankers and hedge fund managers trade fantastic volumes of derivatives, fed through to the real economy with shocking speed. Within weeks of the Lehman Brothers bankruptcy, jobs

The disease Russia didn't catch

How much worse would Russia's financial crisis have been, if financiers who wanted to expand the domestic derivatives market had got their way? Luckily, we don't know.

Internationally, the over-the-counter derivatives market (private, unregulated transactions between financial institutions) had swelled to a mind-boggling volume of $683 trillion (notional amounts outstanding) in mid-2008; the exchange-based derivatives market (transactions regulated through exchanges) was $82.7 trillion. And a key driver of the 2008 financial meltdown in the United States was the perception that investment banks and other financial institutions face massive losses on derivatives based on the US mortgage market – losses that were sometimes greater than their original investments.

While Russian banks may have dabbled in international derivatives markets, there was little such opportunity at home. According to Micex, the largest Russian stock exchange – which had been lobbying for a legal framework for derivatives trading to be put in place – the exchange-based derivatives market was in 2007 worth just 17 per cent of GDP in Russia, compared with 6,026 per cent in North America and 2,577 per cent in Western Europe.

Sanction for derivatives markets has been withheld by Russian politicians with bad memories of the 1998 crisis. While the crisis originated in the sale of the infamous treasury bills to banks, those purchases were largely financed by derivatives trading. When the pyramid collapsed, Russian banks failed to settle with foreign banks a particular type of derivatives – nondeliverable forward contracts (NDFs), that is, contracts to lock in a ruble exchange rate agreed in advance. The courts subsequently ruled that NDF contracts were a form of gambling, and the foreign banks lost their money.

During the 2000s, a Russian parliamentary working group advised by PriceWaterhouseCoopers, the international accountancy firm, came up with draft laws to regulate derivatives markets, but not all the necessary changes were made. In 2006–07 parliament amended the gambling law, to scrap the definition of derivatives trading as gambling, but the change was vetoed by the Federation Council. In 2008, only a few of the least complex derivatives were traded on Russian exchanges. The trading volumes were tiny.[25]

were being destroyed and lives disrupted in another world, where millions of people live in constant danger of poverty. Economic forecasts for the 'emerging markets' deteriorated even faster than for the rich countries. By February the IMF was forecasting that the East Asian economies would contract by 2.6 per cent in 2009. In China, within four months of the Wall Street crash, the government stated that 20 million of the 100 million migrant workers who have moved to industrial areas in recent years had returned home. Japan, whose conservative banks had avoided the worst of the financial mess, found in December 2008 that the exports on which its industries depend had fallen 35 per cent year on year. State bankruptcy stalked dozens of countries: eastern and central Europe appeared particularly vulnerable. In October 2008, before Lehman's derivatives traders had collected their last pay cheques, several governments negotiated rescue packages with the IMF. Ukraine, whose economy is like Russia's, but without oil, was at the head of the queue.

The Russian oil boom had left its economy and finances better able to cope with a crisis than many countries'. Its foreign debt was the weak spot – equal to 31 per cent of GDP, compared to China's 11 per cent and Brazil's 12 per cent. Ukraine's foreign debt was proportionally greater than Russia's, at 56 per cent of GDP. But the ratio of central bank reserves to months' worth of imports – a measure used to indicate to how well a country can deal with changing terms of trade and devaluation – was 23 for Russia, compared to China's 18, Brazil's 15 and Ukraine's 4.5. And Russia's budget surplus, of 7.7 per cent of GDP, also compared well with China's 4 per cent, Brazil's -2.3 per cent and Ukraine's -2 per cent. Nevertheless, the crisis put an end to the oil boom and threw Russia into recession.[26] I outline here its impact on the national finances, on industry, on companies and banks, and on people.

Russia's national finances have been struck a body blow. More than one-third of its foreign exchange and gold reserves – the wealth it accumulated during the oil boom – was used up. In July 2008 the reserves totalled $597 billion (including $162 billion in the sovereign wealth funds); by January 2009, they had fallen by $210 billion to $387 billion (including $225 billion in the sovereign wealth funds). At the time of writing, the government was projecting that reserves would fall to $300 billion by the end of 2009. And the steep fall in the price of oil in late 2008 meant that revenues into the budget will be sharply reduced. In November 2008, the oil companies, still paying some boom-time rates of tax and export duty on lower revenues, threatened to cut exports. They agreed not to do so after oil export duty was reduced. In early 2009 the government was expecting to run a budget deficit of about 7–8 per cent of GDP.

Although after the crisis Russia's foreign exchange reserves remained the world's third largest, the way in which they drained away raised the spectre of large-scale capital flight. To clarify how great the danger was, economists at the Fitch ratings agency tried to estimate where the $210 billion had gone. They reckoned $58 billion had been lost through the depreciation of the sterling and the euro (in which some Russian foreign exchange reserves are kept) against the dollar, leaving $152 billion to account for. Of that, $36 billion was bought by Russian companies to pay off debts (good news about their financial health, because it suggests they rolled over a further $30 billion of payments due). Gross private-sector capital outflow was $94 billion – contributing to the huge net capital outflow shown in Figure 5.1. But, the Fitch economists pointed out, $30 billion of that reflected purchases of cash dollars by Russian households nervous that their ruble savings would lose value. More of the outflow may have been a short-term reaction to the crisis, they argued; pessimists who attribute it mostly to capital flight had yet to prove their case. Aleksei Kudrin, the finance minister, met with tax officials in January 2009 and acknowledged that capital flight had resumed: he told them that a further $40 billion had exited Russia that month.[27] At the time of writing, the scale of capital flight remained unclear. But it was back.

The crisis also brought back devaluation to Russia. Between July 2008 and February 2009, the ruble lost 29 per cent against the dollar/euro basket used by the monetary authorities, and 35 per cent against the dollar – similar to the falls suffered by other large 'emerging market' currencies. The Russian government rejected calls for a one-off devaluation. It was criticised in the western press, on the grounds that the gradual slide of the ruble encouraged speculators to buy foreign currencies. But other commentators said the policy was designed to reassure Russian companies and individuals who had dollar debts or ruble savings, allowing them to adjust their portfolios – and to avoid panic.[28] In any case, living standards in Russia were badly affected.

The impact of the crisis on *industry* was immediate. Industrial production in November 2008 was 8.7 per cent lower than a year before; in January 2009 it was 16 per cent lower than a year before. An epidemic of redundancies, wage cuts and short time ensued. Wage arrears were reported on a scale unprecedented since the 1990s. Between August 2008 and February 2009, the number of registered unemployed increased by 700,000, rising above 2 million; total unemployment including those not registered reached 6 million, according to the state statistics service. Car industry output had by February 2009 fallen by three-quarters. Managers of the gigantic GAZ factory at Nizhny Novgorod, which is controlled by Rusal owner Deripaska, told bankers in March 2009 that it had laid off 30,000 of its 118,000 workers, and another 30,000 would follow. Kamaz, the truck maker, made 7,000 redundant in December. Avtovaz at Togliatti went on to a three-day week. Production fell steeply at the steel mills, and in March 2009 Severstal, Russia's largest steel maker, announced 9,000 redundancies.[29]

Table 5.2 shows the impact of the crisis on industrial production. Statistics are given for two general categories (industrial production as a whole, and processing industries), and for two particularly badly hit sectors.

Russian companies and banks found themselves caught by plunging demand and sales on one hand, and difficulty in repaying or rolling over debts on the other. Their problems were exacerbated by the collapse in their share prices, especially in cases where these shares were used as collateral for loans and were subject to margin calls, as mentioned above. Some of the oligarchs spent early 2009 running back and forth between the Kremlin and the western banks, cutting deals to roll over their debts and if necessary restructure their empires. The most serious problems were concentrated in the metals sector. In February 2009, Deripaska (of Rusal), Potanin (the main owner of Norilsk Nickel), and Alisher Usmanov (main owner of Metalloinvest iron ore and steel group, part owner of Arsenal Football Club in London, head of a key Gazprom subsidiary and reputedly a close friend of Medvedev's) put a plan to president Medvedev to merge their assets into a gigantic state-backed conglomerate. It was refused. Shortly afterwards, Rusal announced that it had agreed with western banks to freeze repayments on $14 billion worth of debts. There were reports that the banks had made similar, smaller deals with the steel companies Evraz, of which Roman Abramovich is the main owner, and Mechel.[30]

In total, Russian banks and companies were thought to have to find about $140 billion in debt repayments to foreign lenders in 2009, and at least $64 billion in 2010, so the game of rollover and restructuring will go on. Those who had money, rather than debts, when the crisis broke, gained advantage – so Mikhail Prokhorov,

Table 5.2 Industrial production, 2008–09

% increase/decrease, year-on-year	Jul 08	Aug 08	Sep 08	Oct 08	Nov 08	Dec 08	Jan 09	Feb 09
Industrial production	3.2	4.7	6.3	0.6	-8.7	-10.3	-16.0	-13.2
Processing industries	4.6	6.5	8.2	0.3	-11.3	-13.2	-24.1	-18.3
Machines and equipment sector	-0.8	19.9	15.8	4.6	-15.0	-17.3	-45.9	-6.0
Vehicles and equipment sector	18.2	11.9	19.3	3.6	-4.8	-23.2	-36.0	-31.0

Source: Rosstat.

having sold his share of Norilsk Nickel to Deripaska just before the crisis, not only replaced him as Russia's richest man, but also bought a stake in Renaissance Capital (mentioned above) and had money to spare. Foreign banks with money moved in, too: in March 2009 Standard Bank of South Africa agreed to buy in to Troika, Russia's second-biggest investment firm after Renaissance, and said it was on the look out for assets being sold by indebted Russian business groups.[31] But overall the credit crunch will weaken the billionaire oligarchs as a group. At the time of writing it seemed likely that some would have to surrender parts of their business to western banks, to state-controlled competitors, or both. Not all of them will survive.

The impacts of the crisis on Russia's *people* have been mentioned throughout this section: redundancies; short time, wage arrears and wage cuts for those who keep their jobs; and a loss of spending power as a result of devaluation. The World Bank's statistics throw harsh light on the extent to which higher living standards were dependent on oil: the average wage in Russia peaked in July 2008, the same month that oil prices peaked (at $755 per month), and fell rapidly from there as the oil boom ended (to $524 per month in February 2009, with the slide accelerated by ruble devaluation).[32] In early 2009, many other gains made in living standards and welfare during the boom were being reversed. The extent of the setback is hard to forecast. So, too, are the ways in which the majority of people will react. These issues are further discussed in the final section of Chapter 9.

6

POWER AND PEOPLE: HOW RUSSIA IS RULED

From the state's relationship with Russia's capitalists, the focus now shifts to the way in which the state rules over society as a whole, and the successes and failures of democracy.

THE WAR THAT MADE PUTIN

Ultimately, states rule by violence. The strengthening of the state in 1999–2002, described in Chapter 4, centred on a diabolical act of violence: the second Chechen war. Putin's image as the Russian soldiers' inspiration was instrumental in getting him elected in March 2000, just as Margaret Thatcher's flag-waving for the UK invasion of the Malvinas islands in 1983 helped her get re-elected. The first Chechen war of 1994–96 had aggravated the fractures pulling the state apart; in contrast, the action that began in 1999 helped to bind demoralised and quarrelsome sections of the security forces to the Kremlin, despite the high cost in terms of casualties among soldiers and civilians. The socialist writer Boris Kagarlitsky, a steadfast public opponent of the war, pointed out that the second Chechen war, 'unlike the first, received almost unanimous support from the Russian "political class"'.[1] It won support from both right-wing liberals and Communist Party leaders. And it strengthened in the armed forces a sense of statehood that had been severely eroded by the chaos of the 1990s. Liudmila Alekseeva, a leader of Russia's human rights movement, told me in an interview:

> The Chechnya war, in which federal troops faced resistance not only from fighters but from the great majority of the civilian population, helped the authorities to undermine democracy.…The soldiers came to consider every Chechen to be

> their enemy; this strengthened their antipathy towards all non-Russians.... Thousands of interior ministry troops, policemen, procuracy officials and others have been for tours of duty in Chechnya. It became a school of cruelty towards not only the enemy but also the civilian population. These *siloviki* often brought this cruelty, this terrible indifference to people's suffering, back to the regions from which they came.[2]

The previous war had ended in August 1996 with a ceasefire agreement that left Chechnya de facto outside Russian state control, and its constitutional status undefined. The Chechen military commander Aslan Maskhadov was elected president of the republic in January 1997, and signed a peace treaty with Yeltsin soon afterwards. Maskhadov faced an impossible task. He had not only to try to rebuild Chechnya's shattered economy and infrastructure, but also to deal with new Islamist and terrorist trends. Shamil Basaev, a field commander during the war, headed a radical opposition influenced by both. In 1998 Maskhadov brought Basaev into government, but the alliance soon broke down. In August 1999 Basaev, together with the Islamist guerrilla Omar Ibn-al Khattab, led an incursion into neighbouring Dagestan. The local population was largely hostile, and by mid-September the insurgents were driven back into Chechnya. In the Moscow political establishment, calls were made for renewed military action against Chechnya. In September 1999, these were amplified a thousand times over after a mysterious series of bombings of apartment blocks – first in the military town of Buinansk, and then in Moscow and the industrial town of Volgodonsk – in which more than 200 Russian civilians were killed.

Putin, then prime minister, sprang into action. He ordered an invasion of Chechnya, which began on 30 September. Previously, Putin had seemed to many an efficient but boring bureaucrat; now, in front of the television cameras, he famously dropped into street slang and promised to pursue the 'terrorists' everywhere (see the box on page 124). His popularity ratings soared. There was no evidence that Chechen forces were responsible for the blasts, but an unprecedented frenzy of anti-Chechen racism seized the pro-Kremlin media. The television presenter Mikhail Leontev called for napalm, poison gas and carpet bombing to be used against the Chechen population. Simultaneously, the Moscow air came alive with rumours, which persist to this day, that elements in the security forces had a hand in the bombings. Putin's political opponents have claimed the blasts were carried out to raise his standing as a fighter against terrorism. The most extreme – and unsubstantiated – version of the story is that Putin himself sanctioned them. I believe the truth lies somewhere in a murky world where FSB agents rub shoulders with hired guns and gangsters, and will probably never be known. There is little doubt that the FSB was prepared to endanger civilians. Shortly after the Moscow blasts, residents of an apartment block in Ryazan caught FSB agents red-handed, placing sacks of explosive in their cellar. The agency claimed, with embarrassment, that it had been conducting a training exercise; the sacks were taken to a military firing range and destroyed.

The story of Mikhail Trepashkin, a lawyer and former FSB officer, also indicates that people in the security services had something to hide. In 2003, two Chechens were tried in secret for transporting explosives used in the Moscow bombings. Trepashkin was due to represent the interests of a victim's family at the hearing. He claims to have compiled details of how a witness had been encouraged by FSB officers to fabricate evidence, and to have learned the identity of an FSB agent involved in the bombings. These assertions were never made in court, because Trepashkin was himself arrested and jailed on charges, which he denies, of possession of firearms and giving away state secrets. He was released in November 2007.[3]

Whatever the truth about the apartment block bombings, there is no doubt that the timing of the invasion of Chechnya had everything to do with the drive to centralise power in Moscow. And it was a ruthless action. A large proportion of the estimated 25,000 deaths in the second Chechen war came in the first few weeks, as towns and villages were bombed heavily, to subdue them before the arrival of ground troops. By the end of January 2000, the federal forces had reached Grozny, the Chechen capital, and several thousand of Maskhadov's and other guerrillas retreated to the hills. Chechnya, despite being part of the Russian Federation, was treated like occupied enemy territory, much as nationalist areas of northern Ireland were in the 1970s.

The Russian federal forces, who in 1994 had arrived with no clear plan for dealing with civilians, this time meted out collective punishment. Villages lived in fear of 'clearances' (*zachistki*) by the army, during which adult men were rounded up and taken to filtration centres for murder, torture or imprisonment. The population was terrorised, and property destroyed and damaged. 'Disappearances', reminiscent of Argentina's 'dirty war' in the late 1970s, became routine. Families were sometimes offered the return of their loved ones, or the bodies, for money. Human rights groups listed 113 'disappearances' in the first 15 months of occupation, and uncovered mass graves. The most notorious of these, containing 51 corpses, was less than a kilometre from the army's main base. 'Civilians are subjected to arbitrary detention, torture, including rape, and ill treatment. Looting and arson of private property are also commonly reported', Amnesty International reported to European parliamentarians in 2002. Almost without exception these crimes have gone unpunished.[4]

'Chechenisation'

In 2003, with Maskhadov's and Basaev's guerrilla forces operating from the hills, the federal forces gained control of sufficient Chechen towns and villages to try to resurrect organs of Russian state power. Moscow had appointed an administration headed by Akhmat Kadyrov, who had been Chechnya's chief mufti (interpreter of sharia law) under Maskhadov, but had in 2000 switched loyalties to the Kremlin. In March 2003, a new constitution for the Chechen republic was approved in a referendum, and in October, a presidential election won comfortably by Kadyrov. The 'rigged' poll marked 'a return to the old Soviet method of total affirmation', under which the number of votes didn't matter, but who was counting them did, the liberal political analyst Lilia Shevstova concluded. Kadyrov was assassinated in May 2004, and although Alu Alkhanov succeeded him as president, his son Ramzan Kadyrov emerged as the real power in the land. Ramzan's initial instrument of rule was a band of 3–4,000 armed men, mostly former guerrillas, labelled the presidential guard. Vladislav Surkov and his team of Kremlin political technologists elaborated a policy of 'Chechenisation' – that is, control by local leaders loyal to the Russian state – and Kadyrov junior was entrusted with its implementation. He had both the ability to get things done, and a reputation for banditry and extreme violence. Credible allegations that he participated in torturing opponents have been published.[5]

In the extraordinary enclave that Chechnya has become, Grozny has been revived from a pile of ruins and made a functioning city. Thousands of former guerrillas switched loyalties to the government. Practically all public criticism of government has been suppressed and some aspects of Islamic law introduced. Tatiana Lokshina, a leading researcher on the Caucasus at Human Rights Watch, told me in an interview: 'Under Kadyrov, Chechnya operates completely outside the Russian legal framework and even outside the Russian cultural framework. Civil society, which emerged during the war, has been completely wiped out.' There are no independent media outlets or nongovernmental organisations (NGOs) in Chechnya; only the bureau of Memorial, the all-Russian NGO, remains, Lokshina explained. Informal but strictly enforced orders have been issued, requiring women to dress modestly – that is, in headscarves in public places – although according to its constitution Russia is a secular state.

'Chechenisation' has also been extended to the conduct of war against the remaining guerrilla forces, and terror against civilians suspected of disloyalty. This reached a peak in 2006, and then reduced as the republic stabilised. Evidence assembled by NGOs suggested that torture and other human rights abuses were 'systemic', and often carried out by forces under Kadyrov's direct command. Memorial documented 277 cases of torture between January 2005 and October 2006, but estimated that the total was likely to be several times higher. At the time of writing, there was no sign that the conflict has run its course. Indeed while Kadyrov has imposed some sort of tyrannical order on Chechnya, the neighbouring republic of Ingushetia has descended into something close to civil war. Since 2007 there has been a sharp rise in attacks on the security forces by armed militants. The response – *zachistki*, disappearances and other terror against civilians – has been terribly reminiscent of Chechnya in 2001–02.[6]

The War, the Army and Russian Society

The brutal resolution of the Chechnya problem redoubled the state's every dictatorial instinct, and its effects rippled out from that state through society. The war not only put some backbone into the disoriented and demoralised security forces, but also left an ugly imprint of racism on them. Some of the vilest manifestations of that racism surrounded the case of Colonel Yuri Budanov, who murdered an 18-year-old Chechen woman, Elza Kungaeva, after a *zachistka* in Tangi-Chu village in March 2000. The autopsy showed that Kungaeva, who had been seized by Budanov and other soldiers during a drunken rampage, was violently raped, beaten and then strangled to death in Budanov's quarters. The rape charge was dropped after some of Budanov's subordinates pleaded guilty to violating Kungaeva's dead body with a spade, but the colonel was found guilty of kidnap and murder and sentenced to ten years in jail. Appeals on the grounds of temporary insanity were unsuccessful and pleas for pardon lodged but then withdrawn. What dismayed opponents of the war and women's groups alike was the level of public support for Budanov. His former commander praised him as 'an asset for Russia'; the defence minister Sergei Ivanov described him as 'a respected officer'; a survey conducted before his trial showed that 50 per cent of respondents thought he should be released; and his every court appearance attracted demonstrations by nationalists.[7] In January 2009, Stanislav Markelov, a lawyer for Kungaeva's family, was shot dead in broad daylight in central Moscow, along with a journalist, Anastasia Baburova; Markelov's colleagues believed he may have been targeted for his commitment to human rights cases generally rather than this one particularly.

The Kungaeva case shone light not only on the immorality of those nationalists who made the sadistic killer of an innocent young woman into a hero, but also on the culture of violence among Russian army officers. Much of this violence is directed against conscript soldiers. All Russian men – except the disabled, some categories of students and those who can bribe their way out of it – serve for two years between the ages of 18 and 27. Many endure a regime of exploitation and bullying (*dedovshchina*) by officers and older conscripts that results in hundreds of deaths, injuries and suicides per year. Humiliating rituals and punishments, confiscation of property and goods and extreme physical and sexual violence are common. In 1994–96, conscripts might have been sent straight to Chechnya, where many were massacred by better trained, better prepared Chechen volunteers. During the second Chechen war, this demoralising and costly practice was ended: most active troops were volunteers, while conscripts served their time away from the front line. Nevertheless, *dedovshchina* remains rampant, striking terror into the heart of every Russian family with teenage sons.[8]

Anti-democratic poison spreads out from Chechnya much further than the security forces. The rigging of the Chechen presidential election of October 2003 became the template for a new type of falsification. The basic principle was ballot stuffing, and specifically, raising both turnout and support for United Russia way above plausible levels, in regions where civil society organisations were weak. In December 2003, in the all-Russian parliamentary elections, war-torn Chechnya – where public services barely functioned and hungry families lived without electricity – registered the

Children in Grozny, the Chechen capital, in front of an apartment block that was being rebuilt, in the summer of 2007. Photo: Tatiana Lokshina.

highest turnout (88.6 per cent) and the highest vote for United Russia (79.8 per cent), compared with national averages of 55.6 per cent and 37.4 per cent respectively. By the 2007 parliamentary election, the technique had been perfected, and deployed across the north Caucasus. Chechnya's turnout (99.4 per cent) and vote for United Russia (99.3 per cent) were again the highest, but were followed closely by Dagestan, Ingushetia, Kabardino-Balkaria and Karachai-Cherkessia, which all scored higher than 90 per cent on both counts. In Chechnya, a veteran local journalist who had been candidate for the Union of Right Forces estimated real turnout at 30 per cent, and in Dagestan the Communist Party brought legal action, alleging 'mass falsification'. The electoral fraud was unmasked most effectively in Ingushetia. The opposition website ingushetiya.ru called on people to file statements to the electoral commission that they had not taken part, and by mid-January 2008 it was reporting that 54.4 per cent of voters had done so.* This ballot stuffing is unlikely to

* In August 2008 Magomed Yevloyev, the owner of ingushetiya.ru and a long-time rival and opponent of Ingush president Murat Zyazikov, was

have altered national election results by itself, but it certainly disenfranchised many of Russia's poorest people and made a mockery of the Kremlin's claims to be developing democracy.[9]

Notwithstanding the corrosive effect of the war on Russian society – the militarism, racism and contempt for democracy that it bred – it has long since lost the support of the majority. Opinion polls show that this support ebbed during 2001–02 and increased only after big terrorist attacks on Russian civilians. In October 2002, the Dubrovka theatre siege in Moscow (see Chapter 4, page 71) caused a brief spike in support for the war, but by May 2003 more than 70 per cent again favoured a peaceful settlement. In September 2004, when security forces ended a much larger siege at a primary school in Beslan, North Ossetia, 334 hostages including 186 children were killed. But this time, the majority remained in favour of a peaceful settlement.[10]

The second Chechen war was waged on a smaller scale than the US and British war on Iraq, but was no less brutal. Like the Iraq war, it was supposedly directed against a government shielding terrorists, but was largely waged against civilians. For the United States and Britain, Iraq was and is about power on an international scale, about upholding their strategic interests in the Middle East. For Russia, the second Chechen war was primarily about power on a national scale and timed according to domestic factors. The Moscow elite used the war as a means to consolidate its grip.

'MANAGED DEMOCRACY' AND ITS LIMITS

Under Putin, the Russian state began to exercise power far more effectively than it had done under Yeltsin. Once federal rule was so savagely restored in Chechnya, there were no substantial threats to Russia's territorial integrity. The high tide of criminal activity had passed and the state almost regained its monopoly on the use of large-scale armed force. The prospect of groups of oligarchs hijacking government for sectional interests, as they had done under Yeltsin, receded. Big business paid more taxes. At the same time, democratic freedoms grabbed by society in the 1990s were eroded. The Kremlin made Parliament, and much of the media, tame and toothless.

---

shot dead while in police custody. His supporters have accused Zyazikov of ordering his death because of his outspoken opposition generally, not the electoral fraud campaign specifically.

Putin is often identified with the 'strong state' – but it would be more accurate to say that he made the state strong only compared with the chaos into which it descended under Yeltsin. Yeltsin's government was lauded in the west, for western political reasons, as democratic, but displayed antidemocratic instincts just as strong as Putin's. Yeltsin's administration closed down and then bombed parliament in 1993, falsified elections on a large scale, and launched the initial conflict in Chechnya. The difference between Yeltsin and Putin was between an ineffective authoritarian and a more effective one, not between a democrat and a dictator.

The Machinery of State

The way that Putin and his colleagues took control of Russia's oil revenues and restored the tax base was described in Chapter 4. Simultaneously, they reorganised and centralised the state apparatus. Putin's assault on the oligarchs and the Primakov–Luzhkov opposition ensured that, from the start, his governments were loyal. Ministerial rebellions were a thing of the past. And the relationship between Moscow and the 83 regions and republics was also transformed. In May 2000, Putin issued a decree dividing Russia into seven large federal districts, headed by presidential envoys. This mechanism ensured the subordination of even the most powerful regional governors to the Kremlin. Federal taxes increased at the expense of regional taxes; the status of regional laws was downgraded; and from September 2004, regional leaders were appointed by the president instead of being elected locally.

These changes were accompanied by a significant influx of *siloviki* into the state apparatus. At the top, the proportion of military personnel in the National Security Council grew to 58 per cent in 2003, from 46 per cent in 1993, and in the government to 33 per cent from 22 per cent. But the *siloviki* advanced most rapidly in the staffs of the seven new presidential envoys; among their deputies, 70 per cent were senior officers in the military or security services, while every third federal inspector supervising individual regions and republics was a *silovik*.

Researchers are divided as to the causes and consequences of these changes. Olga Kryshtanovskaya and Stephen White, who compiled these statistics, concluded that Putin had by 2003 already 'established a network of management based on the military and security services' that controlled 'virtually all the key social processes' and rendered democratic institutions increasingly 'formal' (that is, unreal). Bettina Renz, who conducted another research project on the Russian apparatus, cautioned against assuming that the advance of the *siloviki* was necessarily the result of a conscious policy. She pointed out that Putin, on entering Yeltsin's chaotic Kremlin, had sought to build a power base of people he had worked with before, and trusted. That naturally included many *siloviki*. Renz further cautioned that the *siloviki* were not a homogenous bunch – a point driven home forcefully in 2007, when a dispute between senior *siloviki* spilled out into the public domain. The general prosecutor's office arrested a group of officers in the federal anti-narcotics agency on corruption charges. In response, Viktor Cherkesov, head of the agency and a close ally of Putin's, published an open letter warning that 'feuds within the so-called *chekist* community' would have dire consequences. 'Excesses' by the general prosecutor's office could degenerate into a 'war of all against all'. Then the whole of society would suffer: the caste of *siloviki* had been a hook onto which society had hung in the bad times, and could collapse.[11]

The changes made by Putin at the higher levels of the state administration strike a sharp contrast with the lethargic pace of reform in the lower reaches of Russia's gigantic bureaucracy – in the police stations, the customs service, and the mind-boggling array of federal and local government agencies. Following a pattern established through centuries of Russian history, the bureaucracy has responded to Putin's attempts to trim it by expanding even further. Russia's army of office-based government bureaucrats grew from 600,000 in 1992 to 1.1 million in 2000, and then to 1.6 million by 2007. A survey published in 2005 by Indem, an independent think-tank, showed that corruption among these officials swelled substantially during the oil boom. As soon as the economy got back on its feet and small businesses began to flourish, bribe taking expanded. Corruption by state officials had by 2005 ballooned into a 'market' estimated by Indem to be worth $315 billion, nearly ten times its level in 2001. Indem acknowledged that this astronomical figure – two-and-a-half times larger than the state budget – could be nothing more than an educated guess. It seems to me overestimated. But Indem's research is well grounded and the trend is indisputable. Indem reckoned that the average size of bribes paid by businesses – mostly to executives such as tax inspectors and licensing agents, and on a smaller scale to customs and police officers – spiralled up from $10,000 in 2001 to $136,000 in 2005. Indem also reckoned that the volume of bribes paid by businesses was about a hundred times greater than those paid by private citizens for example, for advantages in health or housing, or for resolving passport registration issues.[12]

Parliament and Parties

The western reader trying to understand the political mechanisms used to rule Russia is faced with a paradox. On one hand, Putin has been an unprecedentedly popular leader, to the extent that popularity can be measured by Russian elections and opinion polls. On the other, the Kremlin has nevertheless felt the need to impose increasingly dictatorial controls over political and civic activity. Putin's support rose from 53 per cent in the 2000 election to 71 per cent in 2004; his successor Dmitry Medvedev polled 71 per cent in 2008. In all cases the Communist party candidate came second, with a steadily decreasing vote. The consensus among independent observers and NGOs is that ballots were rigged (see pages 116–18 above) – but on a small scale, compared for example with the 1996 presidential election. Ballot rigging probably helped Putin to pass the 50 per cent barrier first time round in 2000, but did not in any instance alter the final result. Putin was actually popular, in various ways. Opinion polls recorded that in November 1999 Yeltsin was 'trusted' by 4 per cent of respondents and 'distrusted' by 88 per cent, while in May 2000 Putin was 'trusted' by 41 per cent and 'distrusted' by 39 per cent. Another poll recorded the proportion that 'totally trusted' Putin rising from 15 per cent in 2000 to 19 per cent in 2004, and the proportion 'inclined to trust' him from 48 per cent to 57 per cent.[13]

I have argued throughout that the rising living standards made possible by the oil boom were the main source of Putin's popularity. The sense of stability imparted by Putin – who unlike Yeltsin remained sober in public and coherent at all times – also helped. So did public sympathy both for the second Chechen war and for the assault on the oligarchs. But while the Kremlin nourished this support, it also waged a continuous offensive on democracy beyond the polling booth. I shall deal in turn with the driving of opposition parties out of Parliament, the close supervision of those that remained, state control of television and the attacks on journalism, and the imposition of constraints on civil activism.

The electoral exclusion of parties from Parliament, and discipline of those that remain, may be attributed in part to 'political technology'. This term has been used in the former Soviet Union to describe manipulation of elections and democratic institutions, far beyond what spin doctors are usually able to get away with in the west.[14] Spin doctors fashion and present a message; political technologists also deal in compromising material on opponents, distribute 'black PR' and bribe journalists to vilify opponents. They invent and finance fake political parties, as the CIA's manifold front organisations did in Latin America in the 1960s. When acting for incumbents, political technologists use 'administrative resources' to influence votes (for example, by financing popular measures or corruptly assuring the loyalty of local leaders).

Russian political technology's most sensational creation was the Unity party, which was conjured up in the space of a few weeks after Putin's appointment as premier in 1999. A group of governors fronted Unity, but it was actively supported by the Kremlin's political technologists. Berezovsky, then a Kremlin insider, was intimately involved: ORT television, which he effectively controlled, publicised the new party and discredited the opposition headed by Luzhkov and Primakov. At parliamentary elections three months later, Unity won 23 per cent of the vote, just 1 percentage point behind the Communists. Berezovsky himself was elected to represent Karachaevo-Cherkessia, and his protégé Roman Abramovich was elected governor of the remote province of Chukotka in the Russian far east. Unity's arrival transformed Parliament's relationship with the presidency. Under Yeltsin, Kremlin proposals were constantly blocked by Parliament, where the Communist party and its allies could usually muster a majority. From 1999, Unity could join with the Luzhkov–Primakov bloc, Zhirinovsky's Liberal Democrats and two small right-wing liberal parties to outvote the Communists and their allies. Thenceforth there were no significant Kremlin–Parliament clashes. Two parallel processes now began: election rules were altered to eliminate small parties, and the Kremlin's influence on those that remained was extended.

Measures that favoured large parties included a strict party registration system introduced in 2001, and a 2004 measure banning election blocs bringing together groups of parties. Prior to the 2007 parliamentary elections, the barrier parties had to pass to gain representation was raised from 5 per cent of the vote to 7 per cent. Parliament, which had previously comprised 225 deputies elected from party lists and 225 from geographical constituencies, was now elected entirely from party lists. The most notable victims of these changes were two right-wing liberal parties, the Union of Right Forces and Yabloko. They narrowly failed to pass the 5 per cent barrier in 2003, and the 7 per cent barrier in 2007. (These and other opposition parties are discussed in Chapter 8.) Another measure to protect the large party system was the abolition of the 'against all' category on the ballot paper. This traditional vehicle for protest been used by up to 5 per cent of voters in all previous national elections; in some cases, such as a mayoral election in Vladivostok in 2004, 'against all' protesters won a majority.

The Kremlin's efforts to control parties that remained in Parliament were boosted by Luzhkov and Primakov, who in April 2001 abandoned their opposition stance. Their Fatherland–All Russia bloc merged with Unity to form United Russia, which soon grew into a 'party of power' to which most regional leaders gravitated. In 2003 United Russia took 38 per cent of the votes, comfortably overtaking the Communists, with 13 per cent, to become the largest party in Parliament. United Russia has remained dominant in Parliament ever since, while on the streets its youth movement, Nashi (Ours) – summoned into existence by the political technologists in response to the 'Orange revolution' in Ukraine – has acquired an unpleasant reputation for aggressive demonstrations against perceived foreign enemies.

In 2006, the Kremlin's parliamentary project extended to creating a 'loyal opposition': the Just Russia party headed by Sergei Mironov, chairman of the Federation Council. Just Russia, encouraged by the Kremlin's political technologists, assimilated various left-wing and nationalist parties into a vaguely social democratic mélange. Some United Russia politicians joined too. In early 2007, Anatoly Aksakov, a parliamentary deputy and senior figure in banking circles, quit United Russia and joined Just Russia. Asked in an interview why he had shifted allegiances, he mentioned neither the policies of his old party nor those of his new one, but rather said: 'We need a two-party system here, as they have in the USA.' At the December 2007 elections, United Russia won an overwhelming majority, with 64 per cent of the votes, against 12 per cent for the Communists, 8 per cent for Zhirinovsky's Liberal Democrats and 7 per cent for Just Russia. No other party passed the 7 per cent barrier.[15]

In 2006–07 it was rumoured repeatedly that the Putin administration would press for a change in the Russian constitution, which prevents presidents serving a third term, to allow him to stay on. Some parliamentarians publicly advocated the measure. But it was dropped, and instead Dmitry Medvedev was chosen to succeed Putin. Medvedev had worked as a lawyer with Putin in St

Putin, macho man

Vladimir Putin revels in a macho image. He is a judo black belt, and – in a country where the poor health of men in their 50s is a national scandal – his physical fitness strikes a sharp contrast with Yeltsin, who wore his alcoholism almost as a mark of pride.

Putin is even something of a sex symbol. Just before the 2007 parliamentary elections, the Kremlin released a series of photos of him on a hunting trip, naked from the waist up and all rippling biceps. In some shots he was brandishing a gigantic rifle. A few months earlier, rumours of Putin's sexual prowess were reported across the world. Putin, then 56, was claimed to have had an affair with Alina Kabaeva, then 24, a United Russia parliamentarian and former Olympic rhythmic gymnastics gold medallist who had been voted one of Russia's

Tough guy: the Kremlin released this image of Putin, then president, on a hunting trip in Tyva, in September 2007.
Photo: Reuters/RIA Novosti/Kremlin.

most beautiful women in tabloid press polls. The claim was categorically denied.

There are grounds to suspect that Putin's laddish image is combined with a retrograde attitude to crimes against women. In 2006, a microphone left on inadvertently recorded Putin chatting informally with Ehud Olmert, the Israeli prime minister, about the Israeli president Moshe Katsav, who was facing allegations of rape and sexual assault of up to ten women. Putin told Olmert that Katsav 'turned out to be quite a powerful man.... He surprised all of us. We all envy him.' As a result of the scandal, Katsav resigned, and first avoided the rape charge by a plea bargain, but called off the arrangement in 2009 and was charged with rape and sexual harassment.

Putin's acerbic, sometimes vulgar, one-liners tap into the rich vein of Russian slang and swear words. In 1999, announcing the second Chechen war on television, Putin denounced 'terrorists' and declared: 'we'll soak them in the toilet' ('*my i v sortire ikh zamochim*'). This is a pun on the verb *mochit*, to soak, which also has a slang meaning, to whack or thump. This phrase did more than anything to impress on many Russians the character of their new, and then little known, prime minister. The former Soviet political prisoner Vladimir Bukovsky wrote that the phrase originates from the gulag, where, during rebellions, prisoners would start by killing informers and throwing them into the camps' open toilets. He added: 'And what does Putin know about all that? Nothing.'

More recently, Putin has enjoyed gratuitously insulting the heads of neighbouring states who have fallen out with Russia. In October 2008 he publicly referred to Ukrainian president Viktor Yushchenko as a 'trickster' or 'swindler' ('*mazurik*'). In November 2008 the French press reported that Putin had told president Nicolas Sarkozy of France that he wanted to hang president Mikhail Saakashvili of Georgia 'by the balls'. Subsequently, during a televised phone-in with the public, a caller inquired of Putin whether he really wanted to hang Saakashvili 'by one place'. Putin smiled and responded: 'Why only one?'[17]

Petersburg, was brought to Moscow by Putin in 1999, and soon became deputy head of the presidential administration. During the 2000s he took a series of ministerial and Kremlin posts, and served as Gazprom's deputy chairman, and then chairman. One of his first acts as president was to appoint Putin prime minister. To date Medvedev is assumed to remain a junior partner.

Ideology

When Putin and the Unity party burst on to the scene, they had no mass movement behind them, nor policies to speak of, beyond crushing Chechnya and restoring stability – and did not have an ideology either. Igor Shabdurasulov, a Berezovsky ally and deputy head of the presidential administration during Putin's first few months, said later that ideology 'wasn't necessary [then] from a tactical point of view', and needed time to develop. Then the close relationship formed with the United States in the 'war against terror' began to sour, after the US invasion of Iraq and US support for the Georgian 'Rose revolution' and Ukrainian 'Orange revolution'. Against this background, the Kremlin put together the ideology of 'sovereign democracy', which Putin explained in his 2005 address to the federal assembly.* 'Sovereign democracy' was founded on 'statehood', Putin said. The collapse of the Soviet Union had been 'the greatest geopolitical catastrophe of the century'; the chaos of the 1990s had meant that, up to 2005, restoring stability was the key. Thenceforth mobilisation would be the watchword, against bureaucratic inefficiency and corruption, to strengthen the Russian Federation and to strengthen the legal framework for capitalist free enterprise.[16]

For many Russian liberals and socialists, an important measure by which to judge Putin's 'statehood' is his attitude to Russian history. Before a broader audience, he has played to the ugly nationalism that sees Stalin primarily as an empire builder and architect of Soviet victory over Nazi Germany. Of course Stalin was a dictator, Putin said in a newspaper interview in 2001, but he won the war and 'it would be stupid to ignore that'. And so the Soviet hymn has been reappropriated as the Russian national anthem, with new, un-Soviet words. Putin dismayed human rights groups by waiting

* The president's annual address to both houses of Parliament, similar to the US State of the Union address.

until the final year of his presidency to utter a word about Stalinist repression. And then it was a petulant comparison:

> yes, there were terrible pages of our history, we remember [the Stalinist purges of] 1937. But we didn't use the atomic bomb against civilians. We didn't use chemical weapons.... It's intolerable that guilt should be imposed upon us!

As though one country could deal with its history by scoring points about the crimes of another. Finally, in October 2007, on Russia's memorial day for the victims of political repression, Putin visited the Butova firing range, where 21,000 Muscovites were executed in the late 1930s, and said in a speech: 'We have a great deal to do, to ensure that [this tragedy] is never forgotten.' The words were not accompanied by actions, though. In 2008, historians and educationalists protested against new government-recommended guides for school teachers that emphasised Stalin's role in restoring Russia's imperial might, watered down Gorbachev-era denunciations of repression, and argued that the primary motivation of the terror of the 1930s was 'effective' rule. And in December 2008, riot police burst into the St Petersburg offices of Memorial, the campaign group set up in late Soviet times to support victims of, and archive the history of, the Soviet prison system, and seized computer hard drives containing its entire records of Stalinist atrocities.[18]

The Attack on Democratic Freedoms

Outside Parliament, democratic rights have been eroded consistently in Putin's Russia. The freedoms of speech, assembly and organisation have been pushed back by authoritarianism at the top, and the brutality or indifference of elements in the state.

In respect of *free speech*, Putin's rule began with the campaign to bring the national television stations under state control described in Chapter 4. This ensured that only sanitised news reached most Russian households, which helped to safeguard Putin's electoral majority. For the interested minority that actively seek alternative news sources, the situation has in many respects improved, in the first place because of the Internet. In the print media, some outspoken liberal newspapers of the 1990s, such as *Segodnia*, have closed, and others, such as *Kommersant*, been taken over by Kremlin-friendly owners. The courageous opposition weekly, *Novaya Gazeta*, has flourished – but a very high price has been paid by its journalists, of whom four have been killed to date. Dozens of regional newspapers also shine, regularly standing up to, and exposing, corrupt local politicians. Nadezhda Azhgikhina, a veteran journalist and media freedom campaigner, wrote recently that the pessimism engendered by 'tangible state pressure' and some journalists' 'conformism' must be balanced by optimism about daily acts of courage, especially in the regions.

The most effective means of censorship is the contract killing of outspoken journalists. No evidence has been found linking national political leaders to such killings since colleagues of Dmitry Kholodov, who was bombed to death in 1994, followed the trail back to Yeltsin's defence minister, Pavel Grachev. But the criminal justice system allows those that organise killings, often including law enforcement officers, to act with impunity, the Russian and international journalists' unions say. The murder in October 2006 of Anna Politkovskaya, *Novaya Gazeta*'s heroic writer on Chechnya, received international attention. In February 2009, a jury acquitted three men accused of involvement in Politkovskaya's killing, sparking public outrage – and leaving unchecked a trail of evidence leading, via a shady world inhabited by FSB officers and their criminal contacts, to prominent politicians. Some hired killers have been convicted, but not a single organiser of a journalist's murder – not even in the case of Igor Domnikov, a *Novaya Gazeta* investigative reporter, in which a man was identified as having ordered and paid for the attack, but not tried.

Russia's record for murders of journalists is worse than that of any country except Iraq and Algeria. Between 1993 and 2008, 81 journalists died doing their job, 40 more were killed in suspicious circumstances and 13 disappeared. Journalists well know that their lives are cheap, which gives added menace to the dozens of assaults they face each year – 65, including some near-fatal attacks, were recorded in 2008, for example.[19]

The right to free assembly has almost been extinguished. Local authorities have practically unlimited powers to ban demonstrations, and in 2006–08 used them with increasing regularity against liberal and left-wing demonstrators. But nationalist groups, including some fascist and racist ones, have faced no restrictions when parading arrogantly through Moscow on the new 4 November holiday. This was declared from 2005 to be the 'Day of National Unity', effectively replacing the Soviet holiday on 7 November, the anniversary of the Bolshevik-led revolution of 1917.

Democratic freedoms have also been undermined by government efforts to control Russia's NGOs, of which more than 500,000 were formally registered by 2006. In 2001 a Civic Forum was set up by the Kremlin political technologists, essentially as a means by which government could communicate with, and monitor, the NGOs, but faded because NGOs were split over whether or not to participate. By Putin's second term, a two-pronged approach had been decided upon. First, in 2005, a Public Chamber, empowered to consult with the Kremlin, was established, with one-third presidential nominees (showbiz personalities, oligarchs, lawyers, and so on), one-third from 'national civic associations' and one-third from regional NGOs. Second, a law was passed imposing a mass of complex requirements to register NGOs – a perfect weapon in the hands of bureaucrats who wanted to shut them down. Officials can ban groups that threaten Russia's 'sovereignty' or 'cultural heritage and national interests', in the words of a catch-all clause. Putin railed in his 2004 address to the Federal Assembly against NGOs 'fed by an alien hand', leaving bureaucrats in no doubt about which targets to aim at. Larger NGOs have gone through lengthy court actions to overturn obstructions to registration and many smaller ones have failed. Activists also decry the regular use of antiterrorism laws to threaten opposition movements. Amendments to laws on treason and espionage proposed in late 2008 redoubled such fears: under the new provisions activists sharing information with foreign NGOs could face long jail terms.[20]

To what extent, then, is Putin a dictator? Zbigniew Brzezinski, national security adviser to the US president Jimmy Carter in 1977–81, compared Putin with the Italian fascist leader Benito Mussolini. Putin has 'centralised political power in the name of chauvinism' and 'imposed political controls over the economy without nationalising it or destroying the oligarchs and their mafias', he wrote.[21] Putin's alliance of state and large corporations certainly shares features of Mussolini's. But Mussolini reached the summit of a weak state apparatus via a campaign of violence and intimidation by his blackshirts, and a coup d'etat. He took over at a time of social unrest, in the face of active opposition. Putin, by contrast, was brought in by Yeltsin's kitchen cabinet at a time when social movements were at a low ebb.

Russia's property-owning class might be ready to use large-scale violence against such movements, and the oligarch Petr Aven's statement about Russia needing a Pinochet, mentioned in Chapter 1, is memorable in that context. But no physical repression of opponents on the gigantic scale practised by Pinochet has been seriously contemplated by post-Soviet Russian governments, because of the relative quiescence of the population. Where violence has been required to hold the Russian state together – in Chechnya – it has been meted out with great savagery. But when dealing with popular unrest in Russia proper, Putin and his colleagues have always been relatively cautious. The government works to isolate activists, but remains wary of large-scale movements and ready to make concessions.

Democracy has been rolled back, but its future is yet to be decided – and economic factors will be crucial in shaping that future. Until 2008, mounting authoritarianism was combined with the consistently improving living standards that made Putin popular. The end of the oil boom and the resulting drop in living standards will disrupt that relationship.

Russia's strangest democrat

Boris Berezovsky, the most powerful Yeltsin-era oligarch – who since 2001 has lived in exile in London – has fashioned an image for himself as a 'democratic' opponent of Putin. It is a cautionary tale of how readers of the foreign press can be presented with a back-to-front, upside-down picture. Berezovsky's self-publicising campaign reached its apex in April 2007, when he claimed in an interview with the *Guardian* to be working with elements in the Russian elite to 'use force to change [Putin's] regime'. For observers of Russian politics, Berezovsky's rant was empty: there was no evidence that he had support in Russia, and plenty of evidence that he hadn't. The story nevertheless circulated widely.

In July 2007, Berezovsky followed up by telling British journalists that he had fled London because a Russian hit man had come to the Hilton Hotel to kill him, and that Putin was behind the plot. The story, attributed only to Berezovsky himself, with limited corroboration by an unnamed police source, first appeared in the tabloid, the *Sun*. It was repeated, almost unquestioned, in all the UK broadsheet newspapers.

Only the *Independent* said the timing 'raised suspicions' that it was just 'one more volley' fired by Berezovsky in his war with the Kremlin.

The background to this bizarre episode was the sharp deterioration in UK–Russian government relations following the death in London in November 2006 from polonium poisoning of Aleksandr Litvinenko. From his deathbed, this former FSB agent and employee of Berezovsky's accused Putin of murdering him. The UK authorities decided to prosecute Andrei Lugovoi, a *chekist* and associate of Litvinenko's who met him on the day of his death and appeared to be linked to a trail of polonium traces. The United Kingdom requested his extradition, which was refused. (The anti-British publicity in Russia was as strong as the anti-Russian publicity in Britain, and on the back of it Lugovoi joined Zhirinovsky's Liberal Democrats' list for the December 2007 parliamentary elections. He is now a parliamentary deputy.)

The real cause of Litvinenko's death is unknown. In November 1998, when Putin headed the FSB and Litvinenko worked in it, Litvinenko made public a plan by senior FSB officers to assassinate Berezovsky and others. As a result, Litvinenko was imprisoned, and then released in December 1999. In 2000 he joined Berezovsky in exile in London, and in 2002 published a book about FSB dirty tricks. It repeated the suggestion that Putin may have sanctioned the bombings that led to the second Chechen war, but failed to deal with the obvious point made by the financier George Soros and many others – that Berezovsky, in 1999 far more politically powerful than Putin, could also have done so.

In London Litvinenko was a fish out of water. He received a stipend from Berezovsky and worked as a consultant, selling information about the Russian security services. He collaborated with Mario Scaramella of the Mitrokhin commission, set up by Silvio Berlusconi's right-wing Italian government, ostensibly to examine KGB activities in Italy but actually to smear Berlusconi's political opponents. Litvinenko provided often questionable information for the commission and made dangerous enemies in Italian and Russian criminal networks as a result. In March 2006 the Italian parliament forced Berlusconi to wind up the commission. A month later Romano Prodi, one of Berlusconi's targets, defeated him in a general election.

Litvinenko might have been killed as a result of falling out with former KGB colleagues, or Russian or Italian criminals. But in the United Kingdom and United States he was feted almost universally as a political dissident murdered on Putin's orders, despite the lack of substantial evidence one way or the other.

Berezovsky, whose various foundations make little impact on social movements in Russia, has had one success: in shaping English-language press coverage. Having, in 1996, mobilised power and money to determine the outcome of the presidential election, and when in office revelled in the opaque nexus linking politics and business, he is presented as a democrat. Having done more than anyone to smooth Putin's path to the Kremlin, and sown seeds of the second Chechen war in his confidential dealings with Chechen military formations, he is presented as a principled opponent of Putin's. But as Soros wrote: 'Berezovsky saw the world through the prism of his personal interests. He had no difficulty in subordinating the fate of Russia to his own.'[22]

7

PEOPLE AND MONEY: HUMAN DEVELOPMENT DILEMMAS

Every aspect of Russian people's well-being – from life expectancy to living standards, access to healthcare and education – suffered badly in the 1990s. The return to economic growth in the 2000s brought substantial improvements. Many people were raised out of poverty and average living standards improved. But equally serious problems remained unsolved. The gaps between rich and poor, and between rich and poor regions, widened. The demographic crisis persisted, with death rates still higher than those of the mid-1980s. Health, education and social welfare reforms, guided by right-wing 'market' principles, introduced new inequalities. Worst of all, the government failed to apply Russia's oil windfall to the most pressing problems. Four national projects – on health, housing, agriculture and education – were set up, but often aimed at the wrong targets. The effects of the 2008 financial crash on the state's finances mean that less oil money will be available in future, and chances have been missed. In 2009, unemployment rose, living standards fell, and the associated health and welfare problems began to accumulate again.

THE DEMOGRAPHIC AND HEALTH CRISIS

Russia's worst health statistic – low, and falling, life expectancy – has not improved in the 2000s, despite the oil boom. This is the clearest reflection of the country's formidable health and social problems. In the 1960s, Russia's life expectancy was more or less level with that in developed countries; it is one of the few countries in the world to suffer a decline since then. Now Russian men are dying 15–19 years earlier (at 59 on average), and women 7–12 years earlier (at 73 on average), than those in developed countries.

The death rate, having hit an all-time high in the early 1990s, fell temporarily in the late 1990s, but in the 2000s increased. Mortality among men of working age is three to five times higher, and among women twice as high, as in other countries at similar levels of economic development. The most basic causes are unchanged. Those living on the verge of poverty, and suffering high levels of alcoholism, poor nutrition, lack of healthcare, and psychological stress, are most prone to dying young, a report issued by the UN Development Programme (UNDP) in 2008 said. The health ministry demographer Alla Ivanova told a seminar on the report that the 'low price of human life in the state's eyes', reflected in the lack of finance for healthcare, continued to play a key role.

High death rates have combined with a constantly falling birth rate to produce a sharp decline in Russia's population, and demographers expect this to continue in the coming decades. Political leaders are alarmed: Putin has many times repeated that reversing depopulation is a priority, and in 2007 Dmitry Medvedev, then deputy prime minister, said the prospect of a long-term decline in population 'put the existence of the state into question'. One of Russia's leading demographers, Anatoly Vishnevsky, believes that the problem is not absolute numbers, but the 'serious inconsistencies' between the small size of Russia's population on one hand, and the vastness of its territory and distribution of urban centres on the other. The depopulation of the Russian Far East is an extreme example. But there is a much bigger disagreement between politicians and researchers – about how and when the population decline might be halted.

The government started a natalist programme (that is, encouraging women to have more children) in 2005. After the birth rate increased slightly in 2007, Putin announced that the drive was working, and that within three or four years depopulation could be reversed. But the demographers say that the 2007 statistic was a blip, and that only long-term changes in health and living conditions will depress the death rate and encourage women to have more children. They believe that if long-term trends persist, Russia's population will fall from 142 million in 2008 to 125 million in 2025. A related problem is that a short-term increase in the number of people of working age, relative to pensioners and children, is about to give way to a long-term decrease. In 2006, for every ten people of working age, there were six pensioners and children; by 2025 there will be eight, putting a corresponding burden on health and pension systems.

The declining birth rate goes in waves, the demographers warn. Fewer newborns now means fewer women of childbearing age in 20–25 years' time. And the birth rate fell steeply from 1987, as the then-Soviet economic crisis made young families more uncertain of the future. So in 2007, for every 100 Russian women aged 20–29 (those most likely to become mothers), there were only 75 girls of 10–19 (the most likely mothers in 2017) and just 56 girls of 0–9 (the most likely mothers in 2027). Furthermore, like their counterparts in other industrialised countries, Russian women are often deciding to start families later. They tend to prioritise work above having a large family, even more than women elsewhere – due largely to their high average level of education, researchers believe. In short, many of Russia's young women are exercising their right to choose, and collectively confounding the government's drive to raise the birth rate. The government reckons it can increase the birth rate from its current low level, 1.3 births per woman, up to 1.8 – but still short of the 2.1 needed for natural replacement of the population. Most demographers are doubtful that a rate of 2.1 can be achieved.[1]

In 2006 the government announced improved maternity benefits, and a new scheme under which families receive a 250,000 ruble lump sum on their second child's third birthday. Payments for a third child were mooted. Sociologists and health experts said this was missing the point. Tatiana Maleva at the Independent Institute of Social Policy said the measures would probably only help women who dropped out of the labour force; ways needed to be found to encourage working women to become mothers. UNDP research found that health infrastructure is more important than cash: Russia is short of 1 million pre-school care places, for example. Better housing and secondary health care are key elements, the UNDP argued.

All-round improvements in healthcare and social welfare are not only the most important precondition for increasing the birth rate, they also hold the key to lowering the death rate, the specialists believe. Preventive measures are crucial, and they are the Russian health system's weak point. Reducing alcoholism, which kills about half a million people a year, and heavy smoking, are priorities. So is action on the social conditions that produce high rates of death by 'external causes' (that is, murders, suicides and accidents).

Over the longer term, AIDS will pose the biggest challenge to the health system. In the decade to 2007, the number of registered cases rose from around 1,000 to 405,427; the expert consensus is that the actual number is more than 1 million. Although the primary method of infection in Russia has been by injecting drug use, and most registered sufferers are drug users, specialists have been warning for some years that AIDS is moving over to wider strata of the population, and more frequently being spread via heterosexual intercourse.[2]

Another crucial aspect of Russia's demographic crisis is migration. Historically, Russia has been a destination for migrants from Central Asia and the Caucasus, and these regions continue to provide most immigrants. In the 1990s, an estimated 6.9 million migrants arrived in Russia, while 3.6 million Russians left, mostly to move to the United States, Germany or Israel. Immigration and emigration both fell sharply in the 2000s: official figures say that in 2000–06, 1.4 million people arrived and 600,000 left, but independent researchers say the real figures are at least twice as high. Certainly, many young, educated Russians who had gone to the United States or Europe returned. In addition, there are many millions of temporary migrant workers in Russia, mostly from Ukraine, the Caucasus, Central Asia and China. Russia's main trade union federation estimated that there were 702,500 such arrivals in 2005, but much larger numbers in total – even though the federal migration service's estimate of 10–12 million illegal migrant workers is derided by researchers as exaggerated.

For demographers, immigration is a vital part of the answer to Russia's depopulation question. Migrant workers make a significant contribution to a labour force depleted by demographic trends, as they do in much of western Europe. But Russian politicians have never been prepared to take the bull by the horns and welcome migrants. They prefer to keep their options open, leaving migrants insecure and giving ground to the xenophobic nationalist fringe. The result is that policies and laws look both ways. The 2007 programme on demographic policy envisaged limiting immigration to 160,000–170,000 per year until 2017 – which will minimise the migrant contribution to the economy, demographers warn.

The state has in crucial respects opened the door to racism against migrants by its institutions. A 2002 law made citizenship almost impossible to attain for many migrants. During Russia's diplomatic stand-off with Georgia in late 2006, Georgian nationals were ordered to leave Russia – an order interpreted by many police forces, local authorities and other state agencies as a reason to harass Caucasian and Central Asian migrants in general. At that time post-Soviet Russia experienced its first real pogrom, against Chechen and other Caucasian residents in Kondopoga in north-west Russia. After a fight between Chechens and Russians that led to fatalities, migrants' homes and businesses were attacked by large crowds. In January 2007, the government imposed restrictions on the numbers of non-Russians working in retail outlets, one of the main fields in which Caucasian migrants work.[3]

Russia's relative lack of progress in tackling its demographic crisis during the oil boom is perhaps the single most significant indication of the difficulties that economists call the 'resource curse'. The country's material wealth, which has done so much to benefit its elite, has made no noticeable impact on these grim statistics of life and death.

THE WIDENING GAP BETWEEN RICH AND POOR

During the oil boom, Russia not only failed to improve substantially its people's life expectancy and related measures of health, but also failed to stop the gap between rich and poor widening. In the 1990s, Russia's economy collapsed, and inequalities grew; in the 2000s, the economy recovered, and inequalities grew further. The international background is that in the past two decades the welfare of much of the world's population has improved, but simultaneously, inequality within most countries has increased. Figure 7.1 shows that Russia's Gini coefficient, a standard statistical measure of income distribution,* rose in the late 1990s, paused in 2000–03, then rose again. The second line shows GDP per capita, a measure of national wealth: as it increased, distribution became more unequal.

The Gini coefficient, like all statistics, has its drawbacks. It underestimates the wealth of the rich, because it only measures income, and not possessions. It underestimates the income of some of the poor, because like other statistics it can not count 'grey' (untaxed) earnings – although the proportion of such earnings was certainly falling in Russia between 1995 and 2007. But the main point, that inequality increased during Russia's oil boom, is borne out by research on incomes and nonincome factors such as health,

* The Gini coefficient is a measure of statistical dispersion, defined as a ratio with values between 0 and 1. 0 corresponds to perfect equality (everyone having the same income) and 1 to perfect inequality (one person having all the income and everyone else having zero). Gini coefficients range, approximately, from 0.23 in Denmark to 0.71 in Namibia. Most European countries are between 0.24 and 0.36; the United States is above 0.40.

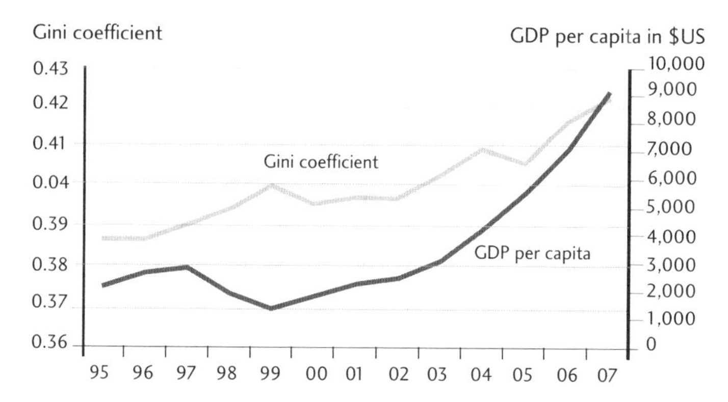

Figure 7.1 As wealth grows, inequality grows, 1995–2007
Source: Rosstat/EBRD.

education, and living and working conditions, which I survey here.

Inequality in Incomes and at Work

Average wages in Russia have risen steeply during the oil boom. Table 7.1 shows that between 2000 and 2007 they rose more than sixfold in dollar terms. Wages also rose more than two-and-a-half times using the federal statistical service's estimate of their value at 1991 prices. In 2006–07, average wages returned to where they had been in 1991, on that measure – although those figures understate the improvement, because they do not reflect the greater availability of goods and services in post-Soviet Russia compared with 1991. But what Table 7.1 also shows is that inequality in incomes – including wages, unearned income, and pensions and other state benefits – has grown. The third column shows the statistical service's 'income differentiation coefficient': the average of the top 10 per cent's income, as a multiple of the average of the bottom 10 per cent's income. It leaped up in the 1990s, and continued to grow in the 2000s. By 2007 the top tenth's average income was 16.8 times greater than the bottom tenth's. And that statistic, again, only counts income, not accumulated wealth.

A big factor driving income inequality is that wages have risen more rapidly than state benefits. Figure 7.2 compares average wages with average pensions: by 2007 average wages were more than four times higher.

However, research on poverty shows that the lowest-paid

Table 7.1 As incomes rise, the gap between rich and poor widens

	Average wages (monthly) in $	in rubles, at 1991 prices	Incomes: average of top 10%, as multiple of average of bottom 10%
1991	n/a	548	n/a
1992	22	369	8.0
1995	103	246	13.5
2000	79	238	13.9
2002	139	332	14.0
2003	179	368	14.5
2004	234	407	15.2
2005	303	459	15.2
2006	391	520	16.0
2007	529	607	16.8

Source: Rosstat.

workers, and especially those with children, are in greater danger than pensioners of being poor. Some of the huge differentials in wages are regional. In 2008 researchers estimated that the average wage in the poorest regions, 7,000 rubles ($250) a month, was about one-sixth of the average in the richest regions, 41,000 rubles ($1,465) a month. Even taking into account that many of the

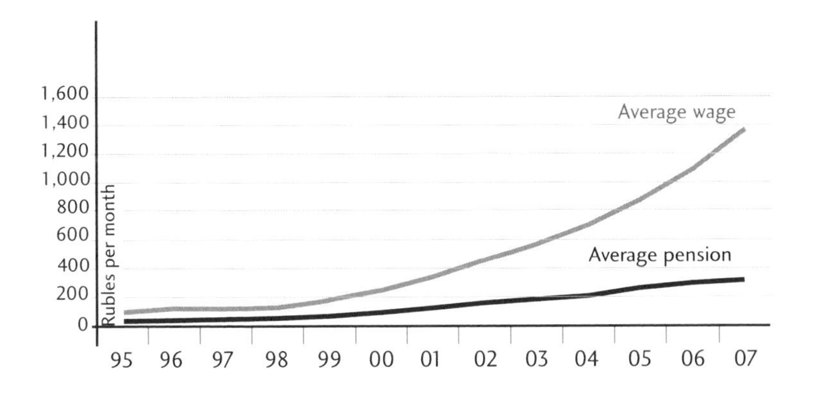

Figure 7.2 Wages rising faster than pensions
Source: Rosstat/Deutsche Bank.

lowest-paid workers live in regions where prices are generally lower than average, they are nevertheless poor by any definition – and have lived in poverty right through the oil boom. The scandalous treatment of these workers has been highlighted by the battle over the minimum wage. This minimum was first established under the labour code that came into force in 2002 – but it was, and remains, less than a quarter of the employed person's subsistence level, which is also set by the government. In 2005, the average wage was 8,550 rubles a month, the employed person's subsistence level 3,255 rubles a month – and the minimum wage just 720 rubles a month. Trade union pressure to raise the minimum wage has met stubborn resistance from Putin (see Chapter 8, page 166).[5]

The growing differentials in wages (which account for more than 70 per cent of incomes) are the main component of differentials in incomes. Wage rates have been impacted by continuing changes in the nature of the workforce, such as the decline of large-scale industry, growth of the service sector and the rise of temporary and informal employment. The move from state ownership to private ownership has continued: in 2007 the proportion of workers in privately owned firms rose from 46 per cent to 56 per cent, and that in state-owned firms fell from 38 per cent to 32 per cent. Large enterprises gave way to small ones, and the number of workers employed in cafés, restaurants and other small trading and service businesses kept rising. By 2007 those in trade and small-scale repair (11.8 million) outnumbered those in processing industry (11.4 million) for the first time. The numbers in education and health (10.6 million), state service (3.5 million), transport (5.4 million) and the natural resources and energy sectors (2.9 million) had not much changed, while the number in agriculture (6.7 million) was continuing to fall. There has been a vast expansion of the 'informal sector' (that is, unregistered businesses employing workers who do not pay tax). Sociologists estimated in 2005 that the informal sector employed 12.1 million workers. There are yawning inequalities in working conditions, too: the trade union federation said in 2005 that more than a quarter of male workers and one-seventh of female workers worked in 'harmful' conditions and that these numbers were rising. There were 2.7 accidents per 1,000 workers in 2007, an improvement on the 5.1 in 2000, but still two or three times higher than in most European countries.[6]

Poverty

The oil boom has lifted millions of people out of poverty in Russia. Table 7.2 shows that more than half of those who in 2000 lived beneath the poverty line set by the federal statistics service had, by 2007, risen above it. But a significant proportion of the population remain poor – 13.4 per cent in 2007 and 10.5 per cent in 2008, according to preliminary estimates. These families are trailing further behind as Russia has become richer. UNDP research showed that 40 per cent of poor households are two-parent families with one or two children, 25 per cent are couples without children, and 30 per cent are the 'traditional poor': that is, families with many children, families with one parent or none, and lone pensioners. The researchers reckoned that only a small minority were in extreme poverty, and said there was cause for hope in that many poor families were not far from the poverty line.

Most worrying is that the heaviest burden of poverty falls on children. Research published by the United Nations Children's Fund in 2006 showed that children are more likely to be poor than adults, children under 6 are more likely to be poor than older children, and that inequalities are being 'consolidated' rather than removed. The number of homeless children and orphans is increasing – and Russia's 'colossal system of orphanages' is as much part of the problem as a solution, Svetlana Aivazova of the Coalition of Women's NGOs told me in an interview. A big obstacle to reform is the social welfare bureaucracy, which has 'an entrenched interest' in keeping the outdated system, and the cashflows through it, unchanged.[7]

Table 7.2 The number of people living below the poverty line

	Millions	% of total
1992	49.3	33.5
1995	36.5	24.8
2000	42.3	29.0
2002	35.6	24.6
2003	29.3	20.3
2004	25.2	17.6
2005	25.2	17.7
2006	21.5	15.2
2007	18.9	13.4

Source: Rosstat.

A demonstration against welfare benefits reforms, January 2006, Izhevsk
Photo: *Den', Izhevsk.*

Regional Inequality

Russia's widening gap between rich and poor is manifested as a widening gap between rich and poor regions. Large differences are hardly surprising, given Russia's huge size, the variation in regional economies, and the way that untrammelled market forces were let loose in the 1990s. What alarms development experts is that the poorer regions have fallen further behind during the oil boom, despite resources being reallocated via the tax system and other government funds. The UNDP concluded from a study in 2007 that 'divisions between regions are increasing', and are 'most marked' in areas in which Russia lags behind developed countries – per capita gross regional product (GRP) and life expectancy. Per capita GRP in the top three regions (Moscow, St Petersburg and the oil-producing region of Tyumen) is between three and nine times greater than the average in the poorest 20 regions. According to the UNDP's collection of development indicators, Moscow is comparable with the Czech Republic and Tyumen with Hungary, while Ingushetia and Tyva are comparable with Guatemala and Tajikistan. Average life expectancy is 71 in Moscow and 56–60 in Tyva, Chita, Amur and Pskov. And in all areas, people living in the countryside are substantially poorer than those living in towns. A report by the World Bank in 2007 admitted that while in strictly economic terms divergence between regions was starting to decline, this was mainly due to some parts of European part of Russia catching up on the very richest – and 'regional disparities will very likely become more severe over the medium and longer term'.[8]

The oil boom exacerbated inequality not only between regions, but also within regions where oil and gas are produced. There is a 'strong, significant and robust relation between inequality and production of hydrocarbons' in the Russian regions, economists at the University of London found in 2007. In particular, the quantity of oil extracted is 'responsible for the increasing gap between the highest percentile of the population with respect to all the remaining four quintiles'.[9] This amounts to further supportive evidence that Russia is afflicted by the 'natural resource curse'.

Inequality in Housing

The chasm between rich and poor is exemplified by the homes in which people in Russia live – and the government's market-oriented approach is making matters worse. At one extreme, builders are grabbing city-centre land to build elite apartments as expensive as those in New York or London. At the other, nearly a quarter of homes have no running water, 15 million people live in prefabs built in the 1950s and 1960s, and 4 million in dormitories or communal flats.

Russia's climate leaves little room for manoeuvre in housing provision. Those who don't have heated accommodation, within solid walls, struggle to survive the winter. The sewers, courtyards and outhouses served up dozens of grisly reminders of that – corpses – in each year of the 1990s slump. The provision of tens of millions of warm but tiny flats to the newly urbanised population was one of the Soviet Union's lasting achievements, and from the 1960s to the 1980s, row upon row of gigantic apartment blocks rose on the outskirts of its cities. Dmitry Shostakovich wrote an opera to celebrate them, and Russia's most popular film ever, *The Irony of Fate*, turns on a joke about everyone's flats being similar. But these flats, still home to most people, are often dilapidated. In the early 1990s, most flats (about 70 per cent) became their residents' private property. The lucky few who lived in big city centres could profit by selling them on, but the change of ownership made little difference to most people. The cost of housing remained close to zero:

Soviet rents had been minuscule, and now there were only charges to pay. Crucially, local government remained responsible for repairs, maintenance and municipal services (gas, electricity, water and heating). These services were safety nets that stayed in place through the 1990s and during Putin's first term; only in 2005, with the adoption of the new housing code, did the price of services start to rise and privatisation begin.

The boom has brought better housing conditions for a better-off minority. Between 1996 and 2003, the long-term trend for the amount of space per person to increase resumed. The proportion of the population living in 25 square metres or more per person rose from 24 per cent to 30 per cent. Some of the worst abuses started to be tackled: the proportion living in less than 9 square metres per person fell slightly, from 7 per cent to 5 per cent, and the proportion of families classed as homeless fell from 15 per cent to 11 per cent. By 2006 it was down to 6 per cent. But more than half of Russia's families still live in housing deemed by the authorities to be too small or lacking basic facilities, and:

- 24 per cent have no running water.
- A further 13 per cent have no running hot water.
- 28 per cent have no direct connection to a sewage pipe.
- 34 per cent have no bath or shower.
- 3 per cent are classified as 'slums' or 'dangerous'.

But the real ticking time-bomb is that Soviet-era apartment blocks are not being refurbished quickly enough. The key statistic is the number of square metres on which capital repairs (restoration of buildings and infrastructure such as gas, water and sewage pipes) are undertaken each year. This sank from 56 million in 1980, to just 11.6 million in 1995 and 3.8 million in 2000. In 2006, five years into the oil boom, it had only recovered to 5.3 million. And prospects have just got even grimmer: housing services, including repairs, were privatised in 2005–08 and service providers are finding ways to avoid undertaking expensive capital repairs.[10] This privatisation has been a major cause of social protest during Putin's second term (see Chapter 9, page 177).

In 2006–07 the government announced plans to spend about $30 billion of its oil money stimulating residential construction and refurbishment under its Accessible Housing programme. But even before the credit bubble burst in late 2008, urban development researchers feared that the emphasis on new build, and mortgages for the middle class, would leave the most serious problems unsolved. In 2006–08 the Russian mortgage market soared from almost nothing, and was estimated at its height to cover 7–8 per cent of the housing market. But most families cannot raise a mortgage. An expert forum at Moscow State University heard that the proportion who could buy 18 square metres per person or more rose from 9 per cent in 2004 to 19 per cent in 2006; the economic crisis will surely bring it down again. The construction businesses – who are in it for the money – gravitate to the minority of paying customers: in 2007 the ten richest regions accounted for 50 per cent of construction, the ten poorest for 0.06 per cent.[11]

SOCIAL POLICY UNDER PUTIN

The health, education and social welfare systems inherited by the Putin administration were in a bad way. In the early 1990s they had been ravaged by the slump and the resultant meltdown of state spending, and by the determination of Yeltsin's extreme pro-marketeers to force as much as possible, as quickly as possible, into the private sector. In the late 1990s, the privatisation mania was constrained by Parliament. But social spending stayed at a pitifully low level, doctors' and teachers' real wages continued to fall – respectively to about 80 per cent and 50 per cent of the average wage – and the services continued to deteriorate.

From 1999, three things changed:

- As the economy improved and tax revenue increased, more money was directed to health, education and social welfare.
- The stalemate between president and Parliament that had paralysed government during Yeltsin's second term was broken.
- The hotch-potch of policies put together by Yeltsin's governments, often with unsuitable advice from the international financial institutions, was replaced by an all-round reform programme drawn up by a team headed by German Gref, Putin's economic development minister.

The reform programme acknowledged the need to mend what was broken in the schools and hospitals, and was able to increase spending at least modestly. But its key principles were adapted from extreme right-wing privatisation credos in the west: as much health, education and social welfare as possible was to be provided by private companies; systems of private medical insurance and privately funded pensions would replace state-funded health and pension provision; the state's role would be to provide basics, to regulate, and to subsidise those who could not afford to pay. Welfare benefits, and housing provision, would be subject to the same principles.[12]

Putin's governments, conscious of public support for the Soviet-era welfare systems and of people's determination to share in the benefits of the oil boom, trod warily. In his first term (2000–04) Parliament passed laws providing for the gradual introduction of medical insurance and privately funded pensions, and for some measure of fee paying in university education. All these measures began to be introduced, but cautiously. The government feared popular reaction – such as the protests that erupted in January 2005, in response to the reform of welfare benefits (see Chapter 9, pages 173–7). That reform was slowed down as a result, and others were paced gently from the start. For example, pension reform was legislated in 2002: alongside the universal state-funded scheme, workers would be encouraged to contribute to private pension funds. But by 2008, fewer than 10 per cent of workers had joined a private scheme, and almost all of these were at above-average income levels.

During Putin's second term, the government's hand was strengthened by the huge volumes of oil money available. The damage done to budget spending in the early 1990s at last began to be reversed. There were substantial pay increases for staff in health, education and other public services. In 2007, a three-year budget was adopted, with priority funds earmarked for 'national projects' in health, education, accessible housing and the development of agriculture. But against the background of mounting social inequality described above, the government faced growing criticism about how the funds that were at long last available should be spent.

In the case of the health system, the government was urged to address widening inequalities of access. In 2008, a study by researchers at the Independent Institute of Social Policy concluded that the system was characterised by 'deep-going differences in the way that various categories of the population – depending on their level of education, income and location – seek different types of medical help'. People in the countryside made extremely little use of outpatient care, particularly by specialists, for example. In some regions, usually poorer ones, the accessibility of free care was limited. There was a 'striking inequality' in the proportion of household income that poor people spent on medicine: 'more than 8 per cent of the population is compelled to shoulder "catastrophic" levels of medical expenses'. The report also said that pay rises had been distributed unevenly through the health service, and that the level of under-the-counter payments for treatment had increased between 2002 and 2007. The much-vaunted 'national projects' will make little difference to the profound institutional and funding problems, Professor Natalia Zubarevich of Moscow State University, a leading social policy researcher, said in an interview. In the health sector, the 'national project' money comprises only 13 per cent of total spending, and is poorly directed, she said. About one-third of the amounts set aside via the 'national project' had been swallowed up by a pay rise for general practitioners, while surgeons and other specialists will receive nothing; another quarter will go on flagship medical centres. Major institutional problems and the inequalities they produce had not been addressed, she warned.[13]

Russia entered the recession of 2009 with many such problems unresolved. The financial strains on the budget, and the human strains on the health, education and social welfare systems, are bound to increase.

8

PEOPLE: PARTIES, UNIONS AND NGOs

In January 2005, the Russian government made changes to the welfare benefit system: benefits in kind, such as free travel and medicine for pensioners, were replaced with money payments or abolished. This sparked the first widespread street demonstrations in Putin's Russia. Only a small minority participated, but they had the support or sympathy of the majority. Government and local authorities hurried to dispel the movement with a combination of concessions, promises and threats.

This episode (which is discussed fully in Chapter 9) highlighted some of the contradictions that make social movements in Russia hard to understand. The demonstrations made the Kremlin extremely nervous. At that time, some in the political elite were terrified that the Georgian 'Rose revolution' of November 2003 and the Ukrainian 'Orange revolution' which began in November 2004 would be repeated in some form in Russia. That did not happen. There were echoes of the Ukrainian events in 2005 in Kyrgyzstan, in the 'Tulip revolution', and in Uzbekistan, in the Ferghana Valley protest movement which ended with the security forces' massacre of protesters at Andijan.* But not in Russia. The revolt by pensioners and other benefit recipients was unexpected, sudden and effective. However, while antigovernment slogans were raised on some of the many demonstrations, no general political movement ensued.

Given that Russia's people have the potential to attenuate, subvert or destroy the power of ruling elites – and that the country's long-term future is largely dependent on how that potential is

* Security forces fired on a crowd of protesters at Andijan on 13 May 2005. The government stated that nine people were killed and 34 injured; credible reports from news organisations and NGOs indicated a death toll between several dozen and 6–700.

realised – these events raised crucial questions. Are Russia's social movements as limited as they seem from a distance? What part might they play in determining broader political change? And how might they react to the hardships threatened by the end of the oil boom? Western journalists all too often conclude, from the absence of national, media-friendly demonstrations like those in Kiev, that the Russian population is sullen, suffering in silence. There are always Russian intellectuals willing to reinforce this misconception with age-old stereotypes of a meek population that neither knows nor cares how to resist the power of their rulers. And after all, Aleksandr Pushkin's *Boris Godunov* – a classic drama of power, with a place in Russian culture comparable to that of *King Lear* in the United Kingdom – ends with the false tsar, Dmitry, usurping the throne, and the haunting stage direction: 'The people are silent.' In this chapter, and the next, I hope to show that nevertheless, Russia's social movements contain the seeds of powerful forces for change.

While the stereotype of a quiescent Russian people hoping for a good tsar is deceptive, it exists for a reason. It was current among Russian intellectuals in the nineteenth century, whose hopes of reforming, or doing away with, the autocratic tsarist regime were frustrated, for one thing, by their inability to communicate meaningfully with the impoverished and largely illiterate peasantry who comprised the overwhelming majority of the population. But the stereotype was overthrown, along with much else, by the three Russian revolutions of 1905, February 1917 and October–November 1917, which drew millions of urban workers, and tens of millions of peasants, into the most far-reaching social uprising Europe had ever seen. These revolutions brought into action an array of collective organisations, from village communes to factory committees and soldiers' and workers' soviets (councils). And these, too, are Russian traditions – although they were quite rapidly dissipated in the retreat from, and defeat of, the revolution in the 1920s and 1930s. It is against this background that the Soviet Union's extraordinarily persistent and pervasive dictatorship developed. That in turn forms the context for the real difficulties of reviving trade union, community and political organisations in post-Soviet Russia.

In the post-war Soviet Union in which much of the adult population of Putin's Russia grew up, collective action, independent of the state and Communist Party, was difficult or impossible. There were no trade unions or community organisations other than those approved by the authorities. There were occasionally spontaneous

'We won't keep quiet!' Workers at the Bummash engineering factory in Izhevsk demanding better conditions in the dormitories where they live, 2006
Photo: *Den', Izhevsk.*

local revolts, which were quickly suppressed. Rebellious trends in youth culture were harder for the authorities to deal with, but any attempt, for example by groups of students, to discuss politics or circulate forbidden reading matter ended in arrests and long terms of imprisonment. I repeat this point, which I made in the Introduction, to remind readers that, as dictatorship eased under Gorbachev, those who sought actively to change their lives, and their country, for the better – be it in trade unions, community groups, journalism or politics – had little tradition or experience to fall back on. Workers formed independent unions where there had been none for two or three generations; people set about political and social activities that had previously been impossible for them or their parents; journalists learned new types of reporting and commentary. The confusion surrounding any and every attempt to articulate working class interests politically was especially intense – hardly surprising, given the way that official Soviet ideology had perverted the meaning of 'socialism', 'communism' and even 'working class'.

The first post-Soviet years brought, along with unprecedented political freedom, new setbacks for all types of collective action. The economic slump had a devastating effect on communities: the social fabric of industrial towns was ripped to pieces. The very material certainties of the late Soviet period – of employment, school education, housing and at least rudimentary healthcare – suddenly vanished. The disruption of stable communities and stable workforces provided the worst possible conditions for collective social or industrial action. The economic boom of the 2000s made potentially for an improvement. This chapter describes the progress of the political opposition, NGOs and trade unions; Chapter 9 deals with the protests over benefits and housing, and other community-based social movements.

THE POLITICAL OPPOSITION

Putin's accession to the presidency in 2000 meant the beginning of the end for the Communist Party of the Russian Federation (CPRF), then post-Soviet Russia's most powerful political party. The blows struck by Putin's political technologists at the CPRF were described in Chapter 6. But these were not the only cause of its decline. Its 'state patriotic' outlook alienated many of its own parliamentary deputies who would have been happy to trade it in for some form of social democracy. And the party's ideology has had little appeal to younger activists, who would be needed to revive it: they have been recruited more successfully by the extreme nationalist parties and by Just Russia, the junior pro-Kremlin party in parliament.

Western readers should bear in mind that the CPRF is quite unlike communist parties in Western Europe. In their heyday, those parties dominated the left wing of the trade union movement and attracted the votes of millions who saw them as a force that could challenge capitalist governments. Even workers who disliked what they knew of the Soviet Union, or disagreed with the communists for other reasons, often admired communist militants for standing up to ruthless employers, corrupt union bosses or the fascists. The CPRF's history is quite different. It rose in 1993 from the ruins of the Communist Party of the Soviet Union, which for two or three generations had a monopoly on political power, industrial management and almost every facet of public life. In the 1960s and 1970s, when French workers might become communists to subvert their bosses, Russian workers joined the party in the hope of being promoted to management. And many of the activists who built the CPRF were lower-level Soviet apparatchiks, embittered by their sudden loss of power and influence. Most CPRF leaders continued to praise Stalin; those that now rued Soviet political repression joined other parties. Nevertheless, the CPRF had gigantic appeal to voters, especially of the older generation. It denounced the impoverishment of the population, lambasted Yeltsin and his oligarchs, and promised a return to the stability and higher living standards that most people in Russia had enjoyed until the early 1980s.

The CPRF's ideology was adapted from that of the Soviet party, although much of the rhetoric about class struggle was shelved. While the CPRF calls for the restitution of the multinational Soviet Union, its Russian nationalism has become ever more strident and its demands for tougher 'antiterrorist' action in Chechnya ever shriller. From its foundation, the CPRF and its leader Gennady Zyuganov worked in the 'red-brown front' with right-wing Russian nationalists (i.e. 'red' communists and 'brown' nationalists). Throughout the 1990s they turned out on anti-Yeltsin street demonstrations in which red flags mingled with the nationalists' often antisemitic placards.

When Putin and his supporters arrived in government in 1999, they stole much of the CPRF's political thunder. Putin was strengthening the state in just the way the CPRF demanded, and before long could offer the prospect of the improved living standards and relative stability its voters craved. Zyuganov's reaction was to dig in, to remind voters that Putin's remained a pro-capitalist regime and to lambast state corruption and bureaucracy. The CPRF's share of the parliamentary election vote fell from 24 per cent in 1999 to 12 per cent in 2007. Membership fell from around half a million in the mid 1990s to 180,000 in 2008.

A succession of CPRF leaders who wanted to rebrand the party as something closer to social democratic have lost the argument. These include Gennady Seleznev, chairman of the Duma from 1996 to 2003, who was expelled in 2002, and Gennady Semigin, a CPRF deputy and multi-millionaire businessman, who was expelled in 2003. The economist Sergei Glazev walked out and joined Dmitry Rogozin's nationalist Rodina party, which formed the basis of an electoral bloc at the 2003 polls, and was given tacit support by the Kremlin in order to draw votes away from the CPRF. Fragments of Rodina were among the groups swept up in 2007 by Just Russia, the 'loyal opposition' mentioned in Chapter 6.[1]

Zyuganov has also dug in ideologically. A new CPRF programme, adopted in November 2008, called for nationalisation, the removal from power of the 'mafia–comprador bourgeoisie' and the revival of the Soviet Union. It also reflected Zyuganov's abiding Stalinism. A long section dedicated to 'saving the nation' briefly expresses regret over the 'breaches of socialist legality and the repressions' of the 1930s and 1940s – a laughably sanitised phrase to describe the executions, mass deportations and slave labour – but insists that the Soviet party's record was overwhelmingly positive. On the 50th anniversary of Nikita Khrushchev's 1956 secret speech, the first denunciation by a Soviet leader of Stalin's crimes, Zyuganov said the speech had done more harm than good. And in 2008 he published an overwhelmingly positive biography of Stalin.[2]

The mixture of socialist terminology and a fierce nationalism situated on, and often over, the border with xenophobia and racism, is characteristic not only of the CPRF but of other so-called 'left' organisations in Russia. This is a phenomenon the western European left has struggled to understand. In the early 1990s, socialists I knew in Moscow had often to explain to western European sympathisers why they would not participate in the 'red-brown' alliance, as a matter of internationalist principle. The visitors often simply did not grasp the extent to which an ugly, reactionary nationalism pervaded the demonstrations. On an official level, the Socialist International (the grouping of social democratic parties) was in 2005 considering an affiliation request from Rodina, when it learned to its surprise that a group of Rodina deputies had, together with some CPRF colleagues, written to the prosecutor demanding a ban on all manifestations of Jewish religion and culture. Rogozin, then Rodina leader, explained that he had no intention of taking action against his antisemitic colleagues, although he disagreed with them.[3]

The 'red-brown' front has declined, along with the CPRF, in the 2000s, but 'left' nationalist groups remain strident. It is worth mentioning the National Bolshevik Party (NBP), mainly because of the astonishing respect accorded by Russian liberal politicians and western journalists alike to Eduard Limonov, its charismatic but politically unpleasant leader. Limonov, who emigrated from the USSR in 1974, became a punk countercultural novelist in the United States and returned to Russia in 1991. After a brief spell in Vladimir Zhirinovsky's Liberal Democratic party, he formed the NBP in 1993. The party's declared aims are 'social justice' via nationalisation, civil and political freedoms, and 'imperial domination' as foreign policy, aimed first at 'the restitution of the empire destroyed in 1991', and specifically the incorporation into Russia of territories with Russian populations in neighbouring countries – Pridnestrovye, Abkhazia, South Ossetia, and so on. In the 1990s the NBP sought notoriety on the 'red-brown' demonstrations: its members dressed in black, carried flags displaying the hammer and sickle on a white circle and red background and shouted 'Stalin! Beria! Gulag!' Limonov advocated a 'Serbian solution' to attacks on Russia's statehood. During the war in former Yugoslavia he befriended the Bosnian Serb war criminal Radovan Karadzic, and was filmed firing a sniper rifle into Sarajevo, the Bosnian capital.[4]

Under Putin, the security forces have clamped down on the NBP. Limonov was jailed from 2001 to 2003, on charges arising from an article calling for an armed attack on Kazakhstan. The NBP organises stunt attacks on politicians and public buildings, and most of its 140-odd 'political prisoners' are participants who received heavy sentences. The courts have declared the NBP 'extremist' and therefore illegal. The NBP's status as a target of state repression, its violent nationalist rhetoric, and its leader's cynical punk prose, have given it a following among young people. The NBP's claim to reject 'any form of xenophobia, antisemitism and racial intolerance' contrasts sharply with the sympathy its officials show to racist gangs. In 2004, for example, after a spate of violent racist attacks in St Petersburg, a group of skinheads named Shultz-88 (the '8s' representing the 'h's in 'heil Hitler'), were tried for brutally assaulting Aram Gasparian, an Armenian. Nikolai Girenko, a prominent antifascist who appeared as a state prosecution witness, was later shot dead, and an extreme racist website claimed he had been 'executed'. But for *Limonka*, the NBP's national newspaper, the skinheads were the victims: it advised them that serving time for such a minor success as beating up Gasparian was a waste of nationalist resources. 'If it's terror, then do it seriously. Like Combat 18 in Great Britain [and other fascist paramilitaries] do', *Limonka* advised.[5]

The NBP's attitude to Nazism is equally generous. Photos of stormtroopers decorate the Khabarovsk branch's website. In a cynical, ironic message to followers in April 1999, Limonov noted the birthdays of Lenin and Hitler, the latter being 'the most mysterious and intriguing of historical figures'. 'Stand equal with great people [such as Hitler]. Don't be small', he wrote. Another article ruminated that 'everyone' in Russia 'needs fascism'.[6] All this would be so much raving from an egotistical eccentric, were it not for the alliance built since 2005 between Limonov and some of Russia's leading right-wing liberals, who perhaps take Limonov more seriously than he takes himself. In 2007 he became a leader, together with liberal politician and former chess champion Garry Kasparov, of the Other Russia opposition movement.

Kasparov's alliance with Limonov epitomises the right-wing

liberals' failure to mount any effective challenge to Putin. The Other Russia was formed in the run-up to the 2007 parliamentary elections, and the heavy police intimidation of the 'Dissenters' Marches' that it organised highlighted state intolerance for public opposition. But Kasparov's project only came to the foreground – and gained an inordinate amount of attention from western journalists – after repeated setbacks for the two established right-wing liberal parties, Yabloko and the Union of Right Forces. Both campaigned strongly on political and media freedom, and both linked these issues to 'economic freedom'. The Union of Right Forces advocates free market and in some cases extreme neoliberal economic policies, while the Yabloko leader Grigory Yavlinsky has taken a social democratic line on economic issues under Putin. The liberal parties' failure to enter Parliament in 2003 and 2007 was mentioned in Chapter 6.

Russia has a small but vigorous antinationalist left, consisting of socialist, Trotskyist, anarchist and 'new left' groups and networks. This left has no national leadership, which some of its participants regard as a virtue, and little national coordination – although since 2005 'social forums', inspired by similar events in the west, have been held. Its strength is its geographically and politically diverse collection of activists, and the wide variety of local campaigns in which it collaborates with trade unions, anti-fascist groups and community movements. In the early 2000s, some sections of the extraparliamentary left campaigned consistently against the war in Chechnya, working closely with human rights activists and leaders of Chechen communities. Although only small numbers were involved, such action demonstrated the possibility of political opposition free of the nationalism that corrodes much of Russia's so-called 'left'.

MOVEMENTS FOR HUMAN RIGHTS AND THE ENVIRONMENT, AND OTHER NGOs

Russia's human rights movement, like its political opposition, bears the stamp of the recent Soviet past. In the 1960s, when civil rights movements of blacks in the US southern states and Catholics in Northern Ireland were at their peak, the USSR's human rights movement comprised minute groups of students and intellectuals, for whom the potential cost of each demonstration organised or bulletin distributed was years in a penal colony. For example six people who protested in Red Square against the Soviet invasion of Czechoslovakia in 1968 were arrested after five minutes, and sentenced to between two and four years in prison or exile. So 1986–88 was a historical turning point: almost all Soviet restrictions on the rights of free speech, assembly and movement were lifted. Political exiles, most notably the physicist Andrei Sakharov, returned home. After years of trying to carve out space for legal, civil, political, industrial and social rights in the Soviet system, the human rights defenders (*pravozashchitniki*) could suddenly work openly.

The early Yeltsin years split the *pravozashchitniki*. Some prominent figures moved into politics. For example Lev Ponomarev and Sergei Kovalev became leading 'democratic' parliamentarians, continuing to support Yeltsin even when he ordered the shelling of Parliament in October 1993, although not for long afterwards. Others kept a sceptical distance. The first Chechen war in 1995–96, and the accompanying onslaught on human rights, was a watershed. Yeltsin had 'crossed a Rubicon that will turn Russia back into a police state', Yelena Bonner, Sakharov's widow, declared. After opposing the war, Kovalev was sacked by parliament as Russia's human rights ombudsman. Yeltsin turned on him and shut down a presidential human rights commission he headed. The Chechen tragedy also brought back into the limelight the soldiers' mothers' movement, one of the most high-profile human rights groups of the Gorbachev period, formed by mothers searching for their sons, or the corpses of their sons, who had been conscripted and sent to fight, first in Afghanistan, then in Chechnya.

History has given the very concept of 'human rights' a wider meaning in Russia than it generally has in the west. Here, most people understand by it political and civil rights – freedom of speech and assembly, the right to equality before the law, and so on – whereas the Russian *pravozashchitniki* assume a much closer link between these rights and economic, social and cultural rights, such as rights at work and in the field of housing, health and education.* This is probably partly a legacy of Soviet times, when ordinary

* The background to the narrower meaning sometimes given to the term 'human rights' in the west is a dispute that erupted, after the United Nations adopted the Universal Declaration of Human Rights in 1948, over how these rights would be written into binding covenants. The controversy was aggravated by the cold war. The western powers, in opposition to the Soviet bloc, insisted that political and civil rights be treated separately from social and economic rights.

people who stood up for economic and social rights had to cross swords with local bureaucrats and – in the absence of effective trade unions or NGOs – might come straight into conflict with the state.[7]

Three main types of human rights organisation have been active in Putin's Russia: campaigners such as the Helsinki group, Memorial and others who focus primarily on research, and those such as Public Verdict who provide legal support to victims of abuses. They work within a much broader spectrum of national NGOs campaigning on social, cultural and political issues, and of local community groups taking up causes from housing rights to the rights of small investors cheated by financial fraud. (An example of NGO activity at the grassroots is given in the box starting on page 158.) The *pravozashchitnik* Liudmila Alekseeva – who became active during the post-Stalin 'thaw' of the late 1950s, emigrated in 1977, and returned to Russia in 1993 – explained in an interview that the older groups focusing on political and civil rights issues have become providers of advice, campaigning support and contacts for the wider movement:

> In Russia, civil and political rights exist in the constitution – but in life, the state does not observe them.... We have to conquer, to win, every right – be it on housing, on allotment gardens, or whatever – in a fight. Quite often, we have to resist encroachments on our social rights through the courts. And quite often we see decisions there in favour of the rich and powerful. Then we go to the media, we go out and demonstrate.... Our understanding of the concept of human rights is wider than in the west ... because our rights, even the most elementary ones, are not observed by the authorities. The laws are not observed.[8]

Environmentalism has produced another army of campaigners. Groups who took up issues such as industrial pollution were among the first to start legal activity under Gorbachev. The Chernobyl disaster of April 1986, when a nuclear reactor in north-west Ukraine exploded, provided a shocking impetus. Much like the human rights campaigners, Soviet-era environmentalists persisted through the 1990s and became the inspiration for a new generation of activists under Putin. Campaigners who focused on the dangers posed by Russia's decrepit nuclear fleet confronted a culture of military secrecy. Aleksandr Nikitin, a former naval safety inspector who contributed to a report by a Norwegian environmental group on Russia's northern fleet, was charged with treason, tried twice, and jailed for long periods, before being acquitted in 2000. Grigory Pasko, a Vladivostok-based journalist who reported the dumping of nuclear waste at sea, spent 33 months in jail from 1999 to 2003 on treason and other charges. Another focus of environmental campaigning has been the defence from pollution of Lake Baikal in eastern Siberia, the world's oldest and deepest freshwater lake. The Baikal Environmental Wave campaign group, set up in 1990 to protest at a paper mill that polluted the lake, in 2006 won a government decision to reroute the East Siberia–Pacific oil pipeline away from the lake's watershed, and in 2009 was mobilising against plans to build a uranium waste dump in nearby Angarsk.[9]

The making of a human rights defender

It was Larisa Fefilova's love and loyalty to her husband Sergei that set her on the path to becoming a *pravozashchitnik*. In March 2005, Sergei was arrested and charged with the murder of Artem Galtsin, son of the regional leader of Putin's United Russia party in Udmurtiya in the Urals.

Police investigating the murder picked up Sergei in a street sweep and terrified him into signing a confession – later withdrawn – that he killed Galtsin with a penknife. In court, Sergei's lawyers pointed out that Galtsin died from a blow to the head with a ribbed instrument, and not a penknife, and that at the time of the killing Sergei had broken his right arm and it was in a cast. But the court was convinced by forensic evidence that Sergei insists was fabricated (a drop of blood on his coat, which police had failed to keep separate from the victim's clothing) and noncredible witnesses (prisoners who claimed Sergei had confessed the murder to them). In December 2005 Sergei was sent down for twelve years.

Larisa, an accountancy clerk with no legal or campaigning experience, swung into action. She brought a case against officers who had allegedly beaten Sergei during questioning, and challenged the court's refusal to hear it. She began to collect evidence for an appeal, and she approached Andrei Galtsin, the victim's father and a powerful local politician. But her attention also turned to the dreadful conditions under which Sergei was imprisoned, first in Udmurtiya's notorious prison no. 1 at Yagul, and after the trial at a prison colony in Mordovia. 'I am extremely worried about Sergei's health', Larisa told me in October 2007. 'He is 20 kilogrammes lighter and has a serious problem with his kidneys. They have failed to treat him correctly and he is being held in a punishment cell.'

On the bus to Yagul for visits, Larisa heard horror stories about its reputation for torture and ill treatment from the mothers, wives and sisters of other prisoners. She formed a local Civil Committee for Prisoners' Defence, to correspond with prisoners and monitor local penal institutions. It linked up with the Moscow-based 'Defend Prisoners Rights' Fund headed by Lev Ponomarev.

In June 2006, the Yagul prison administration faced a serious challenge from the *pravozashchitniki*. Another Moscow-based group, Defend Human Rights, had received letters from prisoners alleging inhumane treatment, and won a decision from the Udmurtiya prosecutor giving access to Yagul for a lawyer, Dzhemal Kaloyan, to investigate. Kaloyan published details of tortures ordered by prison governor Sergei Avramenko and often carried out in his presence. Prisoners were regularly beaten; instructed to squat or do press-ups, and beaten for refusing; and allowed out of their cells only to jog, and beaten if they stopped. Humiliating punishments including being stripped and being ordered to lick the floor. A large number of prisoners had tried to commit suicide, or harmed themselves (for example, by swallowing nails) in attempts to get transferred to prison hospital, from where protests could be posted. Prisoners' belongings were regularly destroyed. Those found smoking were punished by having their cells flooded; in one case they had to live for a week in 5 centimetres of water.

The prison administration launched a counter-attack. Governor Avramenko claimed the report had been inspired by 'criminal structures', to 'destabilise the [prison] regime'. Russia's human rights ombudsman, Vladimir Lukin, sent a representative to Yagul. He wrote to Udmurtiya's prosecutor, stating that the 'special measures' against prisoners were justified, but expressing concern at the number of attempted suicides and the practice of keeping prisoners handcuffed for long periods. He urged the prosecutor to follow personally the cases of those who complained.

Larisa Fefilova and her fellow *pravozashchitniki* tried to arrange to visit Yagul to provide free legal advice, as provided for by law. They were stymied, and when they arranged a public protest against this illegal obstruction, local authorities obstructed that too. As this book goes to press, Sergei remains imprisoned and in poor health.

Yagul is part of one of the largest prison systems in the world. Russia is second only to the United States in terms of prisoners per head of population; in November 2008, there were 893,700 detainees. The levels of tuberculosis, HIV, hepatitis and other infections are high. In the early 2000s, NGOs monitoring the prison service noted improvements: amnesties shortened many inmates' sentences and increased funding enabled prison governors to improve conditions. In 2004 the Helsinki Federation completed the first comprehensive survey of the system. More recently, the situation has deteriorated. At a meeting between Putin and a group of *pravozashchitniki* in January 2007, Valery Borshchev, an official in Lukin's office, said the prison system had 'become closed off'; cooperation between prison officials and *pravozashchitniki* was 'being deliberately destroyed'. Borshchev highlighted two problems at the Lgov penal colony in Kursk, where several hundred prisoners slashed their veins in a protest: prisoners were pressured not to send protest letters, or the letters were stolen, and 'discipline and order brigades' of trusty prisoners had been formed to administer beatings together with prison guards.[10]

WHAT ABOUT THE WORKERS?

The Russian workers' movement is gradually being reborn. It sprang into life in 1989, when striking miners rediscovered the power of grassroots organisation and its political potential. But their movement was too new, and its links with other workers too feeble, for it to withstand the trials of 'shock therapy' and the post-Soviet slump. There was an upsurge of rank and file organisation in the early 1990s. But as the decade wore on, and the nonpayments epidemic grew, demoralisation and desperation spread. Workers were more likely to be blocking roads to demand months' or even years' worth of unpaid wages than to be seeking improvements or pursuing political demands. The post-1998 economic recovery began to open a new chapter. As old economic sectors revived and new ones appeared, industrial disputes began more and more to resemble those in other capitalist countries. There was a rich-looking pie, and workers wanted a bigger share of it. A new generation of activists, most of whom started their working lives in the post-Soviet period, began to breathe life into independent union organisations, and challenged the collaborationist policies of the largest union federation.

Workers' Organisation and the Unions

The damaging legacy of Soviet repression weighed on trade unions perhaps more heavily than any other social organisations. The Soviet dictatorship, exercised in the name of 'socialism' in a fast-industrialising society, was concentrated in workplaces. Readers need to bear in mind the differences between the Soviet trade unions and those in western Europe or the United Kingdom. The Soviet unions were able more effectively to collaborate with the bosses in disciplining workers, because the system was comprehensive. The union officials 'negotiated' with their management colleagues on the workers' behalf, but under precise guidelines set down in advance through Communist Party structures. They worked with managers to achieve production targets, and isolated, and helped to punish, workers who resisted. They administered benefits to working-class families, including holiday passes, access to supplies of cheap food and other consumer goods, and medical and welfare schemes. In the 1970s, as most Russian workers' living standards rose gradually, the trade unions in many respects played a benign and patriarchal role, as did the state itself. But no 'official' union representative ever dreamed of supporting or encouraging workers to take collective action in their own interests, or to place demands on management outside the narrow framework handed down from above. Nor did they protest at the savage repression of isolated workers' protests on one hand, or of attempts to set up independent unions on the other.

There were no collective workers' actions of any size in Russia between the general strike in Novocherkassk, southern Russia, over food price increases in 1962, which ended in a bloody massacre, and the introduction of reforms by Gorbachev in 1986. When Solidarnosc was founded in Poland, in 1980, Soviet workers knew nothing of it and went through no similar experience. So the miners' strikes that exploded against Gorbachev in the summer of 1989 had few traditions to look back on. Pit after pit joined the strike – which soon became national – in defiance of the 'official' Soviet union of coal industry employees. A further national strike in 1991 laid the foundations for large numbers of miners to quit the union and pledge allegiance to the independent mineworkers' union, the Soviet Union's first 'unofficial' union.[11]

In the months leading up to the Soviet Union's collapse, the leaders of the independent mineworkers' union gave strong political support to Boris Yeltsin. The absurdity of this workers' vanguard being tied to his regime, which would soon prevail over such a terrible trashing of workers' living standards, is itself an indication of the confusion that prevailed as the workers' movement emerged from the Soviet 'workers' state'. David Mandel, the Canadian writer and activist, argued that most workers entered the post-Soviet period:

> marked by the legacy of more than half a century of totalitarian oppression. This included traits such as unquestioning submission to authority, coupled with deep cynicism towards authority, lack of solidarity, weak self-confidence and a weakly developed sense of dignity.

The mobilisations under Gorbachev were too limited to have overcome these tendencies, which would be reinforced by the insecurity and demoralisation resulting from Yeltsin's 'shock therapy', Mandel wrote. Most Soviet workers 'remained wedded to values of social justice, egalitarianism and popular democracy' and the right-wing liberals' concept of economic freedom appeared to them 'a logical response to the oppressive bureaucratic regime'. Yeltsin's indoctrination on the virtues of the 'market economy' was facilitated by workers' 'atomisation and almost complete ignorance of capitalist reality (another legacy of the totalitarian system)'.[12]

The dislocation of the workforce, the break-up of communities, unemployment, poverty and nonpayment of wages under Yeltsin were hardly auspicious for the development of the workers' movement. There were strikes. In 1994, the miners, this time largely within the framework of the 'official' union, again took national action, against the late payment of wages. By 1996–97, teachers, hospital staff and other public service workers were striking regularly to demand payment of arrears. The tactic of blocking roads and railways became widespread; some local governments or employers, which had failed to pay wages because they were themselves chasing late payments, encouraged this. During Yevgeny Primakov's spell as prime minister in 1998–99, even the 'official' unions staged protests. But in terms of organisation and collective consciousness, Russian workers lagged behind.

The old 'official' Soviet unions reconstituted themselves in 1990 under the umbrella of the Federation of Independent Trades Unions of Russia (FITUR), and began to swap subservience to management and state in the name of 'socialism' for subservience in the name of 'social partnership'. In 1992–93 the leaders of FITUR formed an alliance with the Union of Industrialists and Entrepreneurs, the employers' lobbying organisation, that lasted through the Yeltsin period. Politically, they soon dropped any idea of forming a labour party and acted jointly with the employers' groups, ending up affiliated to Moscow mayor Yuri Luzhkov's Fatherland party. When that merged into Putin's United Russia in 2001, the FITUR affiliation passed to the latter.[13] Most Russian trade union members, an estimated 28 million, are in traditional organisations linked to FITUR. A small minority, some hundreds of thousands, are in independent unions affiliated to smaller federations including the Confederation of Labour of Russia, the All-Russian Confederation of Labour, Defence (Zashchita) and Sotsprof.

As the economy began to recover in the 2000s, things changed for trade union activists. The improvement in most workers' living standards engendered confidence. In new economic sectors, such as consumer-oriented processing industries and IT, and in some older ones where production was now increasing again, the proportion of young workers – who had no personal recollection of the fear and subservience of the Soviet period – rose. They had no hesitation about organising to improve their wages and conditions. The number of strikes fell sharply as the late payment epidemic subsided, but where activists were at work, grassroots organisation was built, or rebuilt, and shopfloor militancy discovered or rediscovered.

The best indicator of the level of strike activity is the number of working days lost per year. The very sharp decline in working days lost during the 2000s is shown in Table 8.1. Readers should note that this only includes legal strikes – that is, those reported under procedures required by the labour code – and the real figures are higher.

Trade union activists I interviewed reckoned that the economic boom had created better conditions for organisation. Boris Kravchenko, chairman of the All-Russian Confederation of Labour, one of the independent union federations, said an upsurge of trade union activity was to be expected at times of economic growth:

> There are many working people who now have something to lose, who have an improving standard of living. They

Table 8.1 Working days lost per year in legal strikes

1995	1,367,000
1996	4,009,400
1997	6,000,500
1998	2,881,500
1999	1,827,200
2000	236,400
2001	47,100
2002	29,100
2003	29,400
2004	210,900
2005	85,900
2006	9,800
2007	20,500

Source: Rosstat.

> recognise their rights, they want to defend those rights, defend their jobs and defend that increase of their standard of living.

Consequently, there had been an increase in trade union activity by 'fairly well qualified workers with good incomes' in economically strong sectors.[14]

Kirill Buketov, a union activist since the late 1980s, and now the Moscow representative of the international food workers' federation IUF, told me that union organisation had taken a qualitative step forward once the non-payment crisis was left behind and 'real capitalism, with workers getting paid real wages', arrived. Conditions began to change in the food processing sector straight after the 1998 devaluation, when both foreign and Russian capital began to invest heavily, starting with tobacco producers, breweries and confectionery makers:

> Demand rose very quickly; suddenly all the factories were working three shifts; western companies that had previously imported products to Russia decided to produce them here, and began to invest. With this relative economic improvement, a new working class began to take shape, and a new working class consciousness. People could see: companies are coming here and making a nice profit, and they are not sharing it with

> their employees. The employers' attitude to workers changed, too. They simply fired many older workers and took on younger people, often quite highly qualified. These younger people had no experience of working in the Soviet Union. They considered that their wage was their due, their share of the company's revenue. These were much better conditions for union organisation.

The French sociologist Carine Clément, who lives in Russia and works with the Institute for Collective Action, a group that monitors community and protest movements, also highlights the importance of the new, post-Soviet generation, who 'have less thoroughly taken on the ideal that the employer is a kind provider and the state is a caring father'. Her research showed that strikes are often initiated by 'young workers, usually highly qualified, who quite often have some contact with international colleagues, and a broad outlook on life'.[15]

For government and employers, the emergence of workplace relations more closely resembling those in other capitalist countries brought with it the need to constrain union organisation. Once Putin became president, he moved quickly to renew the 'social partnership', under which government, employers and workers would supposedly pull together for the economy's sake. Like similar agreements elsewhere, this became a framework within which union leaders have struck compromises with the employers, disciplined workforces, and discouraged rank and file organisation. The first fruit of the 'social partnership' was a new labour code, approved by parliament in 2001. Although it improved some safety and other workplace measures, strengthened the position of unions' workplace representatives and included provisions for managers who breached the code to be disciplined, it significantly undermined grassroots organisation. Legal strikes had now to be approved by a majority vote of a meeting attended by two-thirds of the labour force, or their representatives, rather than by union members; labour disputes committees were now to be appointed by management and workforce jointly, and in the absence of a joint negotiating body, the law gives sole negotiating rights to a majority organisation, so squeezing out independent unions in favour of FITUR affiliates. Collaborationist unions were strengthened, independent and grassroots organisation obstructed.[16]

Igor Shanin, secretary of FITUR, told me in an interview: 'The "social partnership" is a crucial instrument for protecting workers' living standards. We will continue to press for improvements within that framework.' But when in 2005 FITUR representatives signed a tripartite General Agreement with the government and the employers' organisation, the one issue on which agreement could not be reached was the timetable for raising the minimum wage to the employed persons' subsistence level. In 2005 the minimum wage was 720 rubles ($25) per month, less than a quarter of the employed person's subsistence level of 3,255 rubles ($116) per month. FITUR laid out a timetable to bring the minimum wage to 2,500 rubles per month in 2007 and up to the employed person's subsistence level by 2008 – but the government agreed only to guarantee 1,100 rubles ($39) a month. At the FITUR congress in 2006, Mikhail Tarasenko, president of the miners and metalworkers union, said that the time for 'playing at social partnership' was past. The unions had never been extremist, he pointed out, and had always accepted that 'before dividing the pie, it needs to be baked. But now the pie is baked, and needs to be divided justly.' Putin was in attendance, and denounced Tarasenko's suggestion as 'premature and harmful'.[17]

The struggle over how to divide the pie continues, and the minimum wage continues to lag behind the employed person's subsistence level. In June 2008, with the employed person's subsistence level at 5,024 rubles ($180) per month and rising, the government conceded that from January 2009 the minimum wage would reach 4,330 rubles ($154) a month – a concession, for sure, but one that will still leave millions of Russian workers and their families in dire poverty.[18] Meanwhile a small but determined contingent of trade unionists were taking the battle to divide the pie to their employers by more direct means.

The Strikes of 2007–08

Workers at the Ford factory at Vsevolozhsk near St Petersburg took the lead in realising the potential of industrial militancy. The factory was at the forefront of Russia's car manufacturing boom, churning out the Focus model for the domestic market. Production started in 2002, and from 2005 rose rapidly, reaching 72,000 cars a year in 2007. The workers soon began to demand their share of the factory's handsome profit margin. In late 2005, they responded to plans to raise output by demanding a 30 per cent wage increase and an improved bonus system. A one-week sitdown strike in November that year reduced production by a quarter, but management offered only a 12 per cent increase (compared with 18.5 per cent inflation). The dispute dragged on until March 2006, and ended with the offer of a 16 per cent rise and improvements to the bonus system. But this was just the start. Furious that the FITUR-affiliated auto workers' union had failed to support them, the workers collectively withdrew from it, and with activists at the nearby Caterpillar factory, initiated moves to form an independent car workers' union.

Demand for cars, and production, was still rising. So the Ford factory committee in late 2006 put new demands: for a 30 per cent wage increase (against slightly slower inflation of about 10 per cent), extra long-service payments, maternity and paternity pay, premiums for children's education, and a 7 per cent supplement and 12 extra days' holiday to compensate for arduous conditions for paint shop staff and welders. In February 2007, a mass meeting voted about 1,300 against six to strike, the factory was brought to a standstill for a day, and management caved in to nearly all the demands except on wages, which were increased by 14–20 per cent.

Round three of the dispute came in November 2007. After an intense round of mass meetings and leafleting, the factory committee demanded a 30 per cent wage rise plus other improvements. Again management refused. A one-day warning strike was staged on 7 November. Managers secured a court order postponing further action for two weeks, but to no avail. When the plant's director appealed to a mass meeting, most of the workers got up and walked out. From 20 November the workers went on all-out strike, which ended, with an agreement to continue pay negotiations, on 17 December. In February 2008 wage rises of 16–21 per cent were agreed.[19]

The Ford strikes were unprecedented, in several respects. First, they were offensive actions. Whereas long-drawn-out strikes in the 1990s had essentially been 'hungry revolts', this was a 'struggle for the redivision of profits', as the socialist writer Boris Kagarlitsky observed. The Ford workers were already earning above-average wages, and were driven on in the first place by their knowledge of the sumptuous profits being made in the auto boom. In this sense their action was reminiscent of wages militancy in the British car industry in the 1970s: the more cars the companies needed, the more demands the highly skilled and best-paid workers placed on them. The Ford Vsevolozhsk factory committee chairman and strike leader Aleksei Etmanov explained: 'The factory is exploiting us effectively, but forgetting to increase wages effectively. The capitalist's profit rises, the worker's health is getting ruined.' Andrei

Liapin, Etmanov's counterpart on the factory committee of the GM-Avtovaz joint venture in Togliatti, said that the 'motor boom', with a six-month queue for popular models of cars, had attracted an unprecedented level of foreign investment. 'Besides fantastic demand and consumers who are not over-spoiled, Russia has an abundance of unexpectedly cheap but well-trained labour.'[20]

A second notable feature of the Ford disputes is that the workers were confident enough to proceed in defiance of those labour code provisions that encroached on the right to take collective action, and to break their ties with the collaborationist FITUR. The Ford workers more easily found the road towards independent union organisation because the Vsevolozhsk plant, having started up in 2002, had no traditional union, Petr Zolotarev, leader of the independent union at Avtovaz, Unity, told me in an interview. When the Ford workers called for the formation of an independent union covering the whole auto industry, Unity was one of the first factory organisations to declare support. Factory committees at GM-Avtovaz, the Renault-owned Avtoframos works and the Nokian tyre factory followed suit. In August 2007, the Interregional Union of Auto Industry Workers, as the new grouping was known, met in Moscow and initiated a campaign to raise wages industry-wide.[21]

The events at Ford were at the centre of a wider movement of wages disputes on one hand and a resurgence of independent union organisation on the other. In March 2007, straight after Ford's well-publicised retreat before its workers' offensive, new trade unions were formed at nearby workplaces including a tea-packing plant – Nevskie porogi. The Sotsprof independent union at Heineken's brewery in the city advanced its own 30 per cent wage demand, like Ford, and backed it up with a work to rule. There was some renewed trade union activity in the oil industry, where harsh conditions and geographical distance have made organisation notoriously difficult. A series of protest rallies in October 2006 in the west Siberian oil field, at which independent unions mounted demands for higher wages and improvements to health and safety regimes, led to the formation of an activists' network. There were significant disputes at the Kachkanarsky iron ore mining complex and on the railways. The increased level of strike activity continued into 2008.

Another indicator of the new workers' movement's impact on its enemies is the rising level of intimidation and violence faced by union activists. Apart from the ubiquitous threat of the sack, trade union activists often face beatings, threats and police harassment.

Etmanov, the Ford Vsevolozhsk strike leader, was twice attacked with guns and metal bars. In December 2008, Valentin Urusov, who recruited 1,000 diamond miners at the state-controlled Alrosa company in Yakutia, east Siberia, to an independent union, was sentenced to six years in a labour camp for possession of drugs. Urusov's colleagues insisted he had been framed, and launched an international campaign in his defence. He was released on appeal in May 2009, but jailed again at a further hearing in Yakutia a month later. The campaign continues.[22]

'Where capital goes, conflict goes', Beverly Silver, the historian of international labour, wrote.[23]As capital flew out of Russia in the 1990s, trade unionists, often demoralised or desperate, fought mostly defensive, rearguard actions. In the one-sided boom of the 2000s, labour began to recover confidence. Conflict broke out at Ford, one of the points of entry of foreign capital, in part because FITUR's writ didn't run there and there was no subservient trade union organisation that could discipline the workforce. Strike action by workers at Avtovaz in Togliatti (see box), whose gigantic factory is run by members of Putin's government team, was partly inspired by the Ford strikes. It was successful in bringing wages demand into sharper focus, but did not produce a management climbdown such as that at Ford. Petr Zolotarev, the leader of the independent union at Avtovaz, put it this way:

> Yes, there are grounds to talk about a renaissance of trade union activity. There are changes. But let's be careful: many of these changes are episodic, some of the attempts to set up trade union organisation are quite modest. But the movement is in that direction. It's related to the improvement of economic situation. People feel it's possible to do something. And there are difficulties. The government obstructs the establishment of free trade unions, and prefers to deal with the old FITUR-affiliated unions. That is clear from the wording of the labour code and from the discrimination practised against independent union members.

The Avtovaz workers' battle

No one has felt the Putin government's hostility to trade union organisation more keenly than the car workers at Avtovaz in Togliatti. A protest campaign against poverty-level wages in mid-2007 faced tough repressive action by a new management team put in place by the state corporation Rosoboroneksport.

Avtovaz has long been a front line in the battle between capital and labour. It is the largest car factory in the world, with more than 100,000 employees, and four assembly lines, three of which are more than 2 km long, producing the archetypal Soviet car, the Lada. The plant completely dominates Togliatti's economy. Management and local politicians are as close now as they were in Soviet times. Avtovaz's first strike took place in 1989, when 20,000 workers walked out, demanding a substantial all-round pay increase, supplements for some grades, and indexation. Most Avtovaz workers belonged then, as they do now, to the traditional auto workers' union, ASM – but the 1989 strike catalysed the formation of Unity, the independent union.

Avtovaz's trauma during the 1990s, at the hands of oligarchs and criminals, was referred to in Chapter 5. As car sales increased during the economic boom of the 2000s, the factory's fortunes improved – and workers began to resist management attempts to keep their share of that fortune to a minimum. In 2002, when the new Kalina model was launched, management decided to up the second shift on the third assembly line from eight hours to nine. The ASM consented, despite 90-odd brigade meetings voting against the change. Many workers walked off the job after eight hours before a campaign of intimidation and threats ended the protests. The 2003 collective agreement signalled the cancellation of free welfare benefits, such as medical, cultural and childcare services, and sparked a more widespread protest campaign, supported by Unity. But again ASM sanctioned the changes.

In 2005, Rosoboroneksport took a controlling stake in Avtovaz. A team of administrators arrived from Moscow, headed by Vladimir Artyakov, a member of Putin's circle who worked in the presidential administration in 1997–99 and served as general director of Rosoboroneksport from 2000 to 2005. Artyakov's mandate, apparently, was to bring the local political elite under control, choke off the remaining criminality at Avtovaz, and discipline the workforce. He has headed the Avtovaz board of directors since 2005, and in August 2007 was appointed governor of Samara region.

The new management in 2007 – with the car market

growing and inflation rampant – faced a challenge by assembly plant workers to humiliating pay levels. When I visited Togliatti in October 2007, activists showed me their pay slips: they were taking home around 7,000 rubles ($250) a month, plus about 6,000 rubles ($215) in bonuses. These were subsistence rates. A month's food and rent for an average Togliatti household cost 7,000 rubles. The assembly plant workers were mostly on low grades with little prospect of promotion; labour turnover was at an all-time high.

In March 2007, the pro-Kremlin United Russia party – supported publicly by the Avtovaz top management – fought, and won, the regional parliamentary elections on a slogan of raising wages to 25,000 rubles a month, and pensions to 10,000 rubles a month, by 2010. But, while a fleet of Land Cruisers was bought for the personal use of already highly paid managers, nothing was done to improve wages in the short term. Workers in one of the finishing shops, having lobbied their managers without success, started a work to rule on 9 July. Management had 'not learned to listen to workers', and pay rates 'didn't reflect any Russian or international principles', they complained in a collective letter to Artyakov. They demanded a threefold pay increase, to at least 25,000 rubles a month, and warned that they would strike if it was not granted. Word now spread around the plant and Artyakov received about 10,000 letters from individual workers to the same effect. He announced a 4.5 per cent across-the-board pay increase, so derisory that it just heightened the tension.

On 1 August a group of between 400 and 700 workers struck, stopping one of the main conveyor belts for five hours. A mass meeting on the same day attracted a much larger number, mostly women and young workers. Retribution was swift: the management, having refused to negotiate, now sacked two of the strikers and cut bonus payments to another 67. Later, Avtovaz management promised to index wages to inflation, but refused to raise basic rates.

The courts later refused to reinstate those dismissed, on the grounds that no strike had taken place. Unity announced it would support the victimised workers in challenging that decision, up to the Supreme Court if necessary. Twenty-year-old Anton Vechkunin, a Unity activist, had been arrested in the street before the strike and held for three days without charge. He told me in an interview that the police and factory security guards had 'watched my every move' for several weeks. The officers who arrested him claimed that he had been detained for abusive and disorderly behaviour, a claim he dismissed as 'an insult'.

The strike starkly illuminated the difference between the traditional and independent unions. Nikolai Karagin, the ASM's factory committee chairman and an (unsuccessful) United Russia candidate in the March elections, told workers that stopping work would be illegal. After the strike, he approved the management's disciplinary measures. In an interview with a trade union newspaper, Karagin asserted that the strike would be 'treated not as a strike but as a refusal to work by individuals', and reiterated that he did not support the action.

Most strikers were ASM members, although some quit the union after its failure to back them. It was Unity that supported them, and arranged legal support for those victimised. When workers approached Petr Zolotarev, Unity's president, about their pay demands, he suggested they call on their union, the ASM, to sanction the strike. 'The ASM responded by promising to organise a factory delegates' conference, but this didn't happen', he told me. On the day of the strike, he met with pickets and addressed the mass meeting. 'Workers are often prepared to strike more readily than their trade unions, and that's what happened at Avtovaz', he recalled.[24]

9

PEOPLE: GRASSROOTS MOVEMENTS

Social movements outside the workplace, as well as trade union organisation, revived during Putin's second term as president (2004–08). Nationwide protests were unleashed by public services reforms that threatened vital safety nets for millions of families: the reform of welfare benefits in 2005 and the privatisation of housing services. Community organisations that sprang up during these, and other, protests often outlived the disputes that gave rise to them. Networks have been created, experience accumulated and new methods of organisation worked out. There is potential for social movements embracing a much wider range of issues.

THE WELFARE BENEFITS REVOLT

The reform of welfare benefits and housing services, both of which became the focus of protests in 2005, was part of a broad programme that also envisaged the part privatisation of education and health services, mentioned in Chapter 7. This drive to dismantle much of what remained of the Soviet social welfare system went together with privatisation of the power industry, and the adoption of timetables to raise electricity and gas tariffs to European levels. For the Kremlin, these measures were essential to complete the transition to capitalism. For business, they were welcome opportunities to profit. The reforms could not have been contemplated – even by the most fiendish pro-marketeers – in the 1990s, and were considered too politically risky during Putin's first term. But the economic recovery, and the president's popularity, encouraged the reformers to move ahead in 2004. They confronted opposition from households for whom nonmoney benefits and cheap housing services might well mean the difference between survival and poverty.

The welfare reform aimed to dismantle the Russian system of nonmoney benefits, a Soviet legacy without exact equivalents in the west: free housing, housing services (water, gas, heating, electricity and repairs), public transport, kindergartens, school meals, medicines, health and dental services – and even, for a few, free or subsidised holidays. The benefits went mainly to military or labour veterans, or as incentives to people to move to rural areas or the far north to work. Groups such as the disabled, former political prisoners and victims of the 1986 Chernobyl accident also qualified. A national survey of households conducted in 2003 showed that just over 50 per cent of them received nonmoney benefits. Researchers estimated that nonmoney benefits amounted to 8.5 per cent of the average total income of households receiving them, and 3.6 per cent of the average total income of all households. Although the largest category of recipients was retired employees, and there were more recipients in middle-income than low-income households, those who relied most heavily on the benefits were single women pensioners, retired married couples and single parents. No one pretended the nonmoney benefits were ideal: they did little to counter child poverty or hardship among the unemployed or low-paid workers,

A protest over municipal housing policy, 2007, Izhevsk. Photo: *Den', Izhevsk.*

for example. And during the 1990s, they were simply not available for much of the time in much of Russia – like many monetary benefits. Nevertheless, they provided valuable support to vulnerable sections of the population.[1]

In 2004 Parliament adopted a law that envisaged converting nonmoney benefits to cash payments, transferring responsibility for most of them from central government to the regions, and cutting the number of benefits obligatory under law. The implementation was crassly bureaucratic. Recipients feared that the cash benefits would not keep up with the rising prices of services they lost – which, for many elderly people requiring medicines, for example, turned out to be the case. They also sensed, again correctly, that local authorities would happily cut or abolish benefits not protected by law. Polls in September 2004 indicated that 70 per cent of the population disliked the changes, but the government made no effort to explain them. The reforms came into effect on 1 January 2005, and on 9 January, the first working day of the year for most people in Russia,* protests erupted. Demonstrations and open-air meetings were held in dozens of towns and cities. Roads, including the main Moscow–St Petersburg highway, were blocked. The centre of St Petersburg was blockaded for two days (15–17 January). In Perm, demonstrators were detained by police and the acting governor was imprisoned by protesters in response; in Krasnodar, the deputy governor was trapped by crowds; and in Tomsk, police narrowly saved the regional administrative offices from being overrun. Everywhere, those used to having free transport clashed with bus drivers who tried to enforce the new rules.

The demonstrations were not large by Russian standards, but they had the support or sympathy of the overwhelming majority. Research by the late Yuri Levada, the father of Russian opinion polling, showed that while only 200,000–400,000 people participated in the protests, in January 2005, 41 per cent of the population supported them, a further 41 per cent regarded them 'with understanding', and only 10 per cent were 'against'. Most remarkably, the protests were organised spontaneously – often initiated by groups of middle-aged or elderly people who were directly affected, with young activists joining in. The Communists and other opposition political parties were slower off the mark,

* In the Russian Orthodox calendar, Christmas falls on 7 January. This is a public holiday, and many Russian workplaces close between the New Year and this date.

mobilising only towards the end of January. They coordinated a national day of action, in which an estimated 200,000 people participated, on 12 February.[2]

The demonstrators crossed another barrier: they started by demanding that the ministers directly responsible for the reform be brought to account, and, when the authorities reacted dismissively, often called for then president Putin and his entire government to resign. Some of the Kremlin's political technologists feared, prematurely, that something similar to the Ukrainian 'Orange revolution' could ensue. They started hinting in the press that the demonstrations were inspired by hostile agitators, but soon abandoned that nonsense. Putin rode the storm, presidentially lambasting ministers. The government stood firm on monetisation, but dug into its pockets to mollify discontent, raising pensions and indexing public sector pay ahead of schedule, and awarding supplements to some whose benefits had been monetised. Local authorities, now responsible for supervising the cash benefits, were forced into further concessions where protests were well organised. The protests left an important legacy. In Levada's words:

> The happy, parade-style picture [of the population's attitude to government], the universal 'oh yes, we accept', will not return. Tens of thousands have tasted the 'forbidden fruit', formerly unthinkable and unimaginable, of settling accounts directly with the authorities at all levels. A significantly greater number of people have discovered that such things are possible. The authorities have publicly shown their weakness, daring neither to threaten the 'rebels' nor to admit their mistakes.

The protesters had felt their own weaknesses too, Levada added, paying 'an inevitable price' for lack of organisation, by retreating quite quickly when concessions were offered. But participants in the movement told me in interviews that they had worked to overcome that lack of organisation straight after the protests. Sergei Shchukin, editor of *Den'*, a weekly opposition newspaper based in Izhevsk, explained:

> There were spontaneous meetings against the monetisation of benefits, and ours was the only local paper to cover them. It turned the paper into a sort of open forum. After that, a coordinating council was formed; following each meeting, we published a notice of the next one. That kept the protest

> movement going. These structures were ready when the protests on housing and municipal services began.

Local organisations began to form horizontal networks across Russia. A national Union of Coordinating Councils, drawing together organisations such as those in Izhevsk, was formed.[3]

HOUSING RIGHTS ACTION

A wave of community activity – less concentrated than that over welfare benefits, but longer-lasting – has been triggered by reforms under the 2005 housing code, and especially the privatisation of housing services (repairs, and supply of gas, heating, water and power). Communities have mobilised to demand repairs that should have been done years ago, to defend homeowners' legal rights to a say in housing management, to challenge sharp price increases for services, and to support those squashed into dormitories. The peak of the oil boom, the property prices bubble, and property developers' voracious appetite for space to build, have produced a related wave of protests over land. In some regions, activists have formed networks linking these to other protest groups.

The legal framework for the final stages of housing privatisation was set out in the 2005 housing code, mentioned in Chapter 7. With most flats already granted to residents as private property in the 1990s, the government now sought to create a market in homes, to stimulate the provision of mortgages to the better-off, and to shift responsibility for housing services from local government to private companies. Many of Russia's strongest business empires moved in: the largest housing services companies include RKS, controlled by Viktor Vekselberg's Renova group, which in 2007 had a turnover of more than $1 billion, and Rosvodokanal, owned jointly by Alfa Bank and Deutsche Bank of Germany. The privatisation of housing services has sparked the most vehement protests – in the first place because it was pushed through before the issue of capital repairs to the Soviet-era flats most people live in was resolved. Capital repairs simply ground to a standstill in the 1990s, and most buildings have not been refurbished for more than 30 years. But the 70 per cent of Russians who own their homes are now expected themselves to bear the cost – estimated in 2007 at an average of 60,000 rubles ($2,150) per home. The other 30 per cent, whose homes were slated for privatisation in 2007–10, have a legal clause to hang on to, saying that the seller must undertake capital repairs. In all cases, the housing code leaves residents at the mercy of local authorities whose respect for the law is arbitrary at best. In 2006–07, many authorities handed housing service contracts to private companies which made little or no commitments on capital repairs.

In Izhevsk in the northern Urals, community organisations' representatives told me in October 2007 how they had advised residents to use mass civic action, or legal action, to 'compel the authorities to do their duty' on repairs. There have been both. Protesters were enraged that in 2006, the year before all the town's housing stock was due to pass into private hands, not a kopek had been set aside in the city budget for housing repairs. Svetlana Stichikhina, who heads a residents' committee in her apartment block, told me how she had brought legal action against the privatised housing services company, compelling them to undertake capital repairs. There has also been conflict over the private companies' attempts to impose charges above the levels laid down in federal law.

The Coordinating Council for Civic Action, formed in 2005 in the wake of the campaign over monetisation of benefits, organised more than 60 rallies and pickets in Izhevsk, demanding negotiations with the authorities over housing. Republican and city officials finally deigned to talk to protesters at a meeting in June 2007. When it began, Zinaida Shcherbinina of the General Pensioners Council picked on the issue of the authorities' failure to stick to federal guidelines for metering heat supplies to vent her wrath:

> These are your losses, they're due to your mismanagement. Why should residents pay for broken-down, leaking heat pipes and worn-out buildings that haven't been repaired for thirty or forty years? [4]

The housing code provides for residents in apartment blocks (that is, most of the urban population) either to contract management functions to a commercial agent, or to self-manage their blocks directly (with decisions taken by a general assembly), or via a partnership of property owners or cooperative. The shared problems of living in apartment blocks seem potentially to incline residents to collective democracy, and these organisations can provide a framework for it – so they are loathed by local authority bureaucrats and loved by community activists in equal measure. Vladimir Fershtein, who heads a residents' partnership at blocks on Nagovytsina street in Izhevsk, told me: 'We took matters into our hands and forced the authorities to listen.' The big unresolved battle there is over funding for capital repairs. Stories of bureaucrats who try to silence or threaten or ignore residents' representatives abound. In Togliatti, campaigner Larisa Bozina told me how the city administration has repeatedly and illegally refused to deal with 15 territorial self-management associations, and the local prosecutors' office has tried, but failed, to get the courts to close them down. 'There are no mechanisms for us to assume our legal rights,' she said. Campaigners have compiled a list of more than 250 cases in which authorities that refused to recognise the associations were backed by local courts. In Saratov, the bureaucrats formed their own puppet partnership, supposedly representing 400 apartment blocks, and ignored genuine partnerships set up by residents. In Volgograd, they shut their eyes and ears to all except a commercial agent they had chosen. In other cases, criminal gangs, sometimes with links to local authorities, form false partnerships and try to bully residents into ceding management powers to them.[5]

The bureaucrats are at their most vindictive when dealing with the lowest of the low: millions of residents of dormitories who, under the housing code, are legally entitled to receive their accommodation – often literally no more than a few square metres of floor space and a bed – as private property. Many bureaucrats resist this at all costs, as the dormitories can be useful for accommodating homeless people, refugees or temporary workers. Many dormitories were illegally privatised in the 1990s, and their owners, often with bureaucratic support, raise rents to levels the residents cannot pay, to provide a pretext for eviction. In Perm, dormitory residents staged a tent city protest in the summer of 2008 against high rents and illegal attempts to force them to sign rent agreements. In Izhevsk, dormitory residents won a case against steep rent increases in the local courts, but it was overturned in the notoriously corrupt Udmurtiyan republic courts.[6]

This everyday battle between Russian homeowners on one side, and power and money on the other, will continue for years to come. And since 2005, the battle over capital repairs, housing services and residents' democratic rights has been at the centre of attempts by community and political activists to create national networks. In December 2006, the all-Russian Union of Coordinating Councils organised a day of action to demand 'a housing policy for the people', the repair of outworn buildings at the state's expense, and a series of amendments to the housing code. Organisers estimated that 10,000 people in 30 towns and cities participated. In September 2007, a Russian Movement for Housing Self-Management, comprising an initial 37 local groupings, was formed at a conference in Astrakhan, southern Russia.[7]

Land and freedom

Allotment gardeners in Izhevsk have waged a three-year physical, legal and political battle against a building firm that grabbed their land to build new high-rise blocks. The gardeners at the Liubitel-2 allotments in the Sever suburb have physically obstructed bulldozers, torn down fences and braved physical intimidation from security guards.

Aleksei Ilyin, chairman of the Izhevsk Committee to Defend Allotment Gardeners, told me in an interview in September 2007:

> At every step the authorities say we are obstructing the [government's] Accessible Housing programme. But we are just defending the rights of ordinary people, many of them pensioners, for whom the allotments are one of the most important things in life.

Ilyin had a few weeks previously received a serious shoulder wound and a cut forehead when beaten by security guards during a demonstration.

The Liubitel-2 conflict is typical of many hundreds across Russia, which have pitted communities against developers and construction firms which scheme with corrupt local authorities to acquire allotments, small city-centre parks and garages. Dangerous and unsightly infill development – the construction of new blocks in patches of land separating old ones – is a scourge. The insane building boom was driven by the international property market bubble of 2005–08, which drove land and house prices in almost all Russian cities and towns up to, and sometimes beyond, western European levels. Those who resisted came up against local, national and even international networks of power and money.

Western readers might wonder why the threat to allotments generates such passion. The answer is that in Russia, far more than in other countries, they have played a key role in the lives of the last three or four generations. Once Russian families moved from the countryside, or the slums, into their tiny Soviet-era flats – where you are lucky to have room for a window box – they were usually granted 600 square metres of land outside the city. The allotments provided vital insurance against food shortages, and a place for families to relax at weekends and over the summer.* When I asked Aleksei Ilyin where his commitment to defend his allotment came from, he smiled: 'I'm a peasant at heart.' His family was deported from the southern Urals to Kazakhstan in the 1930s, during Stalin's 'dekulakisation' campaign. In 1977 he travelled to Izhevsk, then a closed city, to study. He took a factory job but spent every spare moment at his perfectly tended allotment.

For the Liubitel-2 gardeners, the immediate enemy is Alians, a company set up in 2003 by Valerii Rogozin, the former deputy mayor of Izhevsk, and his son-in-law Andrei Periakov. Behind Alians, in its turn, stands a larger business group, Komos, controlled by Andrei Oskolkov, a deputy in the Udmurtiya republic parliament, entrepreneur and close friend of Udmurtiya governor Aleksandr Volkov. In June 2008 Komos concluded a 'strategic alliance' with Alians to finance future projects.

Komos, which owns food processing and media businesses as well as a real estate portfolio, expanded rapidly in 2007–08, in part thanks to a $1 billion working capital loan from Sberbank, Russia's main state-owned bank. In 2008 it was in discussion with Cargill, the multinational food corporation, which was considering investing in its animal feedstock factories.

It is no coincidence that Izhevsk's heavy business hitters moved into property. Along with Komos, a key player is the Aspek-Domstroi group, controlled by Viktor Khoroshchavtsev, who represents Udmurtiya in the Federation Council and leads the local branch of United Russia. In keeping with the centralisation of power and money across Russia, Udmurtiya's oil companies passed out of the local elite's hands in the early 2000s and are now controlled by the Kremlin and its allies, as mentioned in Chapter 5. The local elite, cut off from the richest source of revenues, have moved into other spheres in which power can be converted into money.

* The allotment is named colloquially a 'six-hundreder'. Most Russian families have a summer house (dacha) at their allotment: these range from wooden shacks to large brick buildings. Many families spend two months or more at the allotment over the summer; many pensioners spend most of their time there.

The building firms' business plans require a close working relationship with the local authorities. Andrei Konoval, head of Izhevsk's alliance of community groups, explained in a newspaper article that, typically, a builder buys a few allotments, and simply expropriates land set aside for common use. The authorities give him permission to build a residential block. The fact that the adjacent allotments have not sold up doesn't worry either the builder or the authorities. Then the builder applies for a compulsory purchase order for the remaining allotments – and although that's illegal, because private companies cannot under law benefit from such orders, it's granted anyway.

Izhevsk's mayor, Aleksandr Ushakov, had promised in 2006 that no compulsory orders would be issued for allotments in the city. But in January 2007, he signed the orders for land at Liubitel-2 and two other locations. Confrontation climaxed. The gardeners started legal actions against Alians and the city authorities, and physically obstructed the bulldozers.

In 2008, the economic crisis intervened. Alians stopped construction work on the first of its six high-rise blocks; Aleksei Ilyin continued his battle against Alians in the courts; the courts continued to sanction the company's acquisition of land which, for the moment, it could not afford to build on.

The Liubitel-2 battle is part of a national phenomenon. The mighty Moscow administration, renowned for its close connections with the construction industry, has faced a three-year campaign of defiance by allotment owners at the Yuzhnoe Butovo suburb. A compulsory purchase order was used to make way for developers, in contravention of federal law. Some residents were offered modest one-room flats in exchange for picturesque riverside properties.

Campaigners estimate that there are 65 similar cases, involving 86,000 residents, in the Moscow region alone. Another 100 campaign groups in Moscow are fighting infill development and building projects that threaten small parks. In St Petersburg, compulsory purchase orders issued in connection with the Western High Speed Diameter road, the transport ministry's flagship public-private partnership project, were resisted by garage owners who protested at the miserly sums offered. Their spokesman, Dmitry Troyan, was beaten to death in 2006; the murder remains unsolved.[8]

Activists under siege

Even the mildest forms of civic action bring out repressive, paranoid instincts in the Russian law enforcement agencies in Samara, a city of 1.2 million on the Volga. Intimidation of activists and journalists climaxed in May 2007, when then president Putin held a summit with European Union leaders in Samara.

A Dissenters' March was staged to coincide with the summit, although permission for it was only granted after the foreign leaders had protested about heavy-handed police tactics. Supporters from other towns were prevented from travelling to Samara. A week before the summit, police detained Dissenters' March organisers. They were released without charge, but then photos of 30 of them were displayed on 'wanted' posters.

Activists preparing a separate event – an 'intergalactic libertarian forum' in a local community centre – were also targeted. Aleksandr Lashmankin, the forum organiser, was beaten unconscious by two men with baseball bats who stole leaflets for the event and mobile phones. The mayor of Samara, Viktor Tarkhov, forbade the community centre to host the forum. Fifteen would-be participants staged a 'street party', surrounded by 30 police. Lashmankin and another organiser had been detained by police before it even began. In nearby Togliatti, another group – nationalist-leaning activists who had distributed leaflets to soldiers on 9 May,* calling on them not to fight in Chechnya – were arrested.

Journalists were targeted, too. The local offices of the VolgaInform news agency, of *Novaya Gazeta*, Russia's most widely read opposition newspaper, and of Golos, a human rights campaign group, were raided and computers confiscated. Police claimed they were checking for pirate software – a joke in a country where it is ubiquitous in local government, for example. After lengthy legal proceedings, cases against VolgaInform and Golos were dropped, and an apology made. The case against *Novaya Gazeta* resulted in the closure of its local edition in early 2008, despite software licence agreements being presented to the police. Even then the

---

* 9 May is the national holiday marking the Soviet victory over Germany in the Second World War, on which military parades are held in many towns.

vengeful security services were not finished. A year later, *Novaya Gazeta*'s Samara editor, Sergei Kurt-Adzhiev, reported police intimidation of his family.

The Samara security forces renewed their manic harassment of the political opposition in the run-up to the parliamentary elections of December 2007. Four organisers of Kasparov's Other Russia movement were detained for a week. Liudmila Kuzmina of Golos told me that while Russian political leaders claim commitment to democracy, they support laws that empower local security forces to wage witch hunts. 'There is relentless intimidation by the security forces, which is illegal and has not been sanctioned by the courts. The law on NGOs has added to the psychological pressure.'

Before and after the Samara summit, campaigners have broken out of the isolation security forces try to impose, and joined community-based campaigns. The greatest anger has been aroused by property development, which is wrecking historic areas of Samara's town centre, urban parks and lakes, and allotments on the shore of the Volga. Throughout 2007 and 2008, 15 residents' groups have joined with each other, and with young *pravozashchitniki*, to picket the mayor's office. Demonstrations have also been staged against conscription and against the privatisation of the university's library services.

The persistence that campaigners require was brought home to me in an interview with Aleksandr Lashmankin, the 'libertarian forum' organiser. He became a civil activist in 2002, aged 28, when he organised a campaign for the provision of medicines and free diagnosis for AIDS sufferers. Officially there are 33,001 in the Samara region, but he believes there are at least five times as many.

'We came up against a bureaucratic wall,' he said. 'It's in the bureaucrats' personal interest to choke and strangle any civic initiative, and that's what they tried to do.' The hardest thing, he said, was arguing for treatment of AIDS, and proper public information about the condition. Although HIV infection has in this decade spread mainly via sexual activity in the majority heterosexual population, sufferers are victimised by bureaucrats who see them as 'drug users, prostitutes and homosexuals' who had brought it on themselves.

By the mid-2000s, Lashmankin had come to believe that 'if the political situation doesn't change, these things won't change either'. He became active in campaigns against conscription and other human rights protests – and attracted the security services' attention. Despite his unassuming, compassionate character and quietly spoken manner, he found himself made into an 'enemy of the people'. He was repeatedly prevented from travelling from Samara to meet fellow activists.

When he set off to the St Petersburg Social Forum, held in parallel with the G8 summit in July 2006, he was arrested at the bus stop and taken home, missing his train. He travelled to nearby Novokuibyshev to try to get another train from there, and was again detained. Activists' websites logged similar police action in 16 other cities. In December 2006 Lashmankin, anticipating similar trouble, decided to travel to a Dissenters' March in Moscow via Nizhnyi Novgorod. He was detained by security services officers until the event was over.

Samara is not atypical. It is possible to download similar stories of repression in hundreds of Russian cities and towns from human rights organisations' websites.[9]

AN ARRAY OF CAUSES

In this final section I point to some conclusions about the breadth and variety of Russia's social movements, their level of coordination, and their possible future direction.

How broad are the social movements? So far, they embrace only a small proportion of the population. The statistics quoted above, on the protests over welfare benefits reform, are indicative: less than 1 per cent of the population participated, but they had the support or sympathy of the majority. The protests over housing have involved greater numbers, but still a small minority. On the other hand, there are social movements on an ever-wider range of issues. Alongside those described above work the trade union, human rights and environmentalist movements. And new forms of protest keep appearing. For example:

- The environmentalists have been joined by groups opposing the recent construction boom on architectural and aesthetic, as much as social, grounds.[10]
- The soldiers' mothers committees and other longstanding anti-militarist campaigners have been joined by new groups

that defend the rights of conscripted soldiers and/or support conscientious objectors in many towns.

- There has been a revival of student movements, such as the OD Group at Moscow State University, concerned not only with poor living conditions and financing but with the quality of higher education.

Another extraordinary movement, by motorists, burst into life during Putin's second term. It began in the far eastern port of Vladivostok, with protests against government proposals to ban right-hand-drive vehicles. The plans would have outlawed the huge number of secondhand Japanese cars owned by families in the Russian far east, and ruined a thriving import business in which many local people have found work after the closure of manufacturing capacity in the 1990s. In 2005 a nonpolitical lobby group, Freedom of Choice, organised a procession of 3,000 vehicles through Vladivostok sporting orange ribbons, a colour that was supposedly chosen without reference to events in Ukraine but carried an unmistakable message. The movement proved its power over the case of Oleg Shcherbinsky, a railroad worker jailed after a road accident in which the governor of Altai region, Mikhail Yevdokimov, was killed. In August 2005 Shcherbinsky had been turning off a highway in his right-hand-drive car, when Yevdokimov's car tried to overtake at about 200 kilometres per hour and flew off the road. Putin falsely claimed that the involvement of a right-hand-drive car had been a cause of the governor's death, and Shcherbinsky got a four-year jail sentence. Freedom of Choice hit back with a nationwide series of rallies. Sensing a vote winner, the parliamentary speaker Sergei Mironov and then the presidential party United Russia swung behind Shcherbinsky. In March 2006 he was freed on appeal.[11]

As the economic slowdown took hold of Russia in late 2008, one of the government's first measures was to impose import duties of 10–20 per cent on foreign-made cars. The measure, designed to protect domestic manufacturers, took no account of the situation in the far east, where since the collapse of the Soviet Union the local economy has been shaped more by trade links with Japan and Korea than by the government's mainly ineffectual initiatives to revive local industry. The motorists' movement sprang back to life, and in December 2008 several thousand people participated in rallies in a string of far-eastern cities. The authorities' mood had sharply changed since 2006, though: the riot police moved in, between 60 and 200 demonstrators were detained, and twelve journalists covering the event were severely beaten up. A manifesto issued by the organisers called not only for the reduction of import tariffs and support to the car industry, but also for free speech, reduction of housing services tariffs – and the resignation of the government. Previously, the motorists' movement had been categorised by some other activists as of 'the middle class'. Now the point was made that, while the 1990s recession had driven many people in the far east out of jobs and into small businesses, they were anything but a 'middle class' in the European sense. Instead of the possibility of stable employment, they were now being offered blows from police riot sticks.[12]

Coordination and coherence of separate movements is at an early stage. It's worth quoting, again, the sociologist and activist Carine Clément:

> Russia is more and more being divided into two camps. There are those who can make their plans for the future, who feel the effects of stability and the improvement of living standards. And there are those who, despite all the improvements, feel they are in a precarious situation. Something happens – and they can sink. They are not the poorest, but they live just a little above the poverty line. This is the layer of the population that suffers most from the government's social reforms.... Their first reaction to this intervention of the state in their lives is the typical reaction of Soviet citizens in a traditional paternalistic style – to write a letter to whoever's in charge.... And only after that [produces no results] do people begin to think: OK, if the bosses aren't going to do anything, that means they need to do something themselves. And then the embryos of all sorts of new civil structures appear – and these structures have now started, bit by bit, to make contact with each other. It's a very slow process, though.[13]

Those points were made in February 2008, at the very peak of the oil boom. Since then, the very economic changes that could undermine most households' precarious position have become evident. But the coordination and unity of social movements is, as Clément suggests, only at an early stage. Take, for example, Izhevsk, where there has been considerable success at a local level. A Coordinating Council for Civil Action was formed 'to negotiate with the authorities, and participating in amending the

Udmurtiya budget to improve citizens' standard of living' during the welfare protests in 2005. In the following year, the Council moved from being a coalition to being an organising centre. At the end of 2006, the Communist Party, which had traditionally been the strongest political opposition in the town and had until then worked with the Council, backed away from it and tried to organise rival demonstrations. That failed, and the Council was strengthened as a coordinating centre working across political lines. In 2007, after two years of nonrecognition, the local authorities agreed to negotiate with the Council.[14]

Izhevsk is an exception, though. While in many localities single-issue campaign groups have forced authorities to compromise or negotiate, a coordinated approach is rare. That is not to say that activists in different groups are unaware of, or indifferent, to each other's work. On the contrary: as well as the various gatherings (social forums, conferences and so on) already mentioned, Russia's social movements have a magnificent, high-quality Internet presence and a high level of blog use which helps to bind together groups that are geographically distant.[15] (For an example of campaign coordination locally, see the box on page 183 on 'Activists under siege'.)

As for *the future direction of social movements*, a major determinant will be the impact of the economic slowdown on Russia. On the one hand, this may produce a dampening effect on civic activity and organisation of all kinds, for some of the reasons that it did in the 1990s: that is, the daily struggle for survival into which many people are thrown by unemployment, in particular, is often an obstruction to community organisation and civic activism. On the other hand, Russia moves into this economic crisis from a quite different background from that of the early 1990s. Most people's living standards, and expectations, have been rising, albeit slowly – and while democratic rights have been eroded, Putin's rule is a far, far cry from the comprehensive dictatorship of Soviet times. As the recession began to bite in late 2008, Russia's leading business newspaper editorialised that it was those who now had something to lose, as well as those nearer to the poverty line, who might be moved to join protest movements. Arguing for relief for defaulting mortgages, *Vedomosti*'s editors wrote:

> Not to help the middle class now would be dangerous. In 1998, Russians who had still not lost the habits of modest post-Soviet life styles got through the crisis with the usual servility to fate.

> But now they have something to lose: theoretically, 600,000 mortgage payers could lose their flats as a result of failing to make repayments. And those happy owners of cars, fridges and other goods bought with dollar loans, even if they don't lose their property, will spend their time rushing from one foreign exchange booth to another, guessing the rates, hoping to save at least some of their fast-devaluing ruble income on which to live.[16]

The events in Vladivostok, described above, suggest that this is no exaggeration.

The Russian establishment harbours much greater fears, though, about the reaction of the broader mass of working-class people to the economic crisis. In December 2008, a survey recorded that 28 per cent of people have no savings on which to fall back in case of redundancy. The economist Yevgeny Gontmakher, who has headed the government's department of social development (1997–2003) and held a string of other leading social welfare posts, publicly pictured a scenario in which citizens of one of Russia's industrial towns, enraged by a closure of its main factory, occupy buildings and take the local governor hostage. He imagined the example then being followed elsewhere. Such events could happen 'in the very near future', he wrote, in an article headlined 'Novocherkassk-2009', an allusion to the workers' revolt in Novocherkassk in 1962. This articulation of such fears so disturbed the federal media and communications inspectorate that it wrote to the newspaper in which Gontmakher's article appeared, and reminded it of its duty to observe laws against extremism.[17]

In February 2009, when street unrest erupted in the Baltic states of Latvia and Lithuania over state austerity measures, Putin was asked about the prospect of similar protests in Russia at a meeting with United Russia parliamentarians. He emphasised the distinction between lawful and unlawful protests, and that if protesters stepped outside the law, 'the state and society have the right to react and defend themselves'. Without naming the Baltic states, he said Russia would not under any circumstances allow 'the sort of events taking place in other countries'. Given the readiness with which law enforcement agencies have pronounced protest actions illegal, civil society activists feared the worst. Arkady Dvorkovich, an adviser to president Medvedev, told western journalists that the administration was monitoring potential trouble spots, such as factory towns hit by unemployment.[18]

Russian power showed just how nervous it gets about popular reaction to the effects of the economic crisis in June 2009, when Putin made an astonishing visit to the tiny town of Pikalevo in north-west Russia. Pikalevo's single workplace had in 2004 been carved into three: two cement factories and a chemicals plant, owned by Oleg Deripaska and two other oligarchs. In January 2009, as cement prices crashed, all three plants stopped work. After months of being laid off without pay, about 1,000 of Pikalevo's 9,000 workers blockaded the main highway to St Petersburg. Putin flew into town with Deripaska and the other factory owners and commanded, live on television, that they restart operations. They meekly acquiesced. But such populism comes at a cost to power. In the weeks that followed (when this book was already being typeset), activists reported discussions about the need for direct action Pikalevo-style in other towns hit by unemployment. In Altai region in eastern Siberia, a giant tractor factory was occupied and a highway blocked by laid-off construction workers. In Sverdlovsk workers at a stood-down engineering factory formed a council to replace the management.

Spontaneous revolt and civic organisation are not the same. But it seems likely that the end of the oil boom will stimulate both, and bring a turbulence to which an increasing number of people in Russia will react by moving, in one way or another, to take greater control over their lives and thereby take part in shaping the future of their country and much beyond it.

CONCLUSIONS

The interpretation of Putin's Russia that I have presented points to four groups of conclusions, about:

- the legacies left to Russia from the Soviet period
- the character of the Russian oil boom and the recession that is following it
- the evolution of state power under Putin, and its changing relationship with the owners of wealth on one hand and the majority of the population on the other
- Russia's social movements.

Soviet Legacies

The dynamics of power, money and people in Putin's Russia cannot be understood without bearing in mind the legacies of the Soviet period. The first essential Soviet legacy was one of power. In the economy, while Soviet-type workplace relations persisted in some sections of industry and aspects of the Soviet welfare system were maintained by governments wary of popular protest, many of the Soviet system's foundation stones collapsed with incredible speed. In the space of a few years, the suppression of capitalist ownership and the state's near-monopoly of property, trade and commerce disappeared. The near-collapse of the state apparatus, the abolition of market rules and the loosening of capital controls in the 1990s led to a wave of capital flight, probably the most concentrated ever. And yet, as the Soviet economy collapsed and Russia was dragged into the world market, large chunks of the Soviet elite quite easily converted their power in the old system into both power and wealth in post-Soviet capitalism. That power turned out to be a more enduring resource than the state it had headed and the system of Soviet economic rules that it had wielded. Elements of the elite transformed themselves into capitalists, and assumed control of the capitalist state, more easily than might have been expected.

This points to important conclusions about the Soviet system.

Since it had shut out capitalist forms of exploitation in the name of workers' power, previous generations of anticapitalists looked to it as the herald of a better future. For some, this future would mean a system based on state ownership but freed by one means or another from the Soviet political dictatorship; for others, such as Gorbachev, it took the form of a social democratic utopia. But it turned out that the Soviet system was insufficient as the basis for superseding capitalism, and that its state property was easier to unravel than the power of its elite. That is why, as I argued in Chapter 1, the hopes of the international left, of finding alternatives to the nightmare of Yeltsin's forced march to the market, were dashed. Yeltsin's cruel, inhuman policy choices were neither inevitable nor justified – but it is now clear that the road to them was paved as much by late Soviet history as by Yeltsin's notorious advisers. Given how politically and economically bankrupt the Soviet Union was, for decades before its collapse, it is easy to see, with the benefit of hindsight, how it was preparing the ground for the return of capitalism in its insane, unstable late-twentieth-century form.

The second legacy of the Soviet period that remains relevant is the damage done by decades of dictatorship to people's ability to develop social and political movements, to organise for their own interests, and to play a part in shaping society – in other words, to practise democracy in a wide, active sense. Russia emerged from the Soviet Union with virtually no tradition of social and community organisation or of uncensored public discussion. It had an inexperienced working-class movement which had to roll back the effects of decades of collaborationist trade unionism practised in the name of the 'workers' state'. In the 1990s, the combination of this legacy with the shocking effects of the slump obstructed social movements. The main opposition, that of the Communist party, was mounted in the name of the Soviet system, a return to which was impossible. Russian society, and Russian social and political movements, are not free of these shadows of the past even today, and the nationalism and statism prevalent in the so-called 'left' is a reminder of this. The possibilities for superseding these legacies will be a crucial concern of the 2010s.

The Oil Boom and the Recession

The resurgence of state power in Putin's Russia, and the recovery of the economy and of average living standards, were made possible in the first place by the oil boom. From 1999, the revenues from export sales of oil, gas and metals buoyed up the whole economy, helping other industries to recover and stimulating domestic demand. Against this background, Putin and his colleagues took back control of the oil industry, in particular, from the Yeltsin-era oligarchs, increased the tax take and made the state apparatus more effective. But without the economic recovery, much of what Putin did would have been impossible.

During Putin's second term it seemed to the Kremlin that the oil windfall had made it all-powerful. The currency was stabilised, the Russian state debt paid off and a considerable pot of foreign currency reserves accumulated. Internationally, Putin could afford to play the tough statesman, responding vigorously to US aggression in Central Europe and denouncing the 'unipolar' world order. At home, average living standards had returned to, and in many respects exceeded, those of the late Soviet period. In 2006–08, the consumer boom made available cheap credit, cars, electrical appliances, foreign holidays and much else, to millions of better-off Russians. Under these conditions, Putin had more room for manoeuvre politically: unlike Yeltsin, he was supported, or grudgingly accepted, by much of the population.

But the oil boom was lopsided. It was accompanied by a gigantic credit bubble. By mid-2008, the nearly $600 billion of reserves accumulated by the Central Bank was almost matched by the $500 billion borrowed by Russian companies and banks from foreign lenders. Furthermore, the economy remained heavily dependent on commodities and the export revenues they generated – and therefore vulnerable to the price falls that came in 2008–09. And Russia displayed symptoms of 'Dutch disease': that is, manufacturing and agriculture remained uncompetitive in comparison to the commodity-exporting sectors, thus reinforcing the country's dependence on them.

Crucially, the material benefits of the oil boom were mostly gathered in the hands of the property-owning class. The chances provided by the oil windfall to address Russia's crisis of human development were largely lost. As average living standards rose, the gap between the rich and the poor, and between the rich regions and poor regions, widened. Although Russia recovered from extremely high levels of mortality of the early 1990s, little progress was made in tackling its appallingly low life expectancy. The government did too little to address the health and welfare problems that caused it, choosing instead to concentrate fire on the wrong targets, for example with its natalist campaign. The disaster of low life expectancy was clearly related to the misery of Russia's working poor, particularly in industrial areas that had been ravaged by the 1990s slump and had benefited less than others from the oil boom. But Putin's welfare reforms, centred on shifting service provision into the private sector, may end up exacerbating inequalities.

The concept of the 'natural resource curse' explains some of these phenomena, but as I argued in Chapter 3, it takes for granted elements in the bigger picture that should be questioned. First, most writers on the subject assume that natural resources, and indeed whole economies, are bound to remain under the ownership and control either of states or of large privately owned corporations. To my mind, however, socialist forms of common ownership and control – not to be confused with the state ownership and bureaucratic domination practised in the Soviet Union and other largely nationalised economies – are the key to solving these problems. In the aftermath of capitalism's latest and most serious disaster, it is to be hoped that the potential of socialism will begin to be more widely discussed and thought about. Second, the 'natural resource curse' literature says too little about the rich countries' distorted demand for oil, gas and other natural resources, and for exports produced by newly industrialising countries' energy-intensive economies – which have grown sharply with no concern either for human development or for the natural limits of those resources. It is this distortion of the whole of humankind's economic activity that supports the demand for oil and gas and underlies the phenomena associated with the 'natural resource curse'.

The legacy of the world financial crash in 2008, with which the oil boom and credit bubble ended, will play a big part in determining Russia's future. The Russian government has claimed that the oil windfall provided Russia with an economic shield from the worst effects of the financial crash. But it is very far from impervious. The nature of the global financial system into which Russia has so thoroughly integrated is such that capital flows out of weaker economies at times of crisis. The $130 billion outflow of capital from Russia in 2008 is the clearest indication of that. And under conditions of global integration, the shock waves of the financial crisis have ravaged industry across the world, including Russia, with terrifying speed. For Russia's people, all the progress made in terms of human development, living standards and welfare during the boom is now at risk.

State Power under Putin

The centralisation of state power under Putin was in the first place a reversal of the unprecedented collapse of the state under Yeltsin. The state had ceded control of the oil industry to the oligarchs in a chaotic act of surrender; political and military weakness drove it into its disastrous war in Chechnya in 1994–96; its leaders had to rely on oligarch-financed manipulation to win the 1996 election; it had proved unable to collect sufficient taxes to finance its most basic activities, and fell back on issuing treasury bonds, speculation in which played a big part in Russia's 1998 financial crisis. Much of what Putin did in his first term, with the help of the contingent of *siloviki* he brought into the state apparatus, simply restored to the state the functions it fulfils in most capitalist countries but had ceased to do in Russia in the 1990s: collecting taxes, managing the currency, guiding economic policy and so on. This involved disciplining the oligarchs in the interests of the property-owning class as a whole.

The lurid tales in the western press about a 'KGB takeover' are often as one-sided, and reflective of the western business elite's self-interest, as were the claims of a 'mafia state' in the 1990s. Putin's drive to increase the state's role in 'strategic sectors' was not motivated by a wish for large-scale nationalisation: the state even now plays less of a part in the oil industry in Russia than it does in oil states that serve international capitalism most loyally, such as Saudi Arabia, Kuwait and Mexico. Economic policy has been guided throughout the 2000s by right-wing liberal 'market reformers' – Kudrin, Chubais and the rest – who oversaw the creation of domestic capital markets, and continued privatisation and deeper integration with world markets.

The arguments by western commentators who compare the 'dictator' Putin with the 'democrat' Yeltsin are steeped in hypocrisy. Yeltsin ordered the bombing of Parliament when it crossed him, manipulated elections and unleashed mass murder in Chechnya. His authoritarian instincts were limited only by the weakness of the state apparatus that he headed. He was better liked in the west because he was more amenable to US and European financial interests. Democratic freedoms have been rolled back under Putin, not because he wanted to do so more than Yeltsin did, but because he was better at it. That authoritarianism is a very real danger to the social movements and organisations that are the best hope for Russia's future. The violent attacks on activists and journalists, carried out with impunity, and the repressive sanctions used by authorities at all levels, signal real dangers. But any large-scale clash between those movements and the state lies in the future. That is why, as I argued in Chapter 6, Zbigniew Brzezinski's comparison of Putin with Mussolini can not be taken very seriously. Putin disciplined the oligarchs without making any challenge to capitalism as an economic system, in a manner similar to Mussolini's. But Putin and his colleagues – who have shown in the conduct of the second Chechen war the brutality they are prepared to sanction – have in Russia never been faced with the need to crush opposition physically on the scale that Mussolini did.

Social Movements

On one hand I have argued that substantial change is brought about by social movements, through which large numbers of people act collectively to shape their future, taking politics out of the hands of economic and political elites. On the other, the actual movements I have described in Chapters 8 and 9 are embryonic and mostly local. This is a paradox, but it can, and eventually will, be resolved. That resolution is both possible and necessary. Collective participation and social change are not cause and effect, or effect and cause; they are the same thing.

At the start of Chapter 8 I argued that the legacy of Soviet repression – the lack of traditions of organisation and action in communities and workplaces, and in society more generally – is one reason that Russia's social movements have developed so slowly. The Soviet dictatorship, and the workplace paternalism with which it was combined, made collective action all but impossible and bred habits of subservience. And when the Soviet Union collapsed, the 1990s slump, and the social disaster it produced, forestalled any rapid recovery by social movements. The political confusions caused by the false dichotomy between Soviet 'socialism' and capitalism made matters worse – although the crisis now engulfing world capitalism may well provide a clarification of realities that have been obscured by the oil boom and the debt bubble.

What is the real potential of Russia's social movements? The most persistent of them have arisen in response to changes that threaten material benefits that working people perceive to be theirs by right: examples are the demonstrations in January 2005 against the monetisation of welfare benefits, and the protests against municipal services reform and the threat that it implies to decent, affordable housing for most wage earners. At the peak of the boom, the labour movement engaged in battles that – unlike the tormented fights over unpaid wages in the 1990s – bore many similarities to those in other capitalist economies. During the brief period in which capital flowed in to Russia, in 2005–07, labour responded. The Ford strike at St Petersburg was the best example.

I have tried to offer a view of these movements that is just not available via the media, even in the age of the Internet. For example the protests described in Chapter 9 are no less powerful than those that erupted in eastern Europe in the early months of 2009, but – perhaps because they are geographically more distant, and more difficult to contextualise – received only a fraction of the media coverage. Furthermore, the media focuses on spontaneous outbursts of protests – and social movements can not be judged solely on the basis of such events. As I sought to convey in Chapters 8 and 9, Russian civil society has much deeper resources: *pravozashchitniki* with experience stretching back to Soviet times, and stubbornness to match; journalists who challenge officialdom with courage bordering on recklessness; trade union and community activists with fanatical organisational drive. When protests erupted in the early 1990s, their participants had almost no experience to look back to; in the 2010s, that will be different.

For all the Russian government's dictatorial reputation, it has consistently displayed extreme nervousness in the face of social movements. Year after year, it has postponed increases in charges for gas, water and electricity, for fear of provoking a reaction. Authoritarianism is certainly part of the relationship between power and people in Putin's Russia – but, up until now, rising living standards have been, too. This balance has been crucial to the way that Putin has ruled. The economic hardships resulting from the world crisis mean that that relationship will inevitably change. As it does, Russia's social movements will realise some of their potential, in both expected and unexpected ways.

NOTES

Introduction

1 Christopher Xenakis, *What Happened to the Soviet Union? How and why American sociologists were caught by surprise* (Westport, Praeger, 2002), p. 12.
2 On the world economy, Giovanni Arrighi, *The Long Twentieth Century* (London, Verso, 2002), pp. 239–324; Robert Brenner, *The Boom and the Bubble: The US in the world economy* (London, Verso, 2002); A. Glyn, A. Hughes, A. Lipietz and A. Singh, 'The rise and fall of the golden age', in Stephen Marglin and Juliet Shore (eds), *The Golden Age of Capitalism* (Oxford, Clarendon, 1990); Paul Krugman, *The Return of Depression Economics and the Crisis of 2008* (London, Penguin, 2009); David McNally, 'From financial crisis to world slump: accumulation, financialization and the global slowdown' (research paper, 2008); Harry Shutt, *The Trouble With Capitalism: An enquiry into the causes of global economic failure* (London, Zed Books, 1998); Andrew Walter, *World Power and World Money: The role of hegemony and international monetary order* (London, Harvester Wheatsheaf, 1993); John Roberts, *$1000 Billion A Day: Inside the foreign exchange markets* (London, HarperCollins, 1995).
3 Walter, *World Power*, pp. 196–7.
4 Susan Strange, *Casino Capitalism* (Oxford, Blackwell, 1986), p. 18.
5 Arrighi, *The Long Twentieth Century*, pp. 316–17 and pp. 322–3; Stuart Corbridge, Nigel Thrift and Ron Martin (eds), *Money, Power and Space* (Oxford, Blackwell, 1994).
6 Timothy Colton, *The Dilemma of Reform in the Soviet Union* (New York, Council on Foreign Relations, 1986), p. 198.
7 Thane Gustafson, *Crisis Amid Plenty: The politics of Soviet energy under Brezhnev and Gorbachev* (Princeton, Princeton University Press, 1989), pp. 263–86; Stephen Kotkin, *Armageddon Averted: The Soviet collapse, 1970–2000* (Oxford, Oxford University Press, 2001), pp. 15–17.
8 Colton, *The Dilemma*, pp. 37 and 206; Seweryn Bialer, *The Soviet Paradox: External expansion, internal decline* (London, Tauris, 1986); Alan Smith, *Russia and the World Economy: Problems of integration* (London, Routledge, 1993), pp. 156–76.
9 Arrighi, *The Long Twentieth Century*, pp. 323–4.

Chapter 1: From Gorbachev to Yeltsin

1 Egor Gaidar, *Gosudarstvo i evoliutsiia* (St Petersburg, Norma, 1997), p. 159.
2 Ol'ga Kryshtanovskaia, *Anatomiia rossiiskoi elity* (Moscow, A.V. Solov'ev, 2004), pp. 274–304; D. L. Ushakov, *Ofshornye zony v praktike rossiiskikh nalogoplatel'shchikov* (Moscow, Iurist, 1999), pp. 82–3; David Woodruff, *Money Unmade: Barter and the fate of Russian capitalism* (London, Cornell University Press, 1999), p. 66; Alexander Bim, Derek C. Jones and Thomas E Weisskopf, 'Hybrid forms of enterprise organisation in the former USSR and the Russian Federation', *Comparative Economic Studies*, 35:1 (Spring 1993), p. 15 (employment).
3 Anna Akhmedova, 'Ischezaiushchii PSB', *Vedomosti*, 28 February 2007.
4 Juliet Johnson, *A Fistful of Rubles: The rise and fall of the Russian banking system* (London, Cornell University Press, 2000), p. 36.
5 Johnson, *A Fistful of Rubles*, pp. 57–9; David Lane and Cameron Ross, *The Transition from Communism to Capitalism: Ruling elites from Gorbachev to Yeltsin* (London, Macmillan, 1999).
6 'Inside Kremlin as it tightens its grip', *Wall Street Journal*, 19 December 2006; Russian presidential website <www.kremlin.ru>.
7 Ian Traynor, 'Putin urged to apply Pinochet stick', *Guardian*, 31 March 2000; Alfa Bank website <www.alfabank.com>.
8 Naomi Klein, *The Shock Doctrine: The rise of disaster capitalism* (London, Allen Lane, 2007), pp. 219–20 and 239.
9 Peter Reddaway and Dmitri Glinski, *The Tragedy of Russia's Reforms: Market bolshevism against democracy* (Washington, US Institute of Peace Press, 2001), pp. 231–308; Joseph Blasi, Maya Kroumova and Douglas Kruse, *Kremlin Capitalism: Privatizing the Russian economy* (New York, Cornell University Press, 1997), pp. 13–85; Nikolai Shmelev, *V poiskakh zdravogo smysla: dvadtsat' let rossiiskikh ekonomicheskikh reform* (Moscow, Ves' mir, 2006), pp. 242–300.
10 Reddaway and Glinski, *The Tragedy*, p. 253 (my emphasis); Anders Aslund, *Building Capitalism: The transformation of the former Soviet bloc* (Cambridge, Cambridge University Press, 2002), pp. 110–13.
11 Padma Desai, *Conversations on Russia: Reform from Yeltsin to Putin* (Oxford, Oxford University Press, 2006), pp. 291–2 (interview with Boris Jordan); Janine Wedel, *Collision and Collusion: The strange case of western aid to Eastern Europe 1989–1998* (London, Macmillan, 1998), pp. 121–4, and 'Harvard's role in US aid to Russia', *Boston Globe*, 25 March 2006; David McClintick, 'How Harvard lost Russia', *Institutional Investor*, 13 January 2006.
12 Stefan Hedlund, 'Russia and the IMF: a sordid tale of moral hazard', *Demokratizatsiya* 9:1 (2001), pp. 104–6; John Odling-Smee, 'The IMF and Russia in the 1990s' (IMF Working paper 04/155, 2004).
13 L. Abalkin and J. Whalley (eds), 'The problem of capital flight from

Russia', *The World Economy* 22:3 (1999), pp. 421–4; William Cooper and John Hards, 'Russian capital flight, economic reforms and US interests: an analysis', Congressional Research Service report RL30394 (10 March 2000); L. L. Fituni, *Tenevoi oborot i begstvo kapitala* (Moscow, Vostochnaia literatura, 2003), pp. 34–6 and 55–5; L. Grigoryev and A. Kosarev, *Capital Flight: Scale and nature* (Moscow, 2000).

14 Simon Pirani, '$150bn capital flight ravages Russia', *Observer*, 16 May 1999.

Chapter 2: From Yeltsin to Putin

1 Anatol Lieven, *Chechnya: Tombstone of Russian power (*London, Yale University Press, 1998).

2 Lieven, *Chechnya*, p. 170.

3 David Hoffman, *The Oligarchs: Wealth and power in the new Russia* (New York, Public Affairs, 2003), pp. 296–324; Chrystia Freeland, *Sale of the Century: The inside story of the second Russian revolution* (London, Little Brown, 2000), pp. 161–81; Ira Lieberman and Rogi Veimetra, 'The rush for state shares in the "Klondyke" of wild east capitalism', *George Washington Journal of International Law and Economics* 29:3 (1996), pp. 737–68.

4 Hoffman, *The Oligarchs*, pp. 325–64; and newspaper articles.

5 William Tompson, 'Putting Yukos in perspective', *Post-Soviet Affairs* 21:2 (2005), p. 163.

6 Dale Gray, 'Evaluation of taxes and revenues from the energy sector in … FSU countries', IMF Working Paper 98/34 (1998); Hoffman, *The Oligarchs*, p. 205.

7 Vadim Volkov, *Violent Entrepreneurs: The use of force in the making of Russian capitalism* (London, Cornell University Press, 2002); Richard Behar, 'Capitalism in a cold climate', *Fortune*, 12 June 2000; Metal Bulletin Research, *A Strategic Assessment of the Aluminium Industry in the CIS* (London, 1997); *Metal Bulletin*, various articles; <www.bykov.info>.

8 Stephen Handelman, *Comrade Criminal: Russia's new mafiya* (London, Yale University Press, 1995), p. 342.

9 Aslund, *Building Capitalism*, pp. 341–3; Andrei Shleifer and Robert Vishny, *The Grabbing Hand: Government pathologies and their cures* (Cambridge Mass., Harvard University Press, 1998), pp. 7–13 and 123–150; Adam Swain, Vlad Mykhnenko et al., 'Neo-liberalising post-soviet space: corruption and transition', in K. Birch and V. Mykhnenko (eds), *The Rise and Fall of Neoliberalism: The collapse of an economic order?* (London, Zed Books, forthcoming).

10 London School of Hygiene and Tropical Medicine Adult Mortality in Russia project. UN Development Programme, *Demographic Policy in Russia: From reflection to action (life expectancy)*. Rosstat (Federal State Statistics service) website <www.gks.ru> (population).

11 UNICEF, *A Decade of Transition: Regional monitoring report no. 8* (Florence, 2001), pp. 47–52; excess deaths are counted as those that would not have occurred had mortality remained at its 1989 level. Vladimir Shkolnikov et al., 'Changes in life expectancy in Russia in the mid 1990s', *The Lancet*, 24 March 2001; World Bank, *Dying Too Young* (2005); Tatiana Maleva, 'Prostykh reshenii slozhnykh problem ne sushestvuet', *Ekonomika Rossii,* 21:22, 2006; Desai, *Conversations on Russia*, pp. 310–21 (interview with Anatoly Vishnevsky).

12 David Stuckler et al., 'Mass privatisation and the post-communist mortality crisis', *The Lancet*, January 2009; Jeffrey Sachs, letter, *Financial Times*, 19 January 2009.

13 Rosstat; Olga Kislitsyna, 'Income inequality in Russia during transition' (EERC working paper 03/08).

14 Linda Cook, *Postcommunist Welfare States: Reform politics in Russia and Eastern Europe* (London, Cornell University Press, 2007), pp. 62–83.

15 Simon Clarke, 'A very Soviet form of capitalism? The management of holding companies in Russia', *Post-Communist Economies,* 16:4 (2004), pp. 405–22.

16 Aslund, *Building Capitalism* (pp. 5 and 451 quoted) and *How Capitalism Was Built* (Cambridge, Cambridge University Press, 2007); David Woodruff, 'The economist's burden', *New Left Review,* 55 (2009).

17 Joseph Stiglitz, *Globalization and its Discontents* (London, Penguin, 2002), pp. 133–65 and 182–5; Peter Nolan, *China's Rise, Russia's Fall* (London, Macmillan, 1995).

18 World Bank, *Making Russia Competitive: Executive summary* (2006); *Russian Economic Report no. 13* (December 2006).

19 Krugman, *The Return of Depression Economics*, p. 97.

20 Woodruff, *Money Unmade*; Shmelev, *V poiskakh zdravogo smysla*, pp. 281–93.

21 Hoffman, *The Oligarchs*, p. 412.

22 Johnson, *A Fistful of Rubles*, pp. 212–17; OECD, *Economic survey 2000: Russian Federation* (2000) pp. 37–44; Hedlund, 'Russia and the IMF'; CSFB, 1998 Annual Review; newspaper articles.

23 UNCTAD Secretariat and UN Economic Commission for Europe, *The Russian Crisis* (Geneva, October 1998); 'Lex', *Financial Times*, 28 December 1998; letter from Harry Shutt, *Financial Times*, 31 December 1998; Augusto Lopez-Claros, 'The role of international financial institutions during the transition in Russia', in Judith Twigg and Kate Schechter (eds), *Social Capital and Social Cohesion in Post-Soviet Russia* (New York, M.E. Sharpe, 2003), pp. 243–67.

24 OECD, *Economic Survey 2000*, p. 62; Simon Pirani, 'Winter of discontent looms large', *Gemini News Agency*, 27 October 1998.

Chapter 3: Power and Money: The Economic Foundations

1 Accounts Chamber of the Russian Federation, *Bulletin*, various; Paris Club press release, 23 June 2006; Central Bank of Russia

website <www.cbr.ru>; Troika Dialog, *Russia Economic Monthly*, various.

2 Philip Hanson, 'The Russian economic recovery: do four years of growth tell us that the fundamentals have changed?', *Europe-Asia Studies* 55:3 (2003), pp. 365–82.

3 Michael Bernstam and Alvin Rabushka, 'Russia's economic contraction and recovery 1992–2004', in Michael Ellman (ed.), *Russia's Oil and Natural Gas: Bonanza or curse?* (London, Anthem Press, 2006), pp. 55–102.

4 *BP Statistical Review of World Energy.*

5 Amy Myers Jaffe et al., *The Changing Role of National Oil Companies in International Energy Markets.* Baker Institute Policy Report no. 35 (Houston, Baker Institute, 2007); Rosneft company presentation, February 2007; Simon Pirani, 'The worrying wealth of nations', *Emerging Markets*, 21 October 2007.

6 Fiona Harvey, 'Axe fossil-fuel handouts, says Browne', *Financial Times*, 2 November 2008; Greg Muttitt, 'Oil sell-off by stealth' <www.niqash.org> (on Iraq).

7 Hellfire Economics: Multinational companies and the contract dispute over Kashagan (December 2007) and The Kashagan Stitch-Up (January 2008) <www.carbonweb.org> (Kashagan).

8 Rudiger Ahrend and William Tompson, *Realising the Oil Supply Potential of the CIS: The impact of institutions and policies* (Paris, OECD, 2006), pp. 6–8.

9 International Energy Agency, *World Energy Outlook 2004*, pp. 303–4.

10 Ahrend and Tompson, *Realising the Oil Supply Potential*, p. 23; Alfa Bank, 'Russian oil industry – Less taxes, please', research report (Moscow, 14 March 2007).

11 Jonathan Stern, *The Future of Russian Gas and Gazprom* (Oxford, Oxford University Press, 2005), pp. 7–19; 'Gazprom's $69 billion question – when to start developing Yamal gas', *Gas Matters*, October 2004, pp. 27–32.

12 Earth Observation Group, NOAA National Geophysical Data Center, *A Twelve Year Record of National and Global Gas Flaring Volumes* (Boulder, Colo., 2007).

13 Rudiger Ahrend, 'Sustaining growth in a hydrocarbon-based economy', pp. 105–26 in Ellman (ed.), *Russia's Oil and Natural Gas*; Peter Rutland, 'Putin's economic record: is the oil boom sustainable?', *Europe–Asia Studies* 60:6 (2008), pp. 1051–72 (on Russia). Macartan Humphreys, Jeffrey Sachs and Joseph Stiglitz (eds), *Escaping the Natural Resource Curse* (New York, Columbia University Press, 2007); Terry Lynn Karl, *The Paradox of Plenty* (London, University of California Press, 1997); Jeffrey Sachs and Andrew Warner, 'The big rush, natural resource booms and growth', *Journal of Development Economics*, 59:1 (1999), pp. 43–76 (on the natural resource curse generally).

14 Rutland, 'Putin's economic record', p. 1070.

Chapter 4: Power and Money: The State, Oligarchs and Oil

1 Quote from Edward Lucas, 'Back to the Cold War – Putin's Russia threat to Britain', *Daily Mail*, 23 May 2007. Presentational stereotypes tell their own story. An image of Putin in dark glasses, with a shadowy Kremlin behind him, was used on the covers of both Yuri Felshtinsky and Vladimir Pribylovsky's *The Age of Assassins: The rise and rise of Vladimir Putin* (London, Gibson Square, 2008) and an issue of the *Economist* (25–31 August 2007) headlined 'Putin's people: the spies who run Russia'.
2 Reddaway and Glinski, *The Tragedy*, pp. 109–18.
3 Amy Knight, *Spies Without Cloaks: The KGB's successors* (Princeton, Princeton University Press, 1996), pp. 12–27, 32–49, 79–90, 218–21; John Dunlop, *The Rise of Russia and the Fall of the Soviet Empire* (Princeton, Princeton University Press, 1993), pp. 192–206 and 239–60; Yevgenia Albats, *The State Within a State* (New York, Farrar Straus Giroux, 1994), pp. 276–88.
4 Knight, *Spies Without Cloaks*, p. 56.
5 Aleksei Mukhin, *Spetssluzhby Rossii i 'bol'shaia' politika* (Moscow, SPIK-Tsentr, 2000), pp. 17–27; 'Chekistskaia elita v stroiu' <www.whoiswho.ru>, 2001; Iurii Vasil'ev, 'Spetsluzhby gotoviat pokhishchenie Nevzlina', *Moskovskie novosti*, 29 December 2003 (Kondaurov).
6 Knight, *Spies Without Cloaks*, p. 57; Aleksei Khodorych, 'Poslednii dovod zashchity', *Kommersant-Den'gi*, 17 April 2002.
7 'Chekistskaia elita v stroiu' <www.whoiswho.ru> (2001); Anastasiia Dagaeva, 'Deputatu nichego nel'ziia', *Vedomosti*, 8 April 2008 (Lebedev).
8 'The making of a neo-KGB state', *Economist*, 25 August 2007.
9 Il'ia Zhegulev, 'Sozdanie preemnika', *SmartMoney*, 21 April 2008; N. Gevorkian, A. Kolesnikov and N. Timakova, *Ot pervogo litsa: razgovory s Vladimirom Putinym* (Moscow, Vagrius, 2000), pp. 118–28.
10 This interpretation is advanced in Lilia Shevtsova, *Putin's Russia* (Washington, Carnegie Endowment, 2005), pp. 85–6.
11 Lentapedia <www.lenta.ru/lib/> (biographical details); Daniel Triesman, 'Putin's silovarchs', *Orbis*, Winter 2007, p. 143; Olga Kryshtanovskaya and Stephen White, 'Putin's militocracy', *Post-Soviet-Affairs,* 19:4 (2003), p. 300; Peter Baker and Susan Glasser, *Kremlin Rising: Vladimir Putin's Russia and the end of revolution* (New York, Scribner, 2005), pp. 251–3.
12 Felshtinsky and Pribylovsky, *The Age of Assassins*, pp. 6–7; Edward Lucas, *The New Cold War: How the Kremlin menaces both Russia and the west* (London, Bloomsbury, 2008), p. 25.
13 Aleksei Germanovich, 'Kapituliatsiia', *Vedomosti*, 15 February 2001, and 'Nekruglyi stol', *Vedomosti*, 26 February 2001.
14 Valerii Paniushkin and Mikhail Zygar, *Gazprom: novoe russkoe oruzhie* (Moscow, Zakharov, 2008), pp. 90–106; Simon Pirani, 'Turner's Russian roulette', *Observer*, 4 February 2001.

15 Mikhail Kozyrev, 'Gde den'gi-to', *Vedomosti*, 21 November 2001; 'Gazprom boss ends Itera affair by buying Purgaz', *Gas Matters*, December 2001, p. 22; 'After the clear-out, Gazprom gropes towards a strategy', *Gas Matters*, March 2002, pp. 23–8.
16 Andrew Scott Barnes, *Owning Russia: The struggle over factories, farms and power* (London, Cornell University Press, 2006), pp. 210–25; William Tompson, 'Putting Yukos in perspective', *Post-Soviet Affairs*, 21:2 (2005), pp. 159–81; <www.khodorkovsky.ru>; <www.rosneft.ru>.
17 E. Mikhailovskaia (ed.), *Rossiia Putina: istoriia bolezni* (Moscow, Panorama, 2004), p. 98; Boris Kagarlitskii, *Upravliaemaia demokratiia* (Ekaterinburg, Ultra-Kul'tura, 2005), p. 507.
18 'Banks push suretyship case on Yukos loan', *Trade Finance*, February 2005, pp. 10–12; Simon Pirani, 'Rosneft sets ambitious targets', *Trade Finance*, July 2005, pp. 13–15; Catherine Belton, 'Investors "made backdoor Yukos approach"', *Financial Times*, 7 September 2007.
19 Svetlana Ivanova et al., '"Iukos" – ne poslednii', *Vedomosti*, 29 October 2004; OECD, *Economic Survey: Russian Federation 2004*, p. 37.
20 Simon Pirani, 'Oligarch? No, I'm just an oil magnate', *Observer*, 4 June 2000; Andrei Panov, 'Za transfertnye tseny – v tiur'mu', *Vedomosti*, 17 May 2005.
21 World Bank, *From Transition to Development: A country economic memorandum for the Russian Federation* (2005), pp. 60–3; Peter Oppenheimer and Sergiy Maslichenko, 'Energy and the economy: an introduction', in Ellman (ed.), *Russia's Oil and Natural Gas*, pp. 15–31.
22 Alfa Bank, *Russian Tax Claims*, research report (Moscow, November 2004).
23 Iu. Vitkina and A. Rodionov, *Nalogovye prestupniki epokha Putina. Kto oni?* (Moscow, Vershina, 2007), p. 46; Nikolai Petrakov, *Problemy nalogooblozheniia neftianoi otrasli Rossii. Analiticheskii doklad* (Moscow, Institut problemy rynka RAN, 21 March 2006).
24 IMF Bureau of Statistics, *Government Finance Statistics Yearbook 2007*, Table 922.
25 Dev Kar and Devon Cartwright-Smith, *Illicit Financial Flows from Developing Countries: 2002–2006* (economists' version) (GFI, 2009), Tables 10, 14 and 18; Fitch Ratings, *Russia's Rising Capital Flight and Private External Debt*, 13 June 2005; Abdullah Almounsor, 'A development comparative approach to capital flight: the case of the Middle East and North Africa, 1970–2002', in Gerald Epstein (ed.), *Capital Flight and Capital Controls in Developing Countries* (Cheltenham, Edward Elgar, 2005), pp. 234–61.
26 'Isskustvo balansa', *Vedomosti*, 24 September 2002; letter from Anatolii Reshetnikov, *Vedomosti*, 27 September 2002; 'Question time for Rusal', *Metal Bulletin*, 7 October 2002; 'Tolling lives to survive another day', *Metal Bulletin*, 1 September 2003; letter from Robin

Adams, Resource Strategies, to the Russian prime minister, 24 July 2003; Dmitry Simakov, 'Veshch' nedeli: spasibo tollingu', *Vedomosti*, 4 August 2006; Dmitry Kazmin et al., 'Tolling bez ofshorov', *Vedomosti*, 29 July 2008. Gleb Stoliarov, 'Rusal sporit s gorniakami', *Vedomosti*, 28 March 2008; 'Zaiavlenie NPGR o situatsii na "Sevuralboksitrud"', 16 April 2008 <www.ktr.su>; 'Bastoval – teper' ukhodi', *Trud*, 19 August 2008 (Sevuralboksitrud).

27 Ian Rutledge, *The Sakhalin II PSA: A production 'non-sharing' agreement* (Sheffield, SERIS, November 2004); Timothy Fenton Krysiek, *Agreements From Another Era: Production sharing agreements in Putin's Russia, 2000–2007* (Oxford, OIES, November 2007).

28 Elena Mazneva, 'Nominaty "Gazproma"', *Vedomosti*, 30 April 2008; Ed Crooks, 'BP seeks more joint ventures in Russia', *Financial Times*, 23 July 2007; Ed Crooks, 'Schroder a vital link', *Financial Times*, 16 January 2009; other newspaper articles; Krysiek, *Agreements*.

29 Marshall Goldman, *Oilopoly: Putin, power and the rise of the new Russia* (Oxford, Oneworld, 2008), p. 7.

30 Simon Pirani (ed.), *Russian and CIS Gas Markets and their Impact on Europe* (London, Oxford University Press, 2009); Simon Pirani, Jonathan Stern and Katja Yafimava, *The Russo–Ukrainian Gas Dispute of 2009: A comprehensive assessment* (Oxford Institute for Energy Studies, February 2009).

Chapter 5: Power and Money: From Oil Boom to Bust

1 Micex group presentation, 1 October 2008.

2 'Lex: Gazprom', *Financial Times*, 27 April 2006; Simon Pirani, 'The rise and rise of Rosneft', *Energy Focus*, August 2007; Nat Mankelow, 'Maturing market meets western needs', *Financial Times*, 29 October 2007; author's notes (Rosneft annual meeting).

3 Goldman Sachs Global Investment Research, *Russian Banks*, November 2005; Simon Pirani, 'Russian banks', *Credit magazine*, September 2004.

4 Simon Pirani, 'Growing pains', *Emerging Markets*, 19 May 2007; Alfa Bank, *Mortgage Growth Drives Retail Lending,* 27 February 2007; Alfa Bank, *CIS Banks: Time to be choosy,* 18 February 2008.

5 World Bank, *Russian Economic Report* nos 15 (November 2007) and 16 (June 2008).

6 William Tompson, 'Back to the future? Thoughts on the political economy of expanding state ownership in Russia', *Les Cahiers Russe,* no. 6 (2008); *Vedomosti* and the *Moscow Times*, various issues.

7 Nataliia Zubarevich, *Krupnyi biznes v regionakh Rossii: analiticheskii doklad* (Moscow, Pomatur, 2005); *Vedomosti* and *Den'* (Izhevsk), various issues; interview with Sergei Shchukin, 30 September 2007.

8 'Ramki goskapitalizma', *Vedomosti*, 9 July 2007; Igor Ivanov and Andrei Kovalevskii, 'Ponaekhali', *Russkii Newsweek*, 10 April 2008; 'Crisis? What oil crisis?', *Economist*, 7 June 2008.

9 David Mandel, *Labour After Communism* (Montreal, Black Rose Books, 2004), p. 33; Gleb Stoliarov, 'Dvoe iz "kol'tsa"', *Vedomosti*, 10 December 2007; 'Renault priparkovalsia na AvtoVAZe', *Kommersant*, 3 March 2008.

10 'On the offensive', *Financial Times*, 14 May 2008; 'Gunvor, Putin and me' (letter), *Financial Times*, 22 May 2008; Elena Mazneva et al., 'Posledniaia kaplia dlia Timchenko', *Vedomosti*, 23 May 2008; Andrew Higgins et al., 'Secretive associate of Putin emerges', *Wall Street Journal*, 11 June 2008 (on Gunvor). Olga Petrova, 'Khoziain "Rossii"', *Vedomosti*, 16 June 2008; Irina Reznik et al., 'Pomoshniki "Rossii"', *Vedomosti,* 24 July 2008; Elena Mazneva et al., 'Chto pokupaet Timchenko', *Vedomosti*, 7 October 2008; Catrina Stewart, 'Bank Rossiya emerges', *Moscow Times*, 10 July 2008; Boris Nemtsov and Vladimir Milov, *Nezavisimyi ekspertnyi doklad: 'Putin i Gazprom'* (Moscow 2008) (on Rossiya).

11 Capgemini/Merrill Lynch World Wealth Report 2008; Forbes, various issues; Craig Mellow, 'Ruble high rollers', *Institutional Investor*, December 2007; Mikhail Overchenko, 'Milliardery sdulis', *Vedomosti*, 12 March 2009; Gavin Knight, 'From Russia with love', *The London Paper,* 1 November 2007.

12 Committee on the Global Financial System, *Capital Flows and Emerging Market Economies* (BIS website, January 2009), pp. 7–11, 17 and 83.

13 Krugman, *The Return of Depression Economics*, p. 179; World Bank, *Russian Economic Report 17*, p 11; Central Bank of Russia website <www.cbr.ru>; articles in *Trade Finance* magazine by the author (on loans).

14 Deutsche Bank, *Russia's Economics: From fragmentation to integration*, 21 April 2008; Fitch Ratings, *Russia: Global shocks expose weaknesses*, 22 October 2008; Arkady Ostrovsky, 'M Stanley eyes Russian growth', *Financial Times*, 1 June 2004; Peter Larsen, 'Goldman makes measured return to Russia', *Financial Times*, 8 March 2007; Catherine Belton, 'Merrill to expand in emerging markets', *Financial Times,* 24 January 2008.

15 Ol'ga Kuvshinova et al., 'Raznye investitsii', *Vedomosti*, 12 May 2008; Deutsche Bank, *Russia's Economics*; Alfa Bank, *Monitoring Investment Activity in Russia*, research report, 8 February 2007, pp. 4–7; UralSib Bank, *Strategy: Russia in 2008*, 22 January 2008; Deutsche Bank, *Russia: Economics: Dealing with Russia's capital flight* (on returning flight capital).

16 Maria Rozhkova, 'Milliardami zakidaem', *Vedomosti*, 22 May 2007.

17 World Bank, *Russian Economic Report 16*, June 2008.

18 Ol'ga Kuvshinova, 'Evro khuzhe voiny', *Vedomosti*, 22 August 2008; VTB Bank Europe Research, *Economic Flashnote,* 21 August 2008; Andrew Kramer, 'The last days of the oligarchs?', *International Herald Tribune*, 7 March 2009.

19 George Soros, 'America must lead a rescue of emerging economies', *Financial Times*, 28 October 2008.

20 Fitch Ratings, *Russia: Global shocks*; *Kommersant*, 22 September 2008.

21 RIA Novosti, 'Russian billionaire Deripaska gets $4.5 bln state bailout loan', 30 October 2008; Timofei Dziadko, 'Perezaklad na $2 mlrd', *Vedomosti*, 30 October 2008.

22 Nadezhda Ivanitskaia, 'Antikrizisnyi desant', *Vedomosti*, 2 February 2009 (long-term package); Elena Mazneva, 'Neft' na 20 let vpered', *Vedomosti*, 18 February 2009 (Chinese deal).

23 'Putin says $90b stimulus plan', *Bloomberg*, 6 April 2009; Deutsche Bank, *EM Insight: Russia's anti-crisis package*, 30 March 2009; newspaper reports.

24 ITAR-TASS, 31 October 2008; Stefan Wagstyl, 'Putin sees no link to war in market fall', *Financial Times*, 12 September 2008; Robert Skidelsky, 'Crisis hit Russia must scale down its ambition', *Financial Times*, 30 October 2008.

25 Bank for International Settlements, Semiannual OTC Derivatives Statistics, <www.bis.org>; Zhanna Smirnova, *Directing the Derivatives Boom: Micex Group derivatives market presentation* (2008); Tom Fairless, 'Investors pile into Russian derivatives', *Financial News*, 4 July 2008; Tobias Ehinger, 'Trading of Russian derivatives: is the Russian market becoming more mature?', *Eurex*, July 2007; Simon Pirani, 'Russian market needs legal framework', *Futures and Options World*, June 2003.

26 David Pilling, 'Unlucky numbers', *Financial Times*, 10 February 2009; 'The bill that could break up Europe', *Economist*, 28 February 2009; Alfa Bank, *Looking at Russia's Economy in Relative Terms*, 9 October 2008.

27 Fitch Ratings, *Russia: Foreign Reserves, the Rouble and Capital Outflows*, 4 February 2009; 'Capital flight from Russia reaches $40 bn', RIA Novosti, 26 February 2009.

28 Fitch Ratings, *Russia*:, op. cit.; Catherine Belton, 'The Putin defence', *Financial Times*, 29 December 2008.

29 'Russia official jobless up', *Reuters*, 11 March 2009; Ol'ga Kuvshinova, 'Industriia svobodna', *Vedomosti*, 17 February 2009; Gleb Stoliarov, 'Deripaska uvol'niaet', *Vedomosti*, 10 March 2009; 'Severstal' sokrashchaet 9 tysach sotrudnikov', *RIA Novosti*, 11 March 2009.

30 Robin Paxton, 'Mining giant may be hard sell', *Moscow Times*, 25 February 2009; 'Medvedev lays metals merger to rest', *Moscow Times*, 2 March 2009; Iuliia Fedorinova et al., 'Otsrochka na $14 mlrd', *Vedomosti*, 10 March 2009.

31 Fitch Ratings, *Russia*; 'Standard, Troika, to buy troubled assets', *Moscow Times*, 10 March 2009.

32 World Bank, *Russian Economic Report 18* (March 2009).

Chapter 6: Power and People: How Russia is Ruled

1 Boris Kagarlitsky, *Russia Under Yeltsin and Putin* (London, Pluto Press, 2002), p. 239.

2 Interview with Liudmila Alekseeva, 11 March 2008.

3 Kagarlitsky, *Russia Under Yeltsin and Putin*, pp. 230–5; Paul Klebnikov, *Godfather of the Kremlin: Boris Berezovsky and the looting of Russia* (New York, Harcourt, 2000), pp. 302–4; Yuri Felshtinsky and Alexander Litvinenko, *Blowing Up Russia: Terror from within* (New York, SPI Books, 2002), pp. 62–139; Elena Bonner, 'Another Putin show trial', *Wall Street Journal Europe*, 25 November 2004; Marina Lepina, 'Mikhail Trepashkin zanialsia zashchitoi reputatsii', *Kommersant*, 1 April 2008; <www.trepashkin.ru> .

4 Tania Lokshina (ed.), *Zhizn na voine* (Moscow, Demos Centre, 2007), pp. 45–55; Human Rights Watch, *The 'Dirty War' in Chechnya*, March 2001; Human Rights Watch, *Burying the Evidence: The botched investigation into a mass grave in Chechnya,* May 2001; Amnesty International, *Failure to protect or punish: Memorandum to the PACE on the conflict in Chechnya*, January 2002; Memorial website <www.memo.ru>.

5 Liliia Shevstova, *Putin's Russia* (Washington, Carnegie Endowment, 2005), p. 284; RFE/RL, 'What direction for Chechnya?', 8 July 2008; Tom Parfitt, 'The republic of fear', *Sunday Times*, 20 August 2006 (on Kadyrov).

6 Human Rights Watch, 'Widespread torture in the Chechen Republic: briefing paper', 13 November 2006, and *As If They Fell From the Sky': counterinsurgency, rights violations and rampant impunity in Ingushetia* (2008); Mar'iam Magomedova, 'V Ingushetii maniakal'no boiatsia odnogo – ischeznoveniia liudei', *Novye Izvestiia*, 22 September 2008; Memorial website.

7 Peter Baker and Susan Glasser, *Kremlin Rising: Vladimir Putin's Russia and the end of revolution* (New York, Scribner, 2005), pp. 99–120.

8 Anna Politkovskaya, *Putin's Russia* (London, Harvill, 2004), pp. 1–27; Human Rights Watch, *The Wrongs of Passage*, October 2004; Francoise Dauce and Elisabeth Sieca-Kozlowski (eds), *Dedovshchina in the Post-Soviet Military* (Stuttgart, Ibiden-Verlag, 2005).

9 <www.electoralgeography.com> , federal electoral commission website <www.cikrf.ru>; RFE-RL Newsline, 3, 4, 11 and 28 December 2007 and 10 January 2008; Adam Blomfield, 'Putin voting "scam"', *The Independent* (Dublin), 3 December 2007; Golos Association website <www.golos.org>.

10 Iurii Levada, *Ishchem cheloveka* (Moscow, Novoe izdatel'stvo, 2006), p. 126; Kagarlitskii, *Upravliaemaia demokratiia*, p. 506.

11 Olga Kryshtanovskaya and Stephen White, 'Putin's militocracy', *Post-Soviet Affairs* 19:4 (2003), pp. 289–306; Bettina Renz, 'Putin's militocracy? An alternative interpretation', *Europe Asia Studies* 58:6 (2006), pp. 903–24; Viktor Cherkesov, 'Nel'zia dopustit', chtoby voiny prevratilis' v torgovtsev', *Kommersant*, 9 October 2007; Ekaterina Zapodinskaia, 'Iz-pod "dela Gosnarkokontroia" vybivaiut "Trekh kitov"', *Kommersant,* 12 October 2007; 'Ot redaktsii: belaia kost", *Vedomosti*, 2 November 2007 (on intra-siloviki struggles).

12 Deutsche Bank, *Russia's Catch Up Formula*, 29 February 2008; Indem foundation, *Vo skol'ko raz uvelichilas' korruptsiia za 4 goda* <www.anti-corr.ru>; Arkady Ostrovsky, 'Bribery in Russia up tenfold', *Financial Times*, 21 July 2005.
13 Andrew Wilson, *Virtual Politics: Faking democracy in the post-Soviet world* (London, Yale University Press, 2005), pp. 75–7; Golos website; V. K. Levashov, *Sotsiopoliticheskaia dinamika Rossiiskogo obshchestva* 2000–2006 (Moscow, Academia, 2007), p. 48; Levada, *Ishchem cheloveka*, p. 88.
14 Wilson, *Virtual Politics*.
15 Interview with Anatoly Aksakov, 27 June 2007; Richard Sakwa, *Russian Politics and Society* (London, Routledge, 2008), pp. 160–87 (on elections and voting figures).
16 Wilson, *Virtual Politics*, p. 96 (on Shabdurasulov); Aleksei Chadaev, *Putin: Ego ideologiia* (Moscow, 'Evropa', 2006); L. V. Poliakov, *Pro suverennuiu demokratiu* (Moscow, 'Evropa', 2007).
17 Steven Lee Myers, 'Putin is overheard making light of rape', *New York Times*, 19 October 2006, and 'Izrail' ne priznal Romana Abramovicha', *Kommersant*, 19 October 2006 (Katsav); Ukrainska Pravda <www.pravda.com.ua/news>, 12 April 2008 (Saakashvili) and 3 October 2008 (Yushchenko); Vincent Jauvert, 'Sarko le russe', *Le Nouvel Observateur*, 13 November 2008. Thanks to Mike Haynes, who got me thinking about this.
18 'Tsifra nedeli: 1088016', *Vedomosti*, 16 October 2002; 'Ot redaktsii: Den' tirana', *Vedomosti*, 22 December 2004; Kirill Kharat'ian, 'Tsitata nedeli', *Vedomosti*, 26 June 2007; 'Ot redaktsii: razdvoenie amnezii', *Vedomosti*, 31 October 2007; Clifford Levy, 'Nationalism of Putin's era', *New York Times*, 27 November 2008; Liudmila Rybina, 'Esli by na meste Stalina byl ia', *Novaia Gazeta*, 18 September 2008, and other articles; A. V. Filippov, *Noveishaia istoriia Rossii 1945–2006 gg.: kniga dlia uchitelia* (Moscow, Prosveshchenie, 2007), pp. 81–94 (on education).
19 Nadezhda Azhgikhina, 'The struggle for press freedom in Russia', *Europe Asia Studies* 59:8 (2007), pp. 1245–62; 'How free is the Russian media?', *Index on Censorship* 37:1, 2008; International Federation of Journalists website <www.ifj.org>; interviews with representatives of the Russian Union of Journalists and the Glasnost Defence Foundation. In all, 308 journalists died violently or prematurely from 1993–2008; the figures used represent the campaigning organisations' consensus on work-related deaths.
20 Civic Forum website <www.civilforum.ru>; Public Chamber website <www.oprf.ru>; Anastasiia Kornia, 'Dorogoi altruizm', *Vedomosti*, 18 July 2007; Mariia Chertok, 'NKO: zakon ob obshchestvennoi pol'ze', *Vedomosti*, 7 June 2007; Richard Sakwa, *Putin: Russia's choice* (London, Routledge, 2007), pp. 167–74.
21 Zbigniew Brzezinski, 'Moscow's Mussolini', *Wall Street Journal*, 20 September 2004.

22 George Soros, 'Who lost Russia?', *New York Review of Books*, 13 April 2000; Aleksandr Litvinenko, *Lubianskaia Prestupnaia Gruppirovka* (New York, Grani, 2002); Ian Cobain et al., 'UK police investigate tycoon's Russian coup claims', *Guardian*, 13 April 2007; Anne Penketh and Kim Sengupta, 'The plot to kill Boris Berezovsky', *Independent*, 19 July 2007, and other articles; Cathy Scott-Clark and Adrian Levy, 'Why a spy was killed', *Guardian magazine*, 26 January 2008.

Chapter 7: People and Money: Human Development Dilemmas

1 UNDP, *Demographic Policy in Russia: From reflection to action* (2008); World Bank, *Dying Too Young: Addressing premature mortality and ill health ... in the Russian Federation* (2006); Nadezhda Ivanitskaia et al., 'Fantasticheskaia demografiia', *Vedomosti*, 23 May 2007; Desai, *Conversations on Russia*, pp. 310–21; Ol'ga Kuvshinova, 'Rossiia vymiraet', *Vedomosti*, 29 April 2008; Ol'ga Kuvshinova, 'Glavnyi prioritet', *Vedomosti*, 11 February 2008; World Bank, *From Red to Gray: The 'third transition' of aging populations in Eastern Europe and the Former Soviet Union* (Washington DC, 2007).

2 UNAIDS/WHO, *Eastern Europe and Central Asia: AIDS epidemic update, Regional summary* (2008); Murray Feshbach, 'Potential social disarray in Russia due to health factors' (working paper, 2006); Michael Specter, 'The devastation', *New Yorker*, 11 October 2004.

3 Rosstat; World Bank, *Migration and Remittances: Eastern Europe and the Former Soviet Union* (2006); *FNPR v meniaiushchemsia obshchestve: informatsionnyi sbornik ot IV k VI s'ezdu FNPR* (Moscow, 2006), p. 13; RFE-RL, 'New Russian laws create widespread uncertainty', 15 January 2007.

4 K. S. Jomo and Jacques Baudot (eds), *Flat World, Big Gaps: Economic liberalisation, globalisation, poverty and inequality* (London, Zed Books, 2007), p. xvii.

5 *FNPR v meniaiushchem obshchestve*, pp. 10–11; 'Ot redaktsii: soblazn minimuma', *Vedomosti*, 11 April 2008.

6 Rosstat (on industrial sectors). The method of counting workers by industrial sector changed in 2005, making comparisons difficult. Sergei Surkov and Valentina Venedeeva, 'Politika na rynke truda', in Tat'iana Maleva (ed.), *Obzor Sotsial'noi politiki v Rossii, Nachalo 2000-kh* (Moscow, NISP, 2007), pp. 111–57; *FNPR v meniaiushchem obshchestve*, p. 25; ILO press release, 18 November 2008 (on working conditions).

7 Unicef Innocenti Social Monitor, *Understanding Child Poverty in South-Eastern Europe and the CIS* (2006), pp. 2–3; Alina Pishniak, 'Reformy v sfere sotsial'noi podderzhki', in Maleva (ed.), *Obzor Sotsial'noi politiki*, p. 362; interview with Svetlana Aivazova, 4 October 2007.

8 UNDP, *Russia's Regions: National Human Development Report,*

Russian Federation 2006/2007; World Bank, *Russian Economic Report 14* (June 2007), p. 16; Simon Pirani, 'An uncertain future', *Emerging Markets*, 22 October 2007.

9 Tullio Buccellato and Tomasz Mickiewicz, 'Oil and within-region inequality in Russia', Economics Working Paper no. 80 (CSESCE, September 2007).

10 Rosstat; Aleksandra Burdiak and Liliia Ovcharova, 'Dostupnost' zhil'ia: vozmozhnosti naseleniia i podderzhka gosudarstva', in Maleva (ed.), *Obzor Sotsial'noi politiki v Rossii*, pp. 302–30; Tat'iana Sokolova, 'Kto zaplatit za kapital'nyi remont doma?', *Sobstvennik*, November 2006; 'Ot redaktsii: vechnost' remonta', *Vedomosti*, 29 July 2008; Ol'ga Proskurina, 'Vse 240 milliardov srazu ne osvoim', *Vedomosti*, 27 November 2007.

13 <www.urbaneconomics.ru>; Anton Filatov and Bela Liaub, 'Rossiia ne stroitsia', *Vedomosti*, 15 October 2008; Kirill Blokhin, 'Leonid Bandorin: rost ob'emov zhil'ia ne uvelichivaet ego dostupnosti', *Boss magazine*, 10 September 2008.

14 Linda Cook, *Postcommunist Welfare States: Reform Politics in Russia and Eastern Europe* (London, Cornell University Press, 2007), pp. 145–57.

15 S. V. Shishkin (ed.), *Rossiiskoe zdravookhranenie: motivatsiia vrachei i obshchestvennaia dostupnost'* (Moscow, NISP, 2008); interview with Natalia Zubarevich, 10 July 2007.

Chapter 8: People: Parties, Unions and NGOs

1 Kagarlitskii, *Upravliaemaia Demokratiia*, pp. 519–20; <www.lenta.ru>; Natalia Kostenko and Maksim Glikin, 'V Rossii ne byvaet dvukh tsarei', *Vedomosti*, 15 May 2008.

2 *Programma Kommunisticheskoi partii Rossiiskoi federatsii*; 'Ziuganov: XX s'ezd KPSS – "chernaia data" v rossiiskoi istorii', *Trud*, 14 February 2006; G.A. Ziuganov, 'Stalin ob istoricheskom prizvanii russkikh', *Pravda*, 26 September 2008.

3 A. S. Titkov, *Party no. 4. Rodina: Whence and why?* (Moscow, Panorama, 2006); Federation of Jewish Communities press release, 28 June 2005.

4 <www.nazbol.ru>; Andrew Miller, 'Putin's pariah', *New York Times,* 2 March 2008; Keith Gessen, 'Monumental foolishness', *Slate magazine*, 20 February 2003. Pawel Pawlikowski, *Serbian Epics: Bosnia 1992* (film), archived at Records of the International Human Rights Law Institute, HU OSA 304-0-16, and video displayed at <http://www.youtube.com/watch?v=kcCFJAfLTJE> (Sarajevo).

5 'Skinkhedy popali pod redkie stat'i', *Kommersant*, 9 March 2004; 'Delo 'Shul'tsa'', *Limonka* no. 257, September 2004; 'Zub drakona vypal', *Novaia Gazeta*, 12 December 2005; 'Pereneseno slushanie', *RIA Novosti*, 1 July 2005.

6 Eduard Limonov, *Kak My Stroili Budushchee Rossii* (Moscow, 'Yauza', 2004), pp. 117–20, 204 and 499–501.

7 Reddaway and Glinski, *The Tragedy*, pp. 326–8 and 591; Yelena Bonner, 'Yeltsin's betrayal of democracy', testimony to the US Commission on Security and Cooperation in Europe, 19 January 1995; Bill Bowring, 'Sergei Kovalyov: the first Russian human rights ombudsman – and the last?', in Rein Mullerson, Malgosia Fitzmaurice and Mads Andenas (eds), *Constitutional Reform and International Law in Central and Eastern Europe* (The Hague, Kluwer Law, 1998), pp. 235–56; Olivia Ball and Paul Gready, *The No-Nonsense Guide to Human Rights* (London, New Internationalist, 2006), pp. 34–42 (interpretations of human rights).
8 Interview, 3 March 2008.
9 <www.bellona.org> (on Nikitin); <www.sakharov-musem.ru> (on Pasko); <www.baikalwave.eu.org> (on Baikal).
10 Interview with Larisa Fefilova, October 2007; O. P. Dzera, *Polozhenie zakliuchennykh v Udmurtii: Otchet*, published on <www.zaprava.ru>; Nadezhda Gladysh, 'Lav Stori', *Den'* (Izhevsk), 5 July 2007, and other articles in *Den'*; Larisa Fefilova, 'Schastlivyi bilet!?', *Vestnik Fonda 'V zashchitu prav zakliuchennykh'* nos. 6–7, July 2007; Lev Ponomarev, 'Revival of the Gulag? Putin's penitentiary system', *Perspective* (ISCIP), 18:1 (2007); International Helsinki Federation, *Report on Visiting of Closed Institutions in Russian Federation in 2004*; <www.zashita-zk.org>.
11 Samuel Baron, *Bloody Saturday in the Soviet Union: Novocherkassk, 1962* (Stanford, Calif., Stanford University Press, 2001); Viktor Haynes and Olga Semyonova, *Workers Against the Gulag* (London, Pluto Press, 1979); David Mandel, *Perestroika and the Soviet People* (Montreal, Black Rose Books, 1991) (on the Soviet period); Michael Burawoy, Simon Clarke, Peter Fairbrother and Pavel Krotov (eds), *What About the Workers?* (London, Verso, 1993) (on the 1990s).
12 Mandel, *Labour After Communism*, pp. 19–21.
13 Mandel, *Labour After Communism*, pp. 59 and 75.
14 Interview with Boris Kravchenko, 21 February 2007.
15 Interview with Kirill Buketov, 19 February 2007; Carine Clément, 'Pod'em rabochego i profsoiuznego dvizheniia: itogi 2007 goda', <www.ikd.ru>, 28 December 2007.
16 Interview with Boris Kravchenko; Mandel, *Labour After Communism*, pp. 40–1; Oleg Shein, Vystuplenie na mezhdunarodnoi konferentsii po trudovym pravam, Kiev, 26 November 2008; *FNPR v meniaiushchemsia obshchestve*, pp. 6–11; Sarah Ashwin and Simon Clarke, *Russian Trade Unions and Industrial Relations in Transition* (Basingstoke, Palgrave Macmillan, 2003), pp. 62–71 and 106–31.
17 Interview with Igor Shanin, 27 June 2007; *General'noe soglashenie na 2005–2007* gg.; Irina Mysliaeva, *Kakim mozhet byt' sotsial'noe partnerstvo v Rossii* (Moscow, Trudovaia demokratiia, 2000); Andrei Kolesnikov, 'Chleny profsoiuza otrabotali svoe pivo', *Kommersant*, 15 November 2006; <www.gmpr.ru>; Rosstat.

18 'S novym MROTom?', *Solidarnost'*, 18 June 2008; Ol'ga Kuvshinova, 'Tarifnaia gonka', *Vedomosti*, 17 July 2008.

19 Boris Vishnevskii, '"Ford" v fokuse', *Novaia Gazeta*, 15 February 2007; Gleb Stoliarov, 'Profsoiuz meshaet rostu', *Vedomosti*, 19 November 2007; M. Fonov, 'Zabastovka na "Forde". Kak eto bylo', *Solidarnost'*, 16 January 2008; 'Rabochie Ford otkazalis' ot peregovorov s administratsiei', *Vedomosti*, 5 December 2007. I thank the Russia Research Programme at the University of Warwick, which made available research papers on the Ford strike and union organisation at Avtovaz.

20 Sergei Silin, 'Zabastovok budet bol'she', *Solidarnost'*, 13 February 2008; *Svobodnyi profsoiuz* no. 1, 2007, pp. 10–12.

21 Iuliia Fedorinova et al., 'Bastuiut vse', *Vedomosti*, 21 August 2007.

22 Petr Biziukov, 'Kratkii informatsionnyi obzor protestnoi i zabastovochnoi aktivnosti', 24 September 2008, and other articles on <www.ikd.ru>; 'Na lidera profsoiuza "Ford" Alekseia Etmanova sovershено povtornoe napadenie', <www.ikd.ru>, 15 November 2008, and other articles.

23 Beverly Silver, *Forces of Labor: Workers' movements and globalization since 1870* (Cambridge, Cambridge University Press, 2003), p. 41.

24 Interviews with Petr Zolotarev, Anton Vechkunin, Anna Perova and other Avtovaz workers, 5–6 October 2007; Carine Clément, 'Komu vygodno polivat' griaz'iu rabochikh Avtovaza?', <www.ikd.ru>, 14 September 2007; Natal'ia Kochemina, 'Zabastovka na "AvtoVAZe": mify i real'nost', *Solidarnost'*, 8 August 2007; 'Obrashchenie profsoiuznogo komiteta OAO "Avtovaz" 'Edinstvo', 17 August 2007; Albert Speranskii, 'Podpolnyi stachkom deistvuet', <www.ikd.ru>, September 2007; <www.profedinstvo.ru>; <www.lenta.ru> (on Artiakov); Mandel, *Labour After Communism*, pp. 128–52.

Chapter 9: People: Grassroots Movements

1 National Survey of Household Living Standards and Participation in Social Programmes (NOBUS), 2003; Liliia Ovcharova and Alina Pishniak, 'Reformy v sfere sotsial'noi podderzhki naseleniia', in Maleva (ed.), *Obzor sotsial'noi politiki v Rossii*, pp. 331–75; Liliia Ovcharova, 'Vlianiie sotsial'nykh transfertov na uroven dokohdnoi obespechennosti domokhoziaistv', *Demoskop Weekly*, 21 March 2005; Evgenii Gontmakher, 'Monetizatsiia – eto mina, zalozhennaia pod budushchee Rossii', <www.polit.ru>, 15 November 2005; Susanne Wengle and Michael Rasell, 'The monetisation of L'goty: changing patterns of welfare politics and provision in Russia', *Europe-Asia Studies* 60:5 (2008), pp. 739–56.

2 Kagarlitskii, *Upravliaemaia Demokratiia*, pp. 534–41; Levada, *Ishchem cheloveka*, pp. 129–39; Aleksandr Brod, *Sotsial'nyi vzryv i obshchestvenno-politicheskie protsessy sovremennoi Rossii*, 25 March 2005.

3 Levada, *Ishchem cheloveka*, p. 138; interview with Sergei Shchukin, 30

September 2007; Carine Clément, 'Pod'em grazhdanskikh protestnykh dvizhenii', <www.ikd.ru>, November 2006.

4 Galina Khovanskaia, *Kvartirnyi vopros* (Moscow, Veres, 2007); Sergei Shchukin, 'Kak dobit'sia kapital'nogo remonta nashikh domov', *Zhitel'* (Izhevsk): spetsial'nyi vipusk, 1 June 2006, p. 9; Nadezhda Gladysh, 'Vlasti vynuzhdeny idti na ustupki izhevskim domkomam', *Den'*, June 2007; RKS (<www.roscomsys.ru>) and Rosvodokanal (<www.rosvodokanal.ru>) websites; interviews with Svetlana Stichikhina, 30 September 2007, and Andrei Konoval, 2 October 2007.

5 Interviews with Vladimir Fershtein, 1 October 2007, and Larisa Bozina, 5 October 2007; Soiuz Koordinatsiionnykh Sovetov, *Kak zashchitit' svoi prava pri novom Zhilishchnom Kodekse*, <www.ikd.ru>, September 2007; Andrei Pushkin, 'Tochka zreniia: samoupravlenie ili samolechenie?', *Vedomosti*, 12 November 2007; 'Kto dushit TSZh v Volgograde', *Komsomol'skaia Pravda*, 11 September 2006; Regnum news agency, 6 February 2008; correspondence from Brateevo TSZh.

6 Interview with Andrei Konoval, 2 October 2007; *Obrashchenie sovet 'Permskikh obshchezhitii'*, <www.aglob.info>, June 2008; *Izhevskie Obshchagi*, August 2006; Elena Brantsevich, 'Sabotazh v obshchagakh', *Den'*, 12 April 2007.

7 'Prodolzhaetsia kampaniia SKS "Za narodnuiu zhilishchnuiu politiku"', <www.ikd.ru>, December 2006; Iurii Iudin, 'Sozdano rossiiskoe dvizhenie zhilishchnogo samoupravleniia', <www.tsj.ru>, 5 October 2007; Anton Oleinik, 'ZhKKh: Ekho vzryva', *Vedomosti*, 29 October 2007.

8 Interview with Aleksei Il'in, 29 September 2007; Andrei Konoval, 'Al'ians s "Al'iansom"', *Den'*, 1 February 2007 and other articles in *Den'*; Gennadii Zubov, 'Butovskii sindrom', *Ogonek* no. 15, April 2008; Mariia Bunina, 'Na asfal'te: beskonechnaia istoriia', *Vedomosti*, 13 October 2008 (on housing). '"Komos-Grupp" i Volkov Ltd', *Den'*, 8 November 2007; 'Komos Group to discuss cooperation with Cargill', <www.meatrussia.com>, 18 September 2008; 'Komos privlechet amerikanskie tekhnologii', *Kommersant-Perm*, 23 September 2008, and other articles in *Kommersant-Perm*; press release of PIK group, 5 June 2008; '"Komos-Stroi" proglotil "Alians"?', *Sovershenno Konkretno* (Izhevsk), no. 30, August 2007 (on Izhevsk business groups).

9 Interviews with Liudmila Kuzmina, Aleksandr Lashmankin and others, 7–8 October 2007; articles on <www.samara-may.livejournal.com>, <www.svoboda.tv>, <www.ru.indymedia.org> and <www.ikd.ru>; Dar'ia Grigorian, 'Pered sammitom sazhaiut gazony i aktivistov', *Novaia Gazeta,* 14 May 2008; 'Samara vzialas' za beisbol'nye bity', *Kommersant,* 16 May 2007; Sergei Kurt-Adzhiev, 'V sredu posetil kapital Kazenkin', *Novaia Gazeta*, 4 October 2007; Iuliia Sukhonina, 'Pravozashchitniki soobrazili na troikh', *Kommersant-Nizhny Novgorod*, 1 August 2008.

10 Dmitry Vorobyev and Thomas Campbell, 'Anti-viruses and under-

ground monuments: resisting catastrophic urbanism in St Petersburg', <www.metamute.org>, January 2008.

11 'In a grassroots victory, a driver walks free', *Moscow Times*, 24 March 2006; Arkady Ostrovsky, 'Russian car lobby evolves into juggernaut', *Financial Times*, 14 December 2006.

12 Nabi Abdullaev and Francesca Mereu, 'Far east drivers get leaders to listen', *Moscow Times*, 16 December 2008; Boris Kagarlitskii, 'Vosstanie "srednego klassa" v Primor'e', <www.ikd.ru>, 21 December 2008; Roza Gorn, 'Primor'e: bunt vmesto srednego klassa', <www.ikd.ru>, 22 December 2008.

13 Aleksandr Mekhanik, 'Ideologiia obshchestvennoi bor'by', *Ekspert,* 11 February 2008.

14 Interview with Andrei Konoval, 2 October 2007; Sergei Shchukin, 'Kak zakrugliali stol', <www.ikd.ru>, 5 April 2007.

15 Markku Lonkila, 'The internet and anti-military activism in Russia', *Europe-Asia Studies* 60:7 (2008), pp. 1125–49.

16 'Ot redaktsii: est' chto teriat', *Vedomosti*, 2 December 2008.

17 '28% rossiian ne na chto zhit', <www.vedomosti.ru>, 17 December 2008; Evgenii Gontmakher, 'Stsenarii: Novocherkassk-2009', *Vedomosti*, 6 November 2008; Anastasiia Kornia, '"Vedomosti" preduprezhdeny', <www.vedomosti.ru>, 21 November 2008.

18 'V. V. Putin provel vstrechu s rukovodstvom partii "Edinaia Rossiia"', <www.government.ru>, 27 February 2009; 'Putin vows to allow "legal" protests', Bloomberg, 27 February 2009.

GLOSSARY OF RUSSIAN WORDS AND ABBREVIATIONS

chekist (plural *chekisty*) Derives from *Cheka* (an acronym for *chrezvychainie kommissii*, i.e. special commissions), the security force set up after the 1917 revolution. Its name changed several times before becoming the KGB in 1954. See also *silovik*.

dedovshchina The regime of exploitation and bullying in the Russian army.

FSB An acronym for *Federalnaya sluzhba bezopasnosti*, or Federal Security Service. The KGB's principal successor organisation in post-Soviet Russia.

GKO An acronym for *gosudarstvennye kratkosrochnye obligatsii* (short-term state obligations). The main type of Russian short-term treasury bill.

KGB Stands for *Komitet gosudarstvennoi bezopasnosti*, or Committee of State Security. The powerful security service of the late Soviet period. Formed in 1954 as a result of a security forces reorganisation; dissolved in 1991 with the Soviet Union.

Komsomol An acronym for *Kommunistichesky soyuz molodezhi*, or Communist Union of Youth. The youth organisation of the Communist Party of the Soviet Union.

nomenklatura A word used to describe the Soviet bureaucracy, initially by its opponents. It derived from the name of the Communist party's lists of officials available to fill administrative posts.

perestroika Literally 'restructuring'. The name given to Gorbachev's economic and political reforms.

pravozashchitnik (plural *pravozashchitniki*) An acronym meaning 'human rights defender'.

silovik (plural *siloviki*) This is a broader term than *chekist*. It means literally 'power people', and refers to current or former security services officers in government and the state apparatus, including those from the defence establishment, the interior ministry and other agencies, as well as the KGB/FSB.

zachistka (plural *zachistki*) Literally, 'clearance', 'purge' or 'cleansing'. The name given to repressive search-and-detain operations in Chechnya.

CHRONOLOGY

1985	March	Mikhail Gorbachev elected leader of the Soviet Communist Party.
1986	March	Reform policies announced at Communist Party congress.
1989	July	Soviet miners' strike.
	November	Berlin wall taken down.
1991	June	Boris Yeltsin elected first Russian president.
	August	Attempted coup fails in Soviet Union.
	October	Boris Yeltsin declares 'shock therapy' policy for Russia.
	December	Soviet Union dissolved.
1992	January	Russian government liberalises consumer prices.
	December	'Voucher privatisation' programme launched.
1993	October	Yeltsin's dispute with Parliament culminates in armed assault on Parliament.
	December	Russian constitution adopted by referendum. Parliamentary election; Zhirinovsky's Liberal Democrats do well.
1994	December	First Chechen war begins.
1995	September	'Loans for shares' auctions launched.
1996	June–July	Presidential election; Yeltsin beats Gennady Zyuganov (Communist) on second ballot.
	August	First Chechen war ends; Russia defeated.
1997	August	Financial crisis sweeps East Asia.
1998	August	Russian financial crash.
1999	August	Putin appointed prime minister.
	September	Apartment block bombings in Russia. Second Chechen war launched.
	December	Parliamentary election; Unity, the pro-Putin party, comes second after the Communists.

2000	January	Russia consolidates position in Chechnya and claims victory.
	March	Putin elected president.
	May	Putin creates federal districts, eroding the power of regional elites.
	June–September	Legal actions against Vladimir Gusinsky and his companies; he leaves Russia.
	October	Boris Berezovsky sells key Russian assets and leaves Russia.
2001	January	Putin meets with oligarchs and tells them the new rules of the game.
2002	January	Mineral resources extraction tax introduced, as the government moves to increase tax take from oil and gas sector.
2003	October	Arrest of Mikhail Khodorkovsky, owner of Yukos.
	November	'Rose revolution' in Georgia.
	December	Parliamentary elections; United Russia becomes the largest party, displacing the Communists.
2004	March	Putin elected to serve second term.
	September	Direct election of governors replaced by appointment.
	November	'Orange revolution' begins in Ukraine, leading to rerun of presidential elections.
	December	Yukos production company Yuganskneftegaz sold at bankruptcy auction; by acquiring it state-owned Rosneft becomes Russia's largest oil producer.
2005	January	National protest movement against the reform of welfare benefits.
	December	Change in Gazprom share structure raises foreign stake.
2006	July	Rosneft initial public offering raises foreign stake.
	December	Shell ends dispute with authorities over Sakhalin project and arranges sale of controlling stake to Gazprom.
2007	December	Parliamentary election; United Russia again leads.

2008	March	Russian stock market starts to fall.
	March	Dmitry Medvedev elected president.
	June	Russian power sector privatisation culminates in the dissolution of United Energy Systems.
	July	Oil price reaches its peak, $147 per barrel, and starts to fall. Average wage in Russia, measured in dollars, also peaks and starts to fall.
	August	Russo-Georgian war.
	September	Wall Street banking crisis triggers worldwide financial crisis and economic recession.
2009	January	Russo-Ukrainian gas dispute; supplies to Europe cut for two weeks.

FURTHER READING

Here I recommend a small selection of books and other materials. Many more are cited in the endnotes.

On the Yeltsin period. Peter Reddaway and Dmitri Glinski, *The Tragedy of Russia's Reforms: Market bolshevism against democracy* (Washington, US Institute of Peace Press, 2001); David Hoffman, *The Oligarchs: Wealth and power in the new Russia* (New York, Public Affairs, 2003); Paul Klebnikov, *Godfather of the Kremlin: Boris Berezovsky and the looting of Russia* (New York, Harcourt, 2000); Anatol Lieven, *Chechnya: Tombstone of Russian power* (London, Yale University Press, 1998).

On the economy. Philip Hanson, 'The Russian economic recovery: do four years of growth tell us that the fundamentals have changed?', *Europe-Asia Studies*, 55:3 (2003), pp. 365–82; Andrew Scott Barnes, *Owning Russia: The struggle over factories, farms and power* (London, Cornell University Press, 2006); the World Bank's Russian Economic Reports, available on its Russia webpage (navigate from <http://web.worldbank.org/>); and OECD documents, including the biannual *Economic Survey of Russia* (see <http://www.oecd.org/russia>). Specifically on the oil and gas sector: Michael Ellman (ed.), *Russia's Oil and Natural Gas: Bonanza or curse?* (London, Anthem Press, 2006) and Peter Rutland, 'Putin's economic record: is the oil boom sustainable?', *Europe-Asia Studies* 60:6 (2008), pp. 1051–72.

On politics: Lilia Shevtsova, *Putin's Russia* (Washington, Carnegie Endowment, 2005); Padma Desai, *Conversations on Russia: Reform from Yeltsin to Putin* (Oxford, Oxford University Press, 2006); Richard Sakwa, *Putin: Russia's choice* (Abingdon, Routledge, 2004). Western journalists' accounts include Andrew Jack, *Inside Putin's Russia* (London, Granta, 2004) and Peter Baker and Susan Glasser, *Kremlin Rising: Vladimir Putin's Russia and the end of revolution* (New York, Scribner, 2005).

On social and development issues: Judyth Twigg and Kate Schecter (eds), *Social Capital and Social Cohesion in Post-Soviet Russia* (New York, M.E. Sharpe, 2003); Linda Cook, *Postcommunist Welfare States: Reform politics in Russia and Eastern Europe* (London, Cornell University Press, 2007); the websites of UNDP

Russia <http://www.undp.ru/> and the Independent Institute of Social Policy <http://www.socpol.ru/eng/about/index.shtml>.

Read *Putin's Russia* (London, Harvill Press, 2004) and *A Small Corner of Hell: Dispatches from Chechnya* (Chicago, University of Chicago Press, 2003), by Anna Politkovskaya, the campaigning journalist murdered in 2006; and the soldier/writer Arkady Babchenko's *One Soldier's War in Chechnya* (London, Portobello Books, 2007). The <www.artofwar.ru> website has some items in English.

Among the Russian NGOs and human rights organisations who publish in English on the Web are Memorial <http://www.memo.ru/eng/index.htm>, the Moscow Helsinki Group <http://www.mhg.ru/ english> and the Demos Centre <http://www.demos-center.ru/projects/649C353>. The Glasnost foundation <http://www.gdf.ru/> focuses on media freedom issues. An indispensable source on labour and community movements which publishes only in Russian is <www.ikd.ru>.

Studies on the labour movement include David Mandel, *Labour After Communism* (Montreal, Black Rose Books, 2004); Sarah Ashwin and Simon Clarke, *Russian Trade Unions and Industrial Relations in Transition* (Basingstoke, Palgrave Macmillan, 2003); Simon Clarke, *The Development of Industrial Relations in Russia* (downloadable from <http://www.warwick.ac.uk/fac/soc/complabstuds/russia/documents/ilorep.doc>. There is much material available via the University of Warwick's Russian Research Programme page <http://www.warwick.ac.uk/russia/>.

Of Russian socialist writers, only Boris Kagarlitsky's work is easily available in English. His most recent book is *Russia Under Yeltsin and Putin* (London, Pluto, 2002); he also writes a column in the *Moscow Times*. From western Marxists who theorised the Soviet Union, notable work about what followed it and why includes Hillel Ticktin, 'Political economy of a disintegrating Stalinism', *Critique,* 44 (2008), pp. 73–90, and Simon Clarke's analysis of class relations in the books mentioned above.

News from Russia in English is available from websites including those of the semi-official Novosti news agency <http://en.rian.ru/russia/>, Radio Free Europe <http://www.rferl.org/> and the *Moscow Times* <http://www.themoscowtimes.com/>, a newspaper for expatriate business people. Sites offering analysis include those of the Jamestown foundation <http://www.jamestown.org/> and the Russian Analytical Digest <http://www.res.ethz.ch/analysis/rad/>.

INDEX